DEAR FUTURE EXAM SUCCESS STORY

First of all, **THANK YOU** for purchasing Mometrix study materials!

Second, congratulations! You are one of the few determined test-takers who are committed to doing whatever it takes to excel on your exam. **You have come to the right place.** We developed these study materials with one goal in mind: to deliver you the information you need in a format that's concise and easy to use.

In addition to optimizing your guide for the content of the test, we've outlined our recommended steps for breaking down the preparation process into small, attainable goals so you can make sure you stay on track.

We've also analyzed the entire test-taking process, identifying the most common pitfalls and showing how you can overcome them and be ready for any curveball the test throws you.

Standardized testing is one of the biggest obstacles on your road to success, which only increases the importance of doing well in the high-pressure, high-stakes environment of test day. Your results on this test could have a significant impact on your future, and this guide provides the information and practical advice to help you achieve your full potential on test day.

Your success is our success

We would love to hear from you! If you would like to share the story of your exam success or if you have any questions or comments in regard to our products, please contact us at **800-673-8175** or **support@mometrix.com**.

Thanks again for your business and we wish you continued success!

Sincerely,
The Mometrix Test Preparation Team

Need more help? Check out our flashcards at:
http://mometrixflashcards.com/TExES

Written and edited by the Mometrix Exam Secrets Test Prep Team
Printed in the United States of America

TABLE OF CONTENTS

Introduction

Thank you for purchasing this resource! You have made the choice to prepare yourself for a test that could have a huge impact on your future, and this guide is designed to help you be fully ready for test day. Obviously, it's important to have a solid understanding of the test material, but you also need to be prepared for the unique environment and stressors of the test, so that you can perform to the best of your abilities.

For this purpose, the first section that appears in this guide is the **Secret Keys**. We've devoted countless hours to meticulously researching what works and what doesn't, and we've boiled down our findings to the five most impactful steps you can take to improve your performance on the test. We start at the beginning with study planning and move through the preparation process, all the way to the testing strategies that will help you get the most out of what you know when you're finally sitting in front of the test.

We recommend that you start preparing for your test as far in advance as possible. However, if you've bought this guide as a last-minute study resource and only have a few days before your test, we recommend that you skip over the first two Secret Keys since they address a long-term study plan.

If you struggle with **test anxiety**, we strongly encourage you to check out our recommendations for how you can overcome it. Test anxiety is a formidable foe, but it can be beaten, and we want to make sure you have the tools you need to defeat it.

Secret Key #1 – Plan Big, Study Small

There's a lot riding on your performance. If you want to ace this test, you're going to need to keep your skills sharp and the material fresh in your mind. You need a plan that lets you review everything you need to know while still fitting in your schedule. We'll break this strategy down into three categories.

Information Organization

Start with the information you already have: the official test outline. From this, you can make a complete list of all the concepts you need to cover before the test. Organize these concepts into groups that can be studied together, and create a list of any related vocabulary you need to learn so you can brush up on any difficult terms. You'll want to keep this vocabulary list handy once you actually start studying since you may need to add to it along the way.

Time Management

Once you have your set of study concepts, decide how to spread them out over the time you have left before the test. Break your study plan into small, clear goals so you have a manageable task for each day and know exactly what you're doing. Then just focus on one small step at a time. When you manage your time this way, you don't need to spend hours at a time studying. Studying a small block of content for a short period each day helps you retain information better and avoid stressing over how much you have left to do. You can relax knowing that you have a plan to cover everything in time. In order for this strategy to be effective though, you have to start studying early and stick to your schedule. Avoid the exhaustion and futility that comes from last-minute cramming!

Study Environment

The environment you study in has a big impact on your learning. Studying in a coffee shop, while probably more enjoyable, is not likely to be as fruitful as studying in a quiet room. It's important to keep distractions to a minimum. You're only planning to study for a short block of time, so make the most of it. Don't pause to check your phone or get up to find a snack. It's also important to **avoid multitasking**. Research has consistently shown that multitasking will make your studying dramatically less effective. Your study area should also be comfortable and well-lit so you don't have the distraction of straining your eyes or sitting on an uncomfortable chair.

The time of day you study is also important. You want to be rested and alert. Don't wait until just before bedtime. Study when you'll be most likely to comprehend and remember. Even better, if you know what time of day your test will be, set that time aside for study. That way your brain will be used to working on that subject at that specific time and you'll have a better chance of recalling information.

Finally, it can be helpful to team up with others who are studying for the same test. Your actual studying should be done in as isolated an environment as possible, but the work of organizing the information and setting up the study plan can be divided up. In between study sessions, you can discuss with your teammates the concepts that you're all studying and quiz each other on the details. Just be sure that your teammates are as serious about the test as you are. If you find that your study time is being replaced with social time, you might need to find a new team.

Secret Key #2 – Make Your Studying Count

You're devoting a lot of time and effort to preparing for this test, so you want to be absolutely certain it will pay off. This means doing more than just reading the content and hoping you can remember it on test day. It's important to make every minute of study count. There are two main areas you can focus on to make your studying count.

Retention

It doesn't matter how much time you study if you can't remember the material. You need to make sure you are retaining the concepts. To check your retention of the information you're learning, try recalling it at later times with minimal prompting. Try carrying around flashcards and glance at one or two from time to time or ask a friend who's also studying for the test to quiz you.

To enhance your retention, look for ways to put the information into practice so that you can apply it rather than simply recalling it. If you're using the information in practical ways, it will be much easier to remember. Similarly, it helps to solidify a concept in your mind if you're not only reading it to yourself but also explaining it to someone else. Ask a friend to let you teach them about a concept you're a little shaky on (or speak aloud to an imaginary audience if necessary). As you try to summarize, define, give examples, and answer your friend's questions, you'll understand the concepts better and they will stay with you longer. Finally, step back for a big picture view and ask yourself how each piece of information fits with the whole subject. When you link the different concepts together and see them working together as a whole, it's easier to remember the individual components.

Finally, practice showing your work on any multi-step problems, even if you're just studying. Writing out each step you take to solve a problem will help solidify the process in your mind, and you'll be more likely to remember it during the test.

Modality

Modality simply refers to the means or method by which you study. Choosing a study modality that fits your own individual learning style is crucial. No two people learn best in exactly the same way, so it's important to know your strengths and use them to your advantage.

For example, if you learn best by visualization, focus on visualizing a concept in your mind and draw an image or a diagram. Try color-coding your notes, illustrating them, or creating symbols that will trigger your mind to recall a learned concept. If you learn best by hearing or discussing information, find a study partner who learns the same way or read aloud to yourself. Think about how to put the information in your own words. Imagine that you are giving a lecture on the topic and record yourself so you can listen to it later.

For any learning style, flashcards can be helpful. Organize the information so you can take advantage of spare moments to review. Underline key words or phrases. Use different colors for different categories. Mnemonic devices (such as creating a short list in which every item starts with the same letter) can also help with retention. Find what works best for you and use it to store the information in your mind most effectively and easily.

Secret Key #3 – Practice the Right Way

Your success on test day depends not only on how many hours you put into preparing, but also on whether you prepared the right way. It's good to check along the way to see if your studying is paying off. One of the most effective ways to do this is by taking practice tests to evaluate your progress. Practice tests are useful because they show exactly where you need to improve. Every time you take a practice test, pay special attention to these three groups of questions:

- The questions you got wrong
- The questions you had to guess on, even if you guessed right
- The questions you found difficult or slow to work through

This will show you exactly what your weak areas are, and where you need to devote more study time. Ask yourself why each of these questions gave you trouble. Was it because you didn't understand the material? Was it because you didn't remember the vocabulary? Do you need more repetitions on this type of question to build speed and confidence? Dig into those questions and figure out how you can strengthen your weak areas as you go back to review the material.

Additionally, many practice tests have a section explaining the answer choices. It can be tempting to read the explanation and think that you now have a good understanding of the concept. However, an explanation likely only covers part of the question's broader context. Even if the explanation makes perfect sense, **go back and investigate** every concept related to the question until you're positive you have a thorough understanding.

As you go along, keep in mind that the practice test is just that: practice. Memorizing these questions and answers will not be very helpful on the actual test because it is unlikely to have any of the same exact questions. If you only know the right answers to the sample questions, you won't be prepared for the real thing. **Study the concepts** until you understand them fully, and then you'll be able to answer any question that shows up on the test.

It's important to wait on the practice tests until you're ready. If you take a test on your first day of study, you may be overwhelmed by the amount of material covered and how much you need to learn. Work up to it gradually.

On test day, you'll need to be prepared for answering questions, managing your time, and using the test-taking strategies you've learned. It's a lot to balance, like a mental marathon that will have a big impact on your future. Like training for a marathon, you'll need to start slowly and work your way up. When test day arrives, you'll be ready.

Start with the strategies you've read in the first two Secret Keys—plan your course and study in the way that works best for you. If you have time, consider using multiple study resources to get different approaches to the same concepts. It can be helpful to see difficult concepts from more than one angle. Then find a good source for practice tests. Many times, the test website will suggest potential study resources or provide sample tests.

Practice Test Strategy

If you're able to find at least three practice tests, we recommend this strategy:

Untimed and Open-Book Practice

Take the first test with no time constraints and with your notes and study guide handy. Take your time and focus on applying the strategies you've learned.

Timed and Open-Book Practice

Take the second practice test open-book as well, but set a timer and practice pacing yourself to finish in time.

Timed and Closed-Book Practice

Take any other practice tests as if it were test day. Set a timer and put away your study materials. Sit at a table or desk in a quiet room, imagine yourself at the testing center, and answer questions as quickly and accurately as possible.

Keep repeating timed and closed-book tests on a regular basis until you run out of practice tests or it's time for the actual test. Your mind will be ready for the schedule and stress of test day, and you'll be able to focus on recalling the material you've learned.

Secret Key #4 – Pace Yourself

Once you're fully prepared for the material on the test, your biggest challenge on test day will be managing your time. Just knowing that the clock is ticking can make you panic even if you have plenty of time left. Work on pacing yourself so you can build confidence against the time constraints of the exam. Pacing is a difficult skill to master, especially in a high-pressure environment, so **practice is vital**.

Set time expectations for your pace based on how much time is available. For example, if a section has 60 questions and the time limit is 30 minutes, you know you have to average 30 seconds or less per question in order to answer them all. Although 30 seconds is the hard limit, set 25 seconds per question as your goal, so you reserve extra time to spend on harder questions. When you budget extra time for the harder questions, you no longer have any reason to stress when those questions take longer to answer.

Don't let this time expectation distract you from working through the test at a calm, steady pace, but keep it in mind so you don't spend too much time on any one question. Recognize that taking extra time on one question you don't understand may keep you from answering two that you do understand later in the test. If your time limit for a question is up and you're still not sure of the answer, mark it and move on, and come back to it later if the time and the test format allow. If the testing format doesn't allow you to return to earlier questions, just make an educated guess; then put it out of your mind and move on.

On the easier questions, be careful not to rush. It may seem wise to hurry through them so you have more time for the challenging ones, but it's not worth missing one if you know the concept and just didn't take the time to read the question fully. Work efficiently but make sure you understand the question and have looked at all of the answer choices, since more than one may seem right at first.

Even if you're paying attention to the time, you may find yourself a little behind at some point. You should speed up to get back on track, but do so wisely. Don't panic; just take a few seconds less on each question until you're caught up. Don't guess without thinking, but do look through the answer choices and eliminate any you know are wrong. If you can get down to two choices, it is often worthwhile to guess from those. Once you've chosen an answer, move on and don't dwell on any that you skipped or had to hurry through. If a question was taking too long, chances are it was one of the harder ones, so you weren't as likely to get it right anyway.

On the other hand, if you find yourself getting ahead of schedule, it may be beneficial to slow down a little. The more quickly you work, the more likely you are to make a careless mistake that will affect your score. You've budgeted time for each question, so don't be afraid to spend that time. Practice an efficient but careful pace to get the most out of the time you have.

Secret Key #5 – Have a Plan for Guessing

When you're taking the test, you may find yourself stuck on a question. Some of the answer choices seem better than others, but you don't see the one answer choice that is obviously correct. What do you do?

The scenario described above is very common, yet most test takers have not effectively prepared for it. Developing and practicing a plan for guessing may be one of the single most effective uses of your time as you get ready for the exam.

In developing your plan for guessing, there are three questions to address:

- When should you start the guessing process?
- How should you narrow down the choices?
- Which answer should you choose?

When to Start the Guessing Process

Unless your plan for guessing is to select C every time (which, despite its merits, is not what we recommend), you need to leave yourself enough time to apply your answer elimination strategies. Since you have a limited amount of time for each question, that means that if you're going to give yourself the best shot at guessing correctly, you have to decide quickly whether or not you will guess.

Of course, the best-case scenario is that you don't have to guess at all, so first, see if you can answer the question based on your knowledge of the subject and basic reasoning skills. Focus on the key words in the question and try to jog your memory of related topics. Give yourself a chance to bring the knowledge to mind, but once you realize that you don't have (or you can't access) the knowledge you need to answer the question, it's time to start the guessing process.

It's almost always better to start the guessing process too early than too late. It only takes a few seconds to remember something and answer the question from knowledge. Carefully eliminating wrong answer choices takes longer. Plus, going through the process of eliminating answer choices can actually help jog your memory.

Summary: Start the guessing process as soon as you decide that you can't answer the question based on your knowledge.

How to Narrow Down the Choices

The next chapter in this book (**Test-Taking Strategies**) includes a wide range of strategies for how to approach questions and how to look for answer choices to eliminate. You will definitely want to read those carefully, practice them, and figure out which ones work best for you. Here though, we're going to address a mindset rather than a particular strategy.

Your odds of guessing an answer correctly depend on how many options you are choosing from.

Number of options left	5	4	3	2	1
Odds of guessing correctly	20%	25%	33%	50%	100%

You can see from this chart just how valuable it is to be able to eliminate incorrect answers and make an educated guess, but there are two things that many test takers do that cause them to miss out on the benefits of guessing:

- Accidentally eliminating the correct answer
- Selecting an answer based on an impression

We'll look at the first one here, and the second one in the next section.

To avoid accidentally eliminating the correct answer, we recommend a thought exercise called **the $5 challenge**. In this challenge, you only eliminate an answer choice from contention if you are willing to bet $5 on it being wrong. Why $5? Five dollars is a small but not insignificant amount of money. It's an amount you could afford to lose but wouldn't want to throw away. And while losing $5 once might not hurt too much, doing it twenty times will set you back $100. In the same way, each small decision you make—eliminating a choice here, guessing on a question there—won't by itself impact your score very much, but when you put them all together, they can make a big difference. By holding each answer choice elimination decision to a higher standard, you can reduce the risk of accidentally eliminating the correct answer.

The $5 challenge can also be applied in a positive sense: If you are willing to bet $5 that an answer choice *is* correct, go ahead and mark it as correct.

Summary: Only eliminate an answer choice if you are willing to bet $5 that it is wrong.

Which Answer to Choose

You're taking the test. You've run into a hard question and decided you'll have to guess. You've eliminated all the answer choices you're willing to bet $5 on. Now you have to pick an answer. Why do we even need to talk about this? Why can't you just pick whichever one you feel like when the time comes?

The answer to these questions is that if you don't come into the test with a plan, you'll rely on your impression to select an answer choice, and if you do that, you risk falling into a trap. The test writers know that everyone who takes their test will be guessing on some of the questions, so they intentionally write wrong answer choices to seem plausible. You still have to pick an answer though, and if the wrong answer choices are designed to look right, how can you ever be sure that you're not falling for their trap? The best solution we've found to this dilemma is to take the decision out of your hands entirely. Here is the process we recommend:

Once you've eliminated any choices that you are confident (willing to bet $5) are wrong, select the first remaining choice as your answer.

Whether you choose to select the first remaining choice, the second, or the last, the important thing is that you use some preselected standard. Using this approach guarantees that you will not be enticed into selecting an answer choice that looks right, because you are not basing your decision on how the answer choices look.

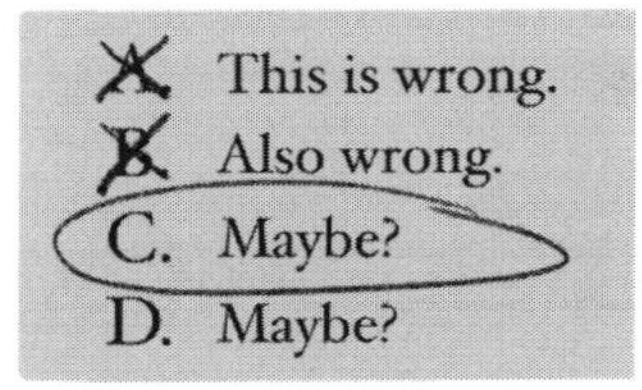

This is not meant to make you question your knowledge. Instead, it is to help you recognize the difference between your knowledge and your impressions. There's a huge difference between thinking an answer is right because of what you know, and thinking an answer is right because it looks or sounds like it should be right.

Summary: To ensure that your selection is appropriately random, make a predetermined selection from among all answer choices you have not eliminated.

Test-Taking Strategies

This section contains a list of test-taking strategies that you may find helpful as you work through the test. By taking what you know and applying logical thought, you can maximize your chances of answering any question correctly!

It is very important to realize that every question is different and every person is different: no single strategy will work on every question, and no single strategy will work for every person. That's why we've included all of them here, so you can try them out and determine which ones work best for different types of questions and which ones work best for you.

Question Strategies

⊘ Read Carefully

Read the question and the answer choices carefully. Don't miss the question because you misread the terms. You have plenty of time to read each question thoroughly and make sure you understand what is being asked. Yet a happy medium must be attained, so don't waste too much time. You must read carefully and efficiently.

⊘ Contextual Clues

Look for contextual clues. If the question includes a word you are not familiar with, look at the immediate context for some indication of what the word might mean. Contextual clues can often give you all the information you need to decipher the meaning of an unfamiliar word. Even if you can't determine the meaning, you may be able to narrow down the possibilities enough to make a solid guess at the answer to the question.

⊘ Prefixes

If you're having trouble with a word in the question or answer choices, try dissecting it. Take advantage of every clue that the word might include. Prefixes can be a huge help. Usually, they allow you to determine a basic meaning. *Pre-* means before, *post-* means after, *pro-* is positive, *de-* is negative. From prefixes, you can get an idea of the general meaning of the word and try to put it into context.

⊘ Hedge Words

Watch out for critical hedge words, such as *likely, may, can, often, almost, mostly, usually, generally, rarely*, and *sometimes*. Question writers insert these hedge phrases to cover every possibility. Often an answer choice will be wrong simply because it leaves no room for exception. Be on guard for answer choices that have definitive words such as *exactly* and *always*.

⊘ Switchback Words

Stay alert for *switchbacks*. These are the words and phrases frequently used to alert you to shifts in thought. The most common switchback words are *but, although*, and *however*. Others include *nevertheless, on the other hand, even though, while, in spite of, despite*, and *regardless of*. Switchback words are important to catch because they can change the direction of the question or an answer choice.

✓ Face Value

When in doubt, use common sense. Accept the situation in the problem at face value. Don't read too much into it. These problems will not require you to make wild assumptions. If you have to go beyond creativity and warp time or space in order to have an answer choice fit the question, then you should move on and consider the other answer choices. These are normal problems rooted in reality. The applicable relationship or explanation may not be readily apparent, but it is there for you to figure out. Use your common sense to interpret anything that isn't clear.

Answer Choice Strategies

✓ Answer Selection

The most thorough way to pick an answer choice is to identify and eliminate wrong answers until only one is left, then confirm it is the correct answer. Sometimes an answer choice may immediately seem right, but be careful. The test writers will usually put more than one reasonable answer choice on each question, so take a second to read all of them and make sure that the other choices are not equally obvious. As long as you have time left, it is better to read every answer choice than to pick the first one that looks right without checking the others.

✓ Answer Choice Families

An answer choice family consists of two (in rare cases, three) answer choices that are very similar in construction and cannot all be true at the same time. If you see two answer choices that are direct opposites or parallels, one of them is usually the correct answer. For instance, if one answer choice says that quantity *x* increases and another either says that quantity *x* decreases (opposite) or says that quantity *y* increases (parallel), then those answer choices would fall into the same family. An answer choice that doesn't match the construction of the answer choice family is more likely to be incorrect. Most questions will not have answer choice families, but when they do appear, you should be prepared to recognize them.

✓ Eliminate Answers

Eliminate answer choices as soon as you realize they are wrong, but make sure you consider all possibilities. If you are eliminating answer choices and realize that the last one you are left with is also wrong, don't panic. Start over and consider each choice again. There may be something you missed the first time that you will realize on the second pass.

✓ Avoid Fact Traps

Don't be distracted by an answer choice that is factually true but doesn't answer the question. You are looking for the choice that answers the question. Stay focused on what the question is asking for so you don't accidentally pick an answer that is true but incorrect. Always go back to the question and make sure the answer choice you've selected actually answers the question and is not merely a true statement.

✓ Extreme Statements

In general, you should avoid answers that put forth extreme actions as standard practice or proclaim controversial ideas as established fact. An answer choice that states the "process should be used in certain situations, if..." is much more likely to be correct than one that states the "process should be discontinued completely." The first is a calm rational statement and doesn't even make a definitive, uncompromising stance, using a hedge word *if* to provide wiggle room, whereas the second choice is far more extreme.

⊘ Benchmark

As you read through the answer choices and you come across one that seems to answer the question well, mentally select that answer choice. This is not your final answer, but it's the one that will help you evaluate the other answer choices. The one that you selected is your benchmark or standard for judging each of the other answer choices. Every other answer choice must be compared to your benchmark. That choice is correct until proven otherwise by another answer choice beating it. If you find a better answer, then that one becomes your new benchmark. Once you've decided that no other choice answers the question as well as your benchmark, you have your final answer.

⊘ Predict the Answer

Before you even start looking at the answer choices, it is often best to try to predict the answer. When you come up with the answer on your own, it is easier to avoid distractions and traps because you will know exactly what to look for. The right answer choice is unlikely to be word-for-word what you came up with, but it should be a close match. Even if you are confident that you have the right answer, you should still take the time to read each option before moving on.

General Strategies

⊘ Tough Questions

If you are stumped on a problem or it appears too hard or too difficult, don't waste time. Move on! Remember though, if you can quickly check for obviously incorrect answer choices, your chances of guessing correctly are greatly improved. Before you completely give up, at least try to knock out a couple of possible answers. Eliminate what you can and then guess at the remaining answer choices before moving on.

⊘ Check Your Work

Since you will probably not know every term listed and the answer to every question, it is important that you get credit for the ones that you do know. Don't miss any questions through careless mistakes. If at all possible, try to take a second to look back over your answer selection and make sure you've selected the correct answer choice and haven't made a costly careless mistake (such as marking an answer choice that you didn't mean to mark). This quick double check should more than pay for itself in caught mistakes for the time it costs.

⊘ Pace Yourself

It's easy to be overwhelmed when you're looking at a page full of questions; your mind is confused and full of random thoughts, and the clock is ticking down faster than you would like. Calm down and maintain the pace that you have set for yourself. Especially as you get down to the last few minutes of the test, don't let the small numbers on the clock make you panic. As long as you are on track by monitoring your pace, you are guaranteed to have time for each question.

⊘ Don't Rush

It is very easy to make errors when you are in a hurry. Maintaining a fast pace in answering questions is pointless if it makes you miss questions that you would have gotten right otherwise. Test writers like to include distracting information and wrong answers that seem right. Taking a little extra time to avoid careless mistakes can make all the difference in your test score. Find a pace that allows you to be confident in the answers that you select.

⊘ Keep Moving

Panicking will not help you pass the test, so do your best to stay calm and keep moving. Taking deep breaths and going through the answer elimination steps you practiced can help to break through a stress barrier and keep your pace.

Final Notes

The combination of a solid foundation of content knowledge and the confidence that comes from practicing your plan for applying that knowledge is the key to maximizing your performance on test day. As your foundation of content knowledge is built up and strengthened, you'll find that the strategies included in this chapter become more and more effective in helping you quickly sift through the distractions and traps of the test to isolate the correct answer.

Now that you're preparing to move forward into the test content chapters of this book, be sure to keep your goal in mind. As you read, think about how you will be able to apply this information on the test. If you've already seen sample questions for the test and you have an idea of the question format and style, try to come up with questions of your own that you can answer based on what you're reading. This will give you valuable practice applying your knowledge in the same ways you can expect to on test day.

Good luck and good studying!

Academic Foundations

History of Medicine

The **history of medicine** includes the following:

- Hippocrates (460 BC–375 BC): Known as the father of medicine, this Greek physician established ethical standards and is known for the Hippocratic oath (which he likely did not write). Hippocrates believed that there were natural causes for disease, such as poor diet, rather than gods' punishment or superstition.
- **Black Death/Great Plague** (1347–1351): Killed between 75 and 200 million people; it is believed to have been caused by *Yersinia pestis.*
- **Leonardo Da Vinci** (1452–1519): An artist, Da Vinci dissected dead bodies (an illegal act) and made extensive drawings and descriptions of anatomical structures.
- **Zacharias Janssen** (1585–1638): A spectacle maker generally credited with creating the compound microscope.
- **William Harvey** (1578–1657): The first person to completely describe the circulatory system and support the idea that there was one circulatory system instead of two.
- **Anton van Leeuwenhoek** (1632–1723): Credited with being the first to use a microscope to observe sperm, red blood cells, protozoa, and bacteria, establishing the basis for bacteriology and refuting the idea of spontaneous generation.
- **Edward Jenner** (1749–1823): Developed a method of vaccination against smallpox using infective material from cowpox (1796).
- **René Laënnec** (1781–1826): Invented the stethoscope in 1816 because he was uncomfortable placing his ear against a woman's chest.
- **James Blundell** (1791–1878): Obstetrician who first successfully treated a patient with a transfusion of human blood in 1818.
- **Crawford Long** (1815–1878): Credited with first using ether as an anesthetic in 1842, but he delayed publication until after William Morton (a dentist) published about his own use of ether and nitrous oxide in 1846.
- **Gregor Mendel** (1822–1884): Considered the father of genetics, described inheritance of genetic traits through the study of pea plants (1856–1863).
- **Paul Langerhans** (1887–1888): Discovered in 1869 that beta cells in the pancreas produce insulin.
- **Louis Pasteur** (1822–1895): Developed the process of pasteurization (1862) to destroy pathogens and vaccines for chicken cholera (1879) and rabies (1885).
- **Robert Koch** (1843–1910): Credited with founding modern bacteriology and discovered bacteria that cause tuberculosis (TB) (1882) and cholera (1883) and the anthrax cycle (1886).
- **Wilhelm Roentgen** (1845–1923): Discovered X-rays in 1895 and their medical applications.
- **Karl Landsteiner** (1868): Classified the ABO blood groups in 1909 as well as other blood groups and identified immunological uses, allowing for safe transfusions.
- **Flu pandemic** (1918–1919): Infected 500 million people worldwide and killed approximately 50 million.
- **Frederick Banting** (1891–1941) and **J.J.R. Macleod** (1876–1935): Credited with the first successful treatment of a patient with insulin in 1922.
- **Sir Alexander Fleming** (1881–1955): Discovered penicillin from mold in 1928.

- **John Hopps** (1919–1998): Developed the first cardiac pacemaker in 1950.
- **James Watson** (1928–)/**Francis Crick** (1916–2004): Created the double-helix model of deoxyribonucleic acid (DNA) in 1953 based on work by Rosalind Franklin and Maurice Wilkins.
- **Jonas Salk** (1914–1995): Developed the first polio vaccine in 1955.
- **Christian Bernard** (1922–2001): Carried out the first heart transplant in 1967.
- **Human immunodeficiency virus/acquired immunodeficiency syndrome (HIV/AIDS) epidemic**: Began in the late 1970s and spread throughout the 1980s. The Pasteur Institute in France identified a retrovirus as the cause in 1983 and the National Cancer Institute in 1984. The first test for HIV was developed in 1985. In 1994, azidothymidine was recommended for treatment, and in 1995, modern drugs were developed. By 2000, at least 33 million people were infected worldwide.
- **Louise Joy Brown** (1978–): First test tube baby (in vitro fertilization [IVF]), born in 1978.
- **Dolly** (sheep) (1996–2003): First cloned mammal in 1996.
- **Ebola outbreak** (2014–2016): Small outbreaks have occurred in Africa since 1976, but the first major outbreak occurred in West Africa in 2014.

Healthcare Reform

The **key legislation** of healthcare reform includes the following:

- **Older Americans Act** (1965): provides community-based serves, such as transportation and meal services, for older adults.
- **Medicare Parts A and B and Medicaid** (1965): provide health insurance for those 65 and older, disabled, and with low income.
- **Consolidated Omnibus Budget Reconciliation Act** (1985): The allows employees to continue paying privately for insurance for 1 year after leaving a job.
- **Emergency Medical Treatment and Labor Act** (1986): requires hospitals/emergency departments to treat and stabilize all patients regardless of their insurance status or ability to pay.
- **Americans with Disabilities Act** (1990): protects the rights of individuals with disabilities.
- **Health Insurance Portability and Accountability Act** (1996): The requires insurance companies to cover preexisting conditions after 1 year and protects patient privacy.
- **State Children's Health Insurance Program** (1997): The provides health care for children whose families are of low income.
- **Patient Protection and Affordable Care Act** (2010): The expanded insurance coverage and expanded Medicaid.

Consumer Protection Measures

- **Pure Food and Drug Act** (1906): Consumer protection act intended to prevent the manufacture, sale, and transportation of adulterated foods, drugs, and alcoholic beverages.
- **Food and Drug Administration** (1906): Consumer protection agency that protects public health through the control and supervision of drugs, vaccines, blood transfusions, medical devices, cosmetics, foods, tobacco, and dietary supplements.
- **Harrison Narcotics Tax Act** (1914): Provides authority for regulation and taxation of production, importation, and distribution of coca/opium products, such as narcotics.
- **Federal Food, Drug, and Cosmetic Act** (1938): Provides authority to the FDA to oversee food, drug, and cosmetic safety.

- **Controlled Substances Act** (1970): Establishes US drug policy and five schedules under which drugs are classified, implemented by the Drug Enforcement Agency (DEA) and the FDA. The DEA, part of the Department of Justice, enforces this act and combats drug smuggling/use.

Medicare

Medicare, a federal health insurance program for those who have social security or bought into Medicare, provides payment to private healthcare providers, such as physicians and hospitals, but limits reimbursement and establishes requirements. Physicians receive 80% of usual customary and reasonable fees if they accept Medicare assignment. If they do not, they can charge up to 115% of what Medicare allows. Patients are responsible for the remaining 20% or up to 115% if the physicians do not accept Medicare. Parts include the following:

- **Medicare Part A**: Hospital insurance that covers acute hospital, limited nursing home care, and/or home health care, as well as hospice care for the terminally ill. There is no premium for this part.
- **Medicare Part B**: Medical insurance that covers physicians, advance practice nurses, laboratory tests, and physical and occupational therapy. Patients must pay an annual deductible as well as monthly payments.
- **Medicare Part D**: Prescription drug plan that covers part of the costs of prescription drugs at participating pharmacies. It is administered by private insurance companies, so monthly costs and benefits vary somewhat.

Medicaid

Medicaid is a combined federal and state welfare program authorized by Title XIX of the Social Security Act to assist people with low income with payment for medical care. This program provides assistance for all ages, including children. Older adults receiving Supplemental Security Income are eligible as are others who meet state eligibility requirements. The Medicaid programs are administered by the individual states, which establish eligibility and reimbursement guidelines, so benefits vary considerably from one state to another. Older adults with Medicare are eligible for Medicaid as a secondary insurance. Covered expenses include inpatient and outpatient hospital services, physician payments, nursing home care, home health care, and laboratory and radiation services. Adults who are legal resident aliens are ineligible for Medicaid for 5 years after attaining legal resident status. Some states pay for preventive services such as home and community-based programs aimed at reducing the need for hospitalization. States may opt to expand Medicaid to include more low-income recipients under the Patient Protection and Affordable Care Act (ACA).

The Patient Protection and Affordable Care Act

The **Patient Protection and Affordable Care Act (ACA)** (2010) aimed to provide insurance coverage for all Americans, who were required to purchase insurance through state and federal exchanges, and it included the expansion of Medicaid. However, the Supreme Court ruled that states were not required to expand Medicaid and could opt out. Additionally, the Republican Party has been opposed to the act and has weakened provisions. Major provisions of the ACA include the following:

- Insurance companies cannot deny coverage of preexisting conditions.
- Premiums for age groups must be the same for all members of the group.
- Premiums for the oldest adults cannot exceed three times the premiums of 18- to 24-year-olds.

- Essential health benefits must be covered, including emergency room visits, hospitalization, mental health care, substance abuse treatment, ambulatory services, laboratory testing, and rehabilitation services.
- Preventive care must be covered, e.g., mammograms, pap smears.
- Caps on annual or lifetime expenses are banned.
- Children can remain on their parents' insurance policy until age 26.

Cultural Influences on Health Care

The ability to understand differences among different **cultures** is an important skill, built on respect for others and knowledge. Some cultures (such as Asians) hold healthcare providers in high esteem and don't question their judgment, whereas others (such as African-Americans) may be more suspicious. It's especially important to understand what the patient believes about illness or health matters. Many cultures use complementary medicine, and the health educator should respect traditional healing and methods as long as the safety of the person is not compromised. Such things as healers, massage, and aromatherapy may provide emotional support to the patient and should be accommodated. If complementary treatment poses a health risk, such as *greta* (a lead-based drink), then the reasons why it should not be used should be clearly stated. Families can be advised that herbs often contain the same chemical compounds found in medications and the patient might have an overdose of an ingredient or a reaction to prescribed medications to encourage them to describe herbal treatments.

Impact of Globalization on Environmental Crises and Epidemics

Globalization may have a profound effect on the following:

- **Environmental crises**: As industrialization moves into developing countries, pollution and stripping of natural resources follows. The increased worldwide demand for goods means that countries are motivated more by monetary gain than by environmental concerns. Forests are decimated and water and air are polluted, but the global community has been unable to reach a worldwide agreement on environmental planning, resulting in increasingly common environmental problems.
- **Epidemics**: Because of the rapid increase in international marketing and travel, it is now almost impossible to completely contain an outbreak that at one time may have been local, such as Ebola (which has killed more than 11,000 people) and HIV (which has killed more than 35 million people). Additionally, health laws and practices vary widely, so not all populations have adequate preventive care or treatment. Thus, any outbreak can pose a worldwide threat. Viruses in particular pose a grave threat because they readily mutate and treatment may be unavailable or inadequate.

Influences of an Agung Population on Health Care

The **aging** population is a concern because advancing age correlates with increased healthcare expenditures because most chronic diseases occur in those older than age 65 (with costs peaking at about age 80). Factors associated with aging and increased costs include end-of-life care, long-term care, and chronic disease and complications (such as ulcer care, cardiac disease, and amputations associated with diabetes). The aging population will require additional healthcare providers (such as primary care and geriatric care physicians, nurses, and personal aides) and facilities (such as hospitals and long-term-care facilities). Funding for Medicare and Medicaid will need to be increased to meet the demand for treatment. Because Alzheimer's disease is primarily a disease affecting older adults, the need for custodial care for patients with dementia will increase. The need for hospice care and palliative care will increase also. Controversial issues, such as physician-assisted suicide, may gain more support as the population ages.

Health Problems in Developed and Developing Countries

Developed countries	Developing countries
The concern is to expand healthcare coverage.	The concern is to have healthcare coverage.
Obesity is a major concern.	Malnutrition is a major concern.
Equipment costs are high.	Equipment is outdated or absent.
Cutting-edge treatments are expensive.	Cutting-edge treatments are not available.
The number of physicians is inadequate.	Many have no access to physicians.
Standards for medical training are high.	Standards for medical training vary widely.
Primary diseases: heart disease, cancer, diabetes, Alzheimer's, stroke, chronic obstructive pulmonary disease (COPD).	Primary diseases: TB, malaria, HIV/AIDS, infectious diarrhea.
Those with the greatest healthcare problems use the most healthcare resources.	Those with the greatest means of paying use the most healthcare resources.
Rates of health literacy are fairly high.	Rates of health literacy are often low.
Immunization rates are high.	Immunization rates vary by country.
Drinking water is usually safe.	Drinking water is often contaminated.
Sanitation standards are high.	Sanitation standards are low.
Working conditions are generally regulated and are relatively safe.	Working conditions are often unregulated and unsafe.

Healthcare Expenditures over Time

Healthcare expenditures have increased markedly since the 1960s. Factors include the following:

- Increased population with an increased need for health care.
- Implementation of government-supported health care: Medicare and Medicaid.
- Increased percentage of older adults in the population.
- Technological advances—expensive equipment and supplies.
- Increased advertising of treatments to consumers, driving demand.
- Development of new—often costly—medications and treatments with lengthy, expensive processes needed to bring drugs to market.
- Increased regulations regarding the testing and approval of drugs and medical devices.
- Market forces driving prices higher.
- Inability of Medicare to negotiate drug prices.
- Uninsured patients—costs are offset by increased prices to insured patients.
- Increased demand for medications and treatments overall.
- Increased use of long-term care for older adults and the disabled.
- Concerns about malpractice driving increased use of imaging and laboratory tests.
- Ongoing international conflicts—Vietnam, Afghanistan, Iraq.

Models of Health Care in Different Cultures

Model	Culture	Description
Beveridge	Great Britain, New Zealand, Spain, Cuba, Scandinavian countries	Government is the sole payer and owns most medical facilities. Physicians may be public or private.

Bismarck	Germany, Belgium, France, Japan, Switzerland, Netherlands	People have insurance through employers and pay part of the cost. Everyone must enroll.
National health insurance	Canada, South Korea, Taiwan	Single-payer system into which everyone must contribute. The government is the sole payer, but healthcare providers are private.
Out of pocket	Most of the developing world (India, Cambodia)	Pay as you go with money or goods or go without care.
Mixed model	United States	VA Health is similar to the Beveridge model, Medicare to national health, employer-provided insurance to Bismarck, Uninsured to out of pocket.

Impact of Biomedical Devices on Health Care

Biomedical devices, such as physiological monitors (heart rate, blood pressure [BP]) and smart pumps, must interface between the patient and the device and then in digital form from the device to the information system, which must aggregate the data, and then to an interface that converts the data to HL7 for transmission to the electronic health record (EHR). Although standardization is occurring, there remain many communication standards, and interfacing with older systems or modified systems may pose problems. Additionally, interface requirements may vary among devices. The following are among the many elements that must be considered in determining the interoperability of biomedical devices: type of device, network connectivity, wired or wireless, type of data, security. Cost is another consideration because electronic equipment is more expensive than manual—although it is often more accurate and time saving—and maintenance costs may also be higher. Implantable biomedical devices, such as heart valves, cardioverter defibrillators, pacemakers, hip replacements, and breast implants are in common use and have extended patients' lives and their quality of life.

Impact of BCMA on Health Care

Bar code medication administration (BCMA) uses wireless mobile units at the point of care to scan the bar code on each unit of medication or blood component before it is dispensed. Scanning ensures that the correct medication and dosage are given to the correct patient, eliminating most point-of-administration medication errors. The BCMA system can also be used for specimen collection. This system requires monitoring and input from the pharmacy because each new bar code must be entered into the system. Additionally, some medications are received in bulk, so when they are dispensed in unit doses, bar codes must be individually attached. Staff must be trained to ensure that BCMA is used properly and consistently. The FDA has required that drug suppliers provide bar codes on the labels of medications and other biological product. BCMA increases safety for patients, and it integrates with the medication administration record and the information system of the organization, providing data for assessment.

Impact of RFID on Health Care

Radio-frequency identification (RFID) is an automatic system for identification that uses embedded digital memory chips, with unique codes, to track patients, medical devices, medications, and staff. A chip can carry multiple types of data, such as expiration dates, patient allergies, and blood types. A chip/tag may, for example, be embedded in the identification bracelet of the patient, and all medications for the patient are tagged with the same chip. Chips have the ability to both read and write data, so they are more flexible than bar coding. The data on the chips can be read by sensors from a distance or through materials such as clothing, although tags don't apply or read well on metal or in fluids. There are two types of RFID:

- Active: Continuous signals are transmitted between the chips and sensors.
- Passive: Signals are transmitted when in close proximity to a sensor.

Thus, a passive system may be adequate for administration of medications, but an active system would be needed to track movements of staff, equipment, or patients.

Impact of EHRs on Health Care

The **electronic health record (EHR)** is a digital computerized patient record that may be integrated with computerized physician/provider order entry (CPOE) systems and clinical decision support systems (CDSS) to improve patient care and reduce medical error. Software applications vary considerably, and standardization has not yet been implemented, so the organization must carefully review current and future anticipated needs as well as the ability of applications to interface with each other to provide for adequate measurements, data collection, reports, retrieval of data, analysis, and confidentiality. Increasingly, physicians in private practice, especially those in large groups, are employing EHRs, which may be different systems than those used in hospitals. Systems can be customized to meet the needs of the organization, but cost and lack of standardization remain barriers for implementation. However, studies indicate that there is a positive correlation between comprehensive EMR systems and patient outcomes. Quantifiable data about cost-effectiveness can be difficult to calculate because savings are often in terms of saved time, fewer interventions, and reduced error.

Impact of PHRs on Health Care

The **personal health record (PHR)** presents an opportunity for patient participation in health care in many ways:

- **Data entry**: Most PHRs allow patients to enter some types of data, although this may vary. Typical data entry includes personal and family health history, use of complementary therapy, and health behaviors (such as diet and exercise). Some also allow entry of health data, such as BP readings, daily blood sugar, and weight.
- **Delegation**: PHRs usually allow the patient to assign a delegate or proxy (such as a caregiver or immediate family member) to access the PHR. In most systems, parents can access information for a child until age 13; the child may assign a parent as proxy after that age, although selected information (such as sexual history, treatment) may be blocked.
- **Messaging**: Many systems allow patients to send secure messages to healthcare providers, in some cases routing them through a triage team.

Impact of CPOE Programs on Health Care

Computerized physician/provider order entry (CPOE) programs are clinical software applications that automate medication/treatment ordering, requiring that orders be typed in a standard format to avoid mistakes in ordering or interpreting orders. CPOE is promoted by Leapfrog as a means to reduce medication errors. About 50% of medication errors occur during ordering, so reducing this number can have a large impact on patient safety. Most CPOE systems contain a CDSS as well so that the system can provide an immediate alert related to patient allergies, drug interactions, duplicate orders, or incorrect dosing at the time of data entry. Some systems can also provide suggestions for alternative medications, treatments, and diagnostic procedures. The CPOE system may be integrated into the information system of the organization for easier tracking of information and data collection. This system is cost-effective, replaces handwritten orders, and allows easy access to patient records.

Impact of CDSS on Health Care

Clinical decision support systems (CDSS) are intended for the end user and comprise interactive software applications that provide information to physicians or other healthcare providers to help with healthcare decisions. The programs contain a base of medical knowledge to which patient data can be entered so an evidence-based inference system can provide patient-specific advice. For example, a CDSS system may be used in the emergency department so that staff can enter symptoms into the program and, based on the information entered, the CDSS program provides possible diagnoses and treatment options. The CDSS system may be used for a variety of purposes, such as the following:

- Record keeping and documentation, such as authorization.
- Monitoring patient treatments, research protocols, orders, and referrals.
- Ensuring cost-effectiveness by monitoring orders to prevent duplication or tests that are not indicated by condition/symptoms.
- Providing support in physician diagnosis and ensuring that treatments are based on best practices.

Role of HHS and CDC in Global Health

The **Centers for Disease Control and Prevention (CDC)**, an agency of the US Department of Health and Human Services (HHS), maintains the Center for Global Health (CGH), whose goal is to protect the health and safety of Americans and to reduce disease worldwide. CGH monitors outbreaks throughout the world, taking measures to prevent their spread, and it provides technical assistance, often in conjunction with the World Health Organization (WHO). CGH trains people from around the world in disease and outbreak investigation and provides response teams to assist countries in outbreak control. CGH carries out research in order to learn more about infectious agents, such as the Zika virus, and to develop immunizations to combat infectious diseases. CGH supports 10 disease detection centers in different countries around the world so that rapid response to outbreaks is possible. CDC works with other countries to develop public health systems and national public health institutes.

Role of WHO in Global Health

The **World Health Organization (WHO)**, established in 1948 and headquartered in Geneva, Switzerland, is charged with directing and coordinating international public health efforts as an agency of the United Nations. WHO focuses on communicable (such as Zika, HIV/AIDS, TB, and malaria) and noncommunicable (diabetes, mental health disorders, injuries associated with violence, vision impairment) diseases, preparedness, surveillance, and response through the provision of leadership and technical support, research, setting of standards, corporate services, and monitoring trends in health. When outbreaks or serious health problems occur, WHO leads the health response. There are currently 194 member states. WHO works in partnerships with other organizations, such as the CDC. WHO maintains a multilingual website with health information for healthcare providers and consumers, such as vaccination requirements for travel, and it issues numerous publications. The WHO issues the *World Health Report*, the *World Health Survey*, and *World Health Day*.

Calculations for Drug Dose, Pounds to Kilograms, and IV Flow Rate

Drug-Dose Calculations

Desired dose and volume/concentration on hand	Milligrams needed ÷ milligrams available in dose × volume per dose = current dose.	If an infant is to receive 65 milligrams of acetaminophen elixir that contains 80 milligrams per 5 mL: 65 mg ÷ 80 mg = 0.8125 × 5 = 4.06 = 4 mL.
Convert pounds to kilograms	Number of pounds ÷ 2.2 kg.	Infant's weight = 16 pounds. 16 ÷ 2.2 = 7.3 kg, rounded to 7 kg.
IV flow rate in drops per minute	Volume (mL) ÷ time (minutes) × drop factor = flow rate. Note: The standard drop factor is 15 drops/mL, but microdrip infusion sets (used with pediatrics or small volumes) have 60 drops/mL.	If a patient is to receive 1,200 mL of D5W in 5 hours (300 minutes), and the drop factor of the infusion set is 15 drops per mL: 1,000 ÷ 300 × 15 = 49.9 = 50 drops/min.

MEDICAL MATHEMATICS

RATE AND RATIO

A **rate** is the number of events per a given population (a rate of three infections per 100 patients) or per a time period (a rate of three infections per 1,000 device days). These figures are expressed as the **ratios** 3:100 and 3:1,000. Rates and ratios are accessible, and, for example, much infection control data is expressed by these statistics. However, data should be stratified, taking risk factors into account, and different rates should be derived for different populations for validity. The **risk ratio** is the ratio of incidence of infection/disease among those who have been exposed compared to the incidence among those who have not been exposed. A risk ratio of 1.0 suggests that there is an equal risk of infection. A higher number suggests the probability that those exposed will have higher rates. Thus, a number of 1.5 shows that the exposed group is 1.5 times more likely to become infected than those not exposed. A lower number suggests that exposure brings less risk of infection (immunity).

Roman Numerals, Rounding Rules, Military Time, and Body Surface Area

Medical Calculations		
Roman numerals (often are used in prescriptions)	I = 1, V = 5, X = 10, L = 50, C = 100, D = 500, and M = 1,000.	IV = 4, V = 5, VII = 7, IX = 9, XII = 12, XLII = 42.
Rounding rules	Round up for >0.5 and down if <0.5, although liquid medications are usually rounded to the closest 10th and injectable medications to the closest 100th if measurement is possible (such as with a syringe).	4.7 rounds up to 5.0. 4.3 rounds down to 4.0.
Military time	24-hour time format beginning with midnight at 0000/00:00 and ending at midnight at 2400/24:00. For hours after noon: 12 + number of hours. 6 p.m. = 1800/18:00.	6 a.m. = 0600/6:00. Noon = 1200/12:00. 6 p.m. = 1800/18:00. For partial hours, 6:36 p.m. = 1836/18:36.
Body surface area	Rule of 9s for adults: 9% head, trunk (front) 18%, trunk (back) 18%, arm 9%, leg 18%, perineum 1%.	Rule of 9s for infants & children: 18% head, trunk (front) 18%, trunk (back) 18%, arm 9%, leg 14%, perineum 1%.

Metric System

In medicine, the **metric system** is used almost exclusively, although height and weight may also be reported in standard measurements (feet, inches, and pounds) because metric measures are not in common use among the general population.

Metric system							
Measure	**Kilo**	**Hecto**	**Deca**	**BASE**	**Deci**	**Centi**	**Milli**
Weight	Kilogram (kg)			Gram (g)			Milligram (mg)
Volume	Kiloliter (kL)			Liter (L)			Milliliter (mL)
Length	Kilometer (km)			Meter (m)			Millimeter (mm)
Value to base	1,000	100	10	1	0.1	0.01	0.001

Using the chart above, 1 gram is equivalent to 1,000 kilograms and 0.001 milligrams. Micro- is also commonly used when calculating doses: a micro is one millionth (0.000001) of the base. Common metric conversions:

- 1 ounce = 30 mL.
- 8 ounces/1 cup = 240 mL.
- 1 quart = 32 oz = approximately 1 liter = 1,000 mL.
- 1 inch = 2.54 cm (generally rounded to 2.5).
- 1 teaspoon = 5 mL, 2 tablespoons = 1 oz.

Measures of Averages

Measures of averages locate the center point of a group of data:

- **Mean** is the average number. However, because the distribution can vary widely, the mean may not give an accurate picture. For example, if compiling data and one unit has 20 infections per 100 and the other has 1 infection per 100, the mean (21 ÷ 2) is 10.5 per 100, which has little validity.
- **Median** is the 50th percentile. For example, consider the following numbers: 1, 3, 7, 9, and 15. The number 7 is the median (middle) number. If there were an even number, the two middle numbers would be averaged: 1, 3, 7, 9, 14, and 15. The numbers 7 and 9 are averaged, so the median is 8. If there is an even distribution, the mean and median will be the same. The wider the difference between the two, the more uneven the distribution will be.
- **Mode** is the number occurring with the highest frequency. There may be bimodal or trimodal numbers.

Measures of Distribution

Measures of distribution show the spread or dispersion of data.

- **Range** is the distance from the highest to the lowest number. The term interquartile denotes the range between the 25th percentile and the 75th percentile. The range is usually reported with the median to provide information about the center point and the dispersion.
- **Variance** measures the distribution spread around an average value. It is often used to calculate the effect of variables. A large variance suggests a wide distribution, and a small variance indicates that the random variables are close to the mean.
- **Standard deviation** is the square root of the variance, and it shows the dispersion of data above and below the mean in equally measured distances. In a normal distribution, 68% of the data are within one deviation (measured distance) of the mean, 95% are within two deviations, and 99.7% are within three deviations.

Steps to Scientific Inquiry

Scientific inquiry is based on numerous steps to use when trying to understand phenomena. The steps to scientific inquiry include the following:

1. Observing a phenomenon: Thinking about the phenomenon and what it might mean.
2. Formulating a question about the phenomenon.
3. Gathering data about the phenomenon: Literature research, interviews, observations.
4. Formulating a hypothesis based on the question. For example, if the question is "Are adolescents better at playing video games than adults?", the hypothesis might be "Adolescents are better at playing video games than adults." The null hypothesis (which suggests that there is no relationship) is "Age does not affect the ability to play video games."
5. Experimenting: Carrying out tests to verify the hypothesis/null hypothesis and retesting to ensure that the results are valid.
6. Analyzing the data: Assessing not only the test results but also the possibility of undetected variables.
7. Reaching a conclusion: Based on analysis of the data.

8. Reporting findings: Usually in writing, but they may also be presented in video format, displays (such as slide shows), and with charts and graphs.
9. Conducting a follow-up evaluation and looking for potential errors in the experimental process or the data.

Data Analysis

Data should be aggregated and summarized for analysis of results, so a process should be established that identifies those responsible (individuals or groups) and the time frame for the processing and reporting of data. As the data are collected, they should be displayed in a manner that demonstrates the type of problems as well as the extent and causes. Having a written report that summarizes the findings and reaches conclusions based on the data is important, but for general comprehension, data should be displayed graphically in ways that make them accessible. When calculating rates of events (e.g., infection, death, or disease), the formula requires a numerator, which is the targeted event (such as wound infections), and a denominator, which is the pool (the total population studied). Statistics must include adequate denominator data for meaningful analysis, and this can require a longer period of time before a report can be generated.

Critical Thinking Skills When Making Decisions

When using **critical thinking skills** to solve problems, the individual must consider the purpose of a decision, how the decision will affect others, what possible choices can be made, what actions can be carried out, take action, and then assess the result of the actions. Techniques that facilitate critical thinking and decision making include the following:

- **Brainstorming**: Through free discussion, one-at-a-time presentation, or written suggestions.
- **Mapping**: Various methods of mapping may be used, including the creation of an affinity diagram.
- **Setting priorities**: Voting, multivoting, or the creation of a prioritization matrix.

The individual must use care to **avoid common logical fallacies**, such as the following:

- **Overgeneralization**: Extending a conclusion beyond what is logical.
- **Hasty generalization**: Jumping to a conclusion without adequate evidence.
- **Post hoc**: Assuming that just because something comes first it is the cause of that which comes second.
- **Appeal to authority**: Assuming that an authority is always correct.
- **False dichotomy**: Stating that there are only two choices and one is not possible, so the other must be the correct choice.

Critical Thinking Skills When Reading Research and Other Articles

There are many steps to **critical reading** and to evaluate research and other articles:

- **Consider the source** of the material. If it is in the popular press, it may have little validity compared to something published in a juried journal.
- **Review the author's credentials** to determine if a person is an expert in the field of study.
- **Determine the thesis,** or the central claim of the research. It should be clearly stated.
- **Examine the organization of the article,** determine whether it is based on a particular theory, and evaluate the type of methodology used.

- **Review the evidence** to determine how it is used to support the main points. Look for statistical evidence and sample size to determine if the findings have wide applicability.
- **Evaluate** the overall article to determine if the information seems credible and useful and should be communicated to administration and/or staff.

Documentation

Documentation is a form of communication that provides information on care was provided or action that was taken. Accurate, objective, and complete documentation of individual care is required by accreditation and reimbursement agencies, including federal and state governments. Purposes of documentation include the following:

- Carrying out professional responsibility.
- Establishing accountability.
- Communicating among health professionals.
- Educating staff.
- Providing information for research.
- Satisfying legal and practice standards.
- Ensuring reimbursement.

Although patient care documentation focuses on progress notes, there are many other aspects to charting. Doctors' orders must be noted, medication administration must be documented on medication sheets, and vital signs must be graphed. Flow sheets must be checked off, filled out, or initialed. Admission assessments may primarily involve checklists, or they may require extensive documentation. The primary issue in malpractice cases is inaccurate or incomplete documentation. It's better to over document than under document, but effective documentation does neither.

Methods of Data Collection

When developing **data collection procedures** to determine needs, the purpose of the data collection, the audience for which the data are intended, the types of questions to be answered, the scope of the research, and the resources available to carry out data collection must be determined.

Method	Issues Regarding Procedures
Direct observation	Observers must be selected and trained as to how to observe and when and how to record observations.
Interviews	Interview questions must be developed and validated and the interviewers must be given practice time.
Questionnaires	The type of questionnaire, the questions, and the Likert scale must be determined as well as the method of distribution (e.g., one on one, group, email, or Internet).
Record review	A form or checklist should be developed to guide the record review, and the records should be selected based on criteria established for the research.
Secondary analysis	The databases to be mined should be selected, and the criteria for the research should be established, including key words, time frames, and populations.

PRINCIPLES OF PHYSICS

The basic **principles of physics** include the following:

- **Constituent/Locality principle** (aka the local principle): An object is influenced only by those things in its immediate environment. So, for example, movement of an object in one area (San Francisco) cannot be influenced by movement of something in another area (Los Angeles). However, quantum physics casts doubt on this principle by suggesting that subatomic particles may behave differently.
- **Causality/Identity principle**: Cause leads to effect; the nature of an object determines the nature of its action (determinism).
- **Covariance principle**: The laws of physics are the same in all frames and transformations.
- **Invariance/Symmetry principle**: An action performed repeatedly yields invariant properties that remain the same regardless of how many times the action is repeated.
- **Equiprobability principle**: With a set of all possible outcomes, each item in the set has an equal probability of occurring as every other item in the set, based on the total number of possible outcomes (the formula is the number of total possible outcomes over the total number in the set).

PRINCIPLES OF CHEMISTRY

ATOMIC STRUCTURE

The basic **principles of chemistry** include the following:

- **Atomic structure**: The atom is comprised of a nucleus, which contains a positively charged proton and an uncharged neutron with a negatively charged electron orbiting around the nucleus. An atom is the smallest particle of matter that comprises an element. Atoms combine to create molecules. A molecule of water, for example, is composed of a compound of two atoms of hydrogen and one atom of oxygen: H_2O.
- **Elements**: Different kinds of atoms, based on the number of protons in the nucleus. For example, nitrogen has seven protons, and oxygen has eight.
- **Atomic stability**: The number of proteins is equal to the number of electrons.
- **Atomic mass**: Protons and neutrons are weighed in terms of atomic mass units (amu), neutrons, or daltons (all are equal to each other) with protons and neutrons approximately equal to one amu, whereas electrons weigh 1/800 amu, so the mass number is based on the number of protons and neutrons; the atomic number is based on the number of protons.
- **Atomic volume**: 99% of an atom is empty space, but the electrons repel other atoms, creating the illusion of solid volume.

PERIODIC TABLE AND ATOMIC VARIATIONS AND REACTIONS

The basic **principles of chemistry** include the following:

- **Periodic table**: Lists all known elements: 117 at the present.
- **Ions**: Atoms with fewer electrons (cations) are positively charged, and atoms with more elections (anions) are negatively charged. Cations are attracted to anions and anions to cations.
- **Isotope**: The same element with the same number of protons but a different number of neutrons, so they have a different atomic mass. Some isotopes are radioactive.
- **Oxidation-reduction reaction**: The oxidation number of the atom, molecule, or ion, based on the number of electrons, changes through gaining or losing electrons, such as occurs in the process of photosynthesis.

- **Acid–base reaction**: Occurs when an acid and a base are mixed, causing neutralization and producing salt and water. A substance is acidic if the reaction results in fewer total hydrogen atoms; it is basic if the reaction results in more total hydrogen atoms.
- **Equilibrium**: A reaction state in which there is no net change in components—forward reactions are equal to reverse reactions.
- **Reaction rate**: Change in concentration over a unit of time.

STATES OF MATTER AND PHASES

The **basic principles of chemistry** include the following:

- States of matter:
    - Solids: Atoms that are packed together create solids, which do not change in shape or volume.
    - Liquids: Atoms that remain close together but are not packed, so they can move about each other, resulting in a changing shape and an unchanging volume.
    - Gas: Atoms that are widely spaced and can move apart if not under pressure. The shape and the volume can change.
    - Plasma: Similar to gas but atoms have lost all or some electrons and positively charged ions move about freely. Plasma is found in stars and is the most common form of matter in the universe but is uncommon on earth.
    - Bose-Einstein condensates: Laboratory-created state of matter in which an element is cooled in order to almost stop molecular movement so the energy cannot transfer, resulting in clumping of atoms to create one giant atom.
- **Phases** result from the addition of energy to matter to cause a change from one state to another: Melting (solid to liquid), freezing (liquid to solid), sublimation (solid to gas), vaporization (liquid to gas), condensation (gas to liquid), and deposition/sublimation (gas to solid).

PRINCIPLES OF BIOMEDICAL SCIENCE

The **basic principles of biomedical science** are based on biology and medicine.

- Biology:
    - Cell theory: All living things are comprised of cells that can only develop from other living cells, and all life begins as one cell. Some remain at one cell—such as bacteria—but others multiply.
    - Homeostasis: A condition in which a living system remains in a steady state, such as through thermoregulation.
    - Evolutionary theory: A population changes over time in response to genetic changes resulting from mutations in the process of natural selection in which traits favorable to survival tend to endure. These changes that promote survival are referred to as adaptations.
    - Gene theory: Traits are inherited through the transmission of genes located on chromosomes, which are comprised of molecules of DNA.
- Medicine:
    - Human body systems, including principles of movement, body function, disease processes, and homeostasis.
    - Medical treatments, laboratory studies, research, medical devices, and innovations.

Hypothesis and Hypothesis Testing

A **hypothesis** should be generated about probable cause based on the information available in laboratory and medical records, epidemiologic study, literature review, and expert opinion. A hypothesis, for example, regarding infection, should include the infective agent, the likely source, and the mode of transmission: "Wound infections with *Staphylococcus aureus* were caused by the reuse and inadequate sterilization of single-use irrigation syringes used during wound care in the intensive care unit."

Hypothesis testing includes data analysis, laboratory findings, and outcomes of environmental testing. It usually includes **case control studies**, with two to four controls picked for each case of infection. They may be matched according to age, sex, or other characteristics, but they are not infected at the time they are picked for the study. **Cohort studies**, whose controls are picked based on having or lacking exposure, may also be instituted. If the hypothesis cannot be supported, then a new hypothesis or different testing methods may be necessary.

Analysis of Hypotheses

A hypothesis is a prediction of an outcome based on the relationship between variables and in response to a research question. Issues to consider when **analyzing the strength of a hypothesis** as part of research include the following:

- Is there a formally stated hypothesis?
- If there is no formally stated hypothesis, is the absence of the hypothesis justifiable by content?
- Is the hypothesis directly targeted at the problem of the research?
- Does the hypothesis seem logical from the literature review and rationale provided?
- Are there at least two variables (simple hypothesis) or more (complex)?
- Is the relationship between dependent and independent variables predicted by the hypothesis?
- Are the variables defined and measurable?
- Is the population/issue under study adequately identified?
- Is the format for testing adequate to determine if the hypothesis is supported or not?
- Is the hypothesis stated as a null hypothesis (there is no relationship between variables) or a research hypothesis (there is a relationship between variables)?
- Is the hypothesis worded clearly and unambiguously?

Hypotheses, Scientific Laws, and Scientific Theories

A **hypothesis** is limited in scope and makes a conclusion about one phenomenon, so even if it is proven to be true, the hypotheses is still too narrow to become a theory or law, although it may be used as evidence to develop either. A **scientific law** is an observation of something that occurs in nature, such as Newton's law of universal gravitation and Boyle's law regarding the relationship between pressure, volume, and temperature of gas. A law doesn't explain the reason or the cause for the observed phenomenon, it may be limited only to that which was observed, and it may not apply in other situations. Most scientific laws can be represented by mathematical equations and are discovered based on repeated experimentation. A **scientific theory**, on the other hand, is a comprehensive explanation of observed natural phenomena, which can be retested repeatedly with similar results and is widely accepted as valid. Examples of scientific theory include the theory of relativity and the big bang theory. However, like laws, conclusions about theories may be subject to change.

Selection of Products and Services

Selection of products and services includes the following:

- **Commitment**: Administration and staff must be committed not only to the financial outlay but to the process of change as with new products/services.
- **Identification of requirements**: Reviewing current status and needs, including making an inventory to determine what is available and what is lacking, and any possible constraints.
- **Identification of user needs**: Assessment of how the products/services will be used through surveys and observations.
- **Assessment of current products/services**: What is available and its costs and benefits.
- **Evaluation of vendors**: Request for information or review of websites and catalogs.
- **Comparison of products/services**: Assessment of differences in terms of costs and benefits to the organization of products/services from different vendors.
- **Training/Implementation considerations**: Those things required in order to use new products/services, such as changes in other equipment, electrical needs, staff training, and safety issues.
- **Contract negotiation/Purchasing**: Making a final decision.

Tools to Display Data

Charts, Tables, and Graphs

Presenting **data** in the form of charts, tables, and graphs provides a visual representation of the data that is easy to comprehend:

- **Line graphs** have an *x* and a *y* axis, so they are used to show how an independent variable affects a dependent variable. Line graphs can show a time series with time usually on the *x* (horizontal) axis. This graph might be used to show the number of infections per week/month.
- **Bar graphs** are used to compare and show the relationship between two or more groups. The graphs can show quantifiable data as bars that extend horizontally or vertically or they are stacked. Bar graphs might be used to show comparison data of different populations or to compare data from one time period to another.
- **Pie charts** are used to show what percentage an item is compared to the whole. A pie chart can show the distribution of infection control resources.
- **Tables** display data in the form of columns and rows, facilitating review of multiple items and the search for patterns.

Run Chart

The **run chart** is a type of line graph with a horizontal *x* axis (independent variables) and a vertical *y* axis (dependent variables, outcomes). The run chart, which provides a running record of a process over time, adds a horizontal median line, calculated according to the number of data points (data points + 1 divided by 2). A run is a sequence of data points on one side of the median line, ending when the line crosses the median. Runs may be color coded. For example, a run chart may plot the number of cases of influenza by month for a one-year period with increased runs indicated by a different color. It's important that data be recorded for a long enough period that normal variations are not misconstrued as significant runs. Run charts (with >25 data points) may demonstrate shifts (≥8 points on one side of the median line), trends (6 data points in the same direction), and patterns (≥8 similar fluctuations). These changes point to specific causes that require investigation.

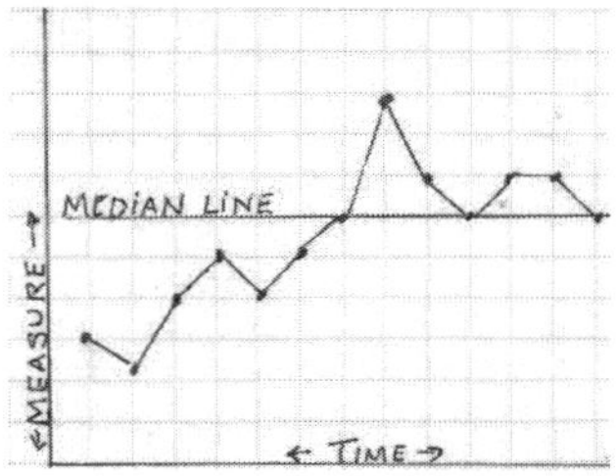

Scattergram

A **scattergram** is a type of graphic display of the relationship between two variables with one variable plotted from the *x* axis and one from the *y* axis. For example, the *x* axis may indicate age, and the *y* axis may indicate admissions to the emergency department. So, a data point is entered for each admission, correlating with age. Analysis of the scattergram, then, can indicate the most common age distributions of patients. The scattergram can be used to test for possible cause-effect relationships, although this type of relationship is not required and the scattergram is not proof of a correlation among data. As the data are plotted, repeat values are circled. With enough input, the data may begin to form a pattern. If this pattern is a straight line, there is evidence that there is a correlation between the two variables.

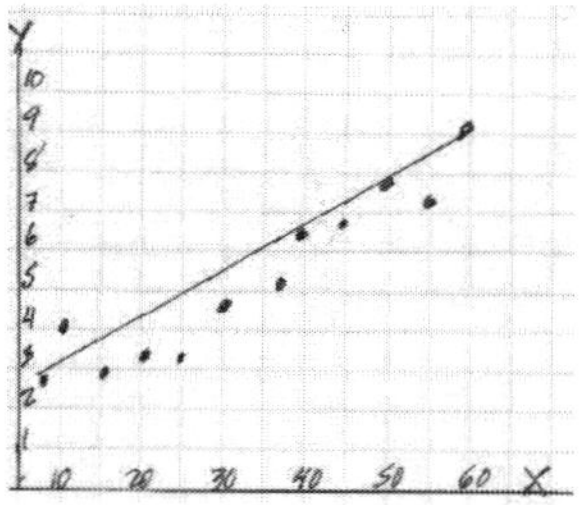

Trending Analysis

Trending analysis is applied to the run chart or control chart. In some cases, the data points of the chart may clearly go upward or downward, indicating a trend, but in other cases, there may be many variations, making the trend difficult to analyze. There are numerous rules applied to trending to help determine if variations are common cause variations or special cause variations:

- **Run** (shift): ≥7 consecutive data points all above or all below the median (run chart) or mean (control chart).
- **Trend**: At least 5 consecutive data points in either ascending or descending order or at least 6 with more than 20 total data points.
- **Cycle**: Up and down variation forming a sawtooth pattern with 14 successive data points, suggestive of a systemic effect on the data. If the trend is related to common cause variation, the variation may be demonstrated with 4–11 successive data points.
- **Astronomical value**: Data point unrelated to other points indicates a sentinel event or special cause variation.

Resources for Keeping Informed About Current Knowledge in Health Sciences

Resources for keeping informed about current knowledge in health science includes the following:

- **Internet**: The government has many websites devoted to current knowledge, such as the CDC site. A valuable online resource is the E-Updates and news from Adolescent Health: Think, Act, Grow provided by the Office of Adolescent Health (HHS). Major news sites, such as CNN, have daily health news. *Medical News Today* provides links to medical news articles.
- **Professional journals**: The *Journal of School Health* and the *American Journal of Health Education* provide health information of particular interest to health educators.
- **Public health/Local health agencies**: These agencies provide updates to the community about issues of current concern, such as outbreaks or emerging infections.
- **Professional organizations**: Organizations such as the American School Health Association and the American Association for Health Education carry out research and provide information and support to members as well as sponsoring state and national conferences, various workshops, and informative websites.

Medical Terminology

Common Medical Abbreviations, Acronyms, and Symbols

Abbreviations/ Symbols	Meaning	Abbreviations/ Symbols	Meaning
ac	before meals	**NPO**	nothing per mouth
pc	after meals	**VS**	vital signs (BP, temperature, pulse rate, respiration rate)
BID	twice daily	**ol or os**	left eye
TID	3× daily	**od**	right eye
QID	4× daily	**ou**	each eye
QOD	every other day	**mL**	milliliter
HS	hour of sleep	**cm**	centimeter
q	every (q 4 hr)	**L**	liter
c/o	complains of	**IM**	intramuscular
hr/hrs	hour/hours	**SQ**	subcutaneous
R/O	rule out	**IV**	intravenous
Dx	diagnosis	**mg**	milligram
Hx	history	**mm**	millimeter
w or c̄	with	**NG**	nasogastric
w/o or s̄	without	**stat**	immediately
BP	blood pressure	**prn**	as needed
TPR	temperature, pulse, and respirations		

Acronym	Meaning
ADHD	attention-deficit hyperactivity disorder
ADLs	activities of daily living
AIDS	acquired immunodeficiency syndrome
BM	bowel movement
CABG	coronary artery bypass graft
CAD	coronary artery disease
CNS	central nervous system
CT	computed tomography

CXR	chest X-ray
DNA	deoxyribonucleic acid
DNR	do not resuscitate
DVT	deep vein thrombosis
ECG/EKG	electrocardiogram
EEG	electroencephalogram
EMG	electromyogram
GERD	gastroesophageal reflux disease
HEENT	head, eyes, ears, nose, and throat
HIV	human immunodeficiency virus
IUD	intrauterine device
ICP	intracranial pressure
MRI	magnetic resonance imaging
NICU	neonatal intensive care
NSAID	nonsteroidal anti-inflammatory drug
OB	obstetrics
PET	positron emission tomography
PID	pelvic inflammatory disease
RNA	ribonucleic acid
ROM	range of motion
URI	upper respiratory infection
UTI	urinary tract infection

Prefixes, Suffixes, and Roots

Medical words are comprised of prefixes, suffixes, and roots in various combinations. The letter o (or i) is often used as a combining form:

Word	Prefix	Root	Suffix
anemia	an (without, less, not)	em (blood)	ia (condition)

The meaning of most medical words is derived by starting with the suffix; thus, anemia means literally a condition with less blood. All words must have at least one root.

Word	Root	o	Root	o	Suffix
gastroenterology	gastr (stomach)	o	enter (intestines)	o	logy (study of)

Common **prefixes** include the following:

Prefix	Meaning	Prefix	Meaning
anti	against	**tachy**	fast
eu	good	**brady**	slow
auto	self	**hemi**	half
ad	toward	**ab**	away from
inter	between	**intra**	within
peri	around	**poly**	many

Common **suffixes** include the following:

Suffix	Meaning	Suffix	Meaning
-ac, -ic, -ary, -al	pertaining to	**-ectomy**	surgical removal

-tion	process	-scopy	scope examination
-phobia	fear	-oma	tumor
-plegia	paralysis	-sis	condition, process
-itis	inflammation	-megaly	enlargement
-otomy	incision	-ectomy	surgical removal

Common **roots** include the following:

Root	Meaning	Root	Meaning
abdomin	abdomen	**my**	muscle
aden	gland	**nas**	nose
arth	joint	**neuro**	nerve
arter/i	artery	**ophthalm**	eye
brach/i	arm	**opt**	vision, sight
carcin	cancer	**or**	mouth
card/i	heart	**oste**	bone
cephal	head	**ot**	ear
chole	bile, gall	**pulmon**	lung
col	colon	**rect**	rectum
cyst	cyst, bladder	**sanguin**	blood
cyt	cell	**sept**	infection
derm	skin	**thorac**	chest
enceph	brain	**trich**	hair
enter	intestines	**ven**	vein
gastr	stomach	**viscer**	viscera
gyn	female	**voc**	voice
hem/hemat	blood	**xer**	dry

SIGNS AND SYMBOLS IN THE MEDICAL FIELD

Sign/Symbol	Interpretation	Sign/Symbol	Interpretation
	Flame: Includes flammable materials and gases and those that are self-heating or self-reactive.		Poison: Includes materials, gases, or substances that are extremely toxic and may result in death or severe illness.
	Corrosion: Includes substances that can cause skin burns, metal corrosion, and eye damage.		Irritant: Includes material, gases, or substances that are irritants to skin, eyes, and/or respiratory tract, acutely toxic, or have a narcotic effect.
	Health hazard: Includes carcinogens, toxic substances, and respiratory irritants.		Biohazard: Includes biological substances, such as body fluids, that pose a threat to humans. Appears on sharps containers that hold contaminated needles.

Medical Eponyms

Medical eponyms are names of diseases, conditions, and signs named after an individual (generally the person who discovered them).

Eponym	Definition	Attribution
Alzheimer's disease	Dementia	Alois Alzheimer identified plaques and tangles in the brain in 1906.
Crohn's disease	Inflammatory bowel disease	Burrill Crohn identified clinical manifestations in 1920.
Cushing syndrome	Primary adrenal gland disease	Harvey Cushing identified the disorder in 1912, publishing in 1932.
Down syndrome	Trisomy 21, genetic disorder	John Down described the syndrome in 1866.
Graves' disease	Hyperthyroidism	Robert Graves described the condition in 1835.
Hashimoto's thyroiditis	Autoimmune thyroid disease	Hakaru Hashimoto identified distinctive goiter characteristics in 1912.
Hodgkin's disease	Lymphoma	Thomas Hodgkin described the disease in 1832.
Huntington's disease	Genetic neurodegenerative disease	George Huntington studied a family with generations of the disorder and published a paper about it in 1872.
Parkinson's disease	Progressive neurological disorder	James Parkinson described the disorder in 1817.
Salmonellosis	Infectious disease	Theobald Smith identified the bacteria in 1885 and named it after the head of the laboratory, Daniel Salmon.
Tay–Sachs disease	Genetic neurological disease	Warren Tay noted eye changes associated with the disorder in 1881, and Bernard Sachs noted cellular changes in 1887.
Tourette syndrome	Tic disorder	Georges Gilles de la Tourette published descriptions of a group of people with this disorder in 1885.
Turner syndrome	Genetic disorder affecting females	Described by Henry Turner in 1938.
Wilms tumor	Kidney tumor	Max Wilms published his findings in 1899.
Zollinger–Ellison syndrome	Gastric disorder caused by tumor	Robert Zollinger and Edwin Ellison discovered the syndrome in 1955.

Medical Terminology Relating to Genetics

Term	Definition
Allele	form of a gene
Autosomal	chromosomes 1–23
Base pairs	form a rung on the DNA ladder
Chromosome	DNA molecule, carries genes
Clustered regularly interspaced short palindromic repeats (CRISPR)	technique for gene editing
DNA	contains genetic material in the cell
Dominant	one gene controls a trait
Gene	unit of heredity

Term	Definition
Genome	complete set of genes
Genotype	individual's unique genome
Haplotype	alleles contributed by a parent
Heterozygous	having two different alleles
Homozygous	having two identical alleles
Karyotype	set of chromosomes
Locus	site where genes are located on the genome
Meiosis	cell division in which one 46-chromosome reproductive cell divides into 4 cells with 23 chromosomes.
Mitosis	cell division in which one 46-chromosome cell divides into two 46-chromosome cells.
Mutation	change in the gene structure
Multifactorial	caused by multiple factors
Phenotype	observable characteristics
Recessive	two genes needed to control a trait
RNA	carries DNA instructions

Medical Terminology Relating to Pathology

Term	Definition
Antibody	proteins produced in an immune response
Antigen	toxin that causes an immune response
Anomaly	abnormal finding
Bacteria	one-celled microorganisms of various shapes (rods, spirals, spheres)
Benign	not dangerous, noncancerous
Biopsy	tissue sample removed from the body
Erythrocyte	red blood cell
Fungus	one-celled or multicelled organisms that produce spores
Gram-negative	staining technique to identify some thin cell-wall bacteria (pink stain)
Gram-positive	staining technique to identify some thick cell-wall bacteria (purple stain)
Hemolysis	breakdown, destruction of red blood cells
Hypoxia	condition with a lack of oxygen
Leukocyte	white blood cell
Negative	disease is not present
Pathogen	disease-causing microorganisms
Positive	disease is present
Purulent	containing pus
Reticulocyte	immature red blood cell
Thrombocyte	platelet
Virus	minute pathogenic agent that can only multiply in the living cells of a host

Medical Terminology Relating to Oncology

Term	Definition
Ablation	destruction of body part/tumor
Adenoma	noncancerous tumor origination in gland-like cells.
Adverse effect	unintended effects of treatment

Aggressive	fast growing, spreading
Baseline	initial measurements
Benign	noncancerous
Cachexia	severe wasting, malnutrition.
Carcinoma	cancer originating in the skin or the tissue lining the organs
Chemotherapy	drugs used to stop the growth of and kill cancer cells.
Grade	classification of tumor according to the degree of abnormality of the cells
Immunocompromised	impaired immune system from treatment or disease
Immunosuppression	damaging to the immune system
In situ	localized at the original site and has not spread
Leukemia	cancer of white blood cells
Malignant	cancerous
Metastasis	spread from the original tumor to other sites in the body
Radiotherapy	high-energy radiation used to kill cancer cells
Sarcoma	cancer originating in bone or supportive or connective tissues (blood, fat, muscles, cartilage)
Satellite tumor	groups of tumor cells near the primary tumor
Stage	extent of the cancer and the amount of spread

Resources to Support Health Education

Resources that support the health educator in compiling evidence-based practice research for the school setting include the following:

- **Local resources**: public health departments, local hospitals, and clinics.
- **Journals**: Health Education Journal, American Journal of Health Education, American Journal of Public Health Research, American Journal of Food and Nutrition, American Journal of Health Promotion, American Journal of Health Education, and American Journal of Health Behavior.
- **Government documents**: The US Government Publishing Office provides materials for all governmental departments.
- **Databases**: State School Health Policy Database, the National Nursing Database, Cumulative Index to Nursing and Allied Health Literature (CINAHL) nursing journal databases, PubMed, Cochrane databases, Educational Resources Information Center (ERIC), and MedlinePlus.
- **Online resources**: CDC (national health education standards); American Alliance for Health, Physical Education, Recreation and Dance; American Academy of Pediatricians; Substance Abuse and Mental Health Services Administration (SAMHSA); Health.gov (guidelines for diet, physical activity, and health literacy); and the Office of Disease Prevention and Health Promotion.

Medical and Dental Dictionaries and Multimedia Resources

Dictionaries include the following:

- **Medical dictionaries**: Taber's Cyclopedic Medical Dictionary, Inductel Med (software), Mosby's Medical Dictionary, Merriam-Webster's Medical Dictionary, Stedman's Medical Dictionary, Dorland's Illustrated Medical Dictionary.
- **Dental dictionaries**: Mosby's Dental Dictionary, Stedman's Medical Dictionary for the Dental Professions, McGraw-Hill Dental Dictionary.

Multimedia resources are available from numerous Internet sites. Some charge a fee, but many are free and can be used with or without credit:

- **Government sites** such as the CDC: Government publications and most photos and illustrations on those sites are copyright free unless otherwise indicated and can be used and copied.
- **Photos and illustrations**: Public Health Image Library, Wikimedia, Unsplash, FreeImages.
- **Clip art/Animated gifs**: Phillip Martin's Clip Art, Classroom Clipart, The Teacher Files.
- **Films**: Movie Licensing USA, Annenberg Learner, PBS Video, The Open Video Project.
- **Various media**: NASA Image Exchange, The Library of Congress, National Science Digital Library.
- **Music**: YouTube, Free Music Archive.

Design and Delivery of Images

Images help to facilitate learning, and visual enhancement (illustrations, photographs) is common in all types of print and digital media. Visualization as part of the learning process is common although not universal, especially in those with learning disabilities. Images transmit information, and the educator must ensure that the image selected transmits the intended message. Although studies show that learning is the same with black and white images as with colored images, most learners prefer colored images. However, for print media, color is more expensive. The size of the image must be considered in terms of cost and use. Important details must be easily discerned. If the image contains words or numbers, these should be easily read. Images may be copyrighted, so the educator must consider whether use is for educational purposes and meets requirements of fair use or is for commercial purposes, which may require permission to use the image or may require payment.

Design and Delivery of Handouts, Flyers, and Other Forms of Documentation

Written **handouts, flyers, or other forms of documentation** are a fixture in classes, but many end up in the wastebasket without ever being used, so thought should be given to providing materials that are useful:

- Handouts that simply copy a slide show presentation or repeat everything in the presentation are less helpful than those that summarize the main points.
- Giving out handouts immediately prior to a discussion ensures that most of the class will be looking at the handout instead of the speaker. Thus, handouts should be placed in a folder or binder and passed out before class so people can peruse them in advance or should be passed out at the end of class.
- Handouts can be used to provide guidance or worksheets for small group discussions.
- Poster-type handouts (with drawings or pictures) that can be placed on bulletin boards are useful.
- Handouts should be easily readable and not smudged copies of newspaper articles or small-print text.
- Journal and other magazine and newspaper articles can be copied for use in classrooms and may be invaluable educational tools.

Use of Electronic/Audiovisual Technology in the Design and Delivery of Educational Materials

Many issues must be considered when teaching and determining the appropriate **electronic/audiovisual materials.** The physical environment is a major consideration, especially when using electronic/audiovisual materials:

- First, everyone in the room must be able to hear and see. In a small room, a television or computer screen may suffice, but in a large space, a projection screen should be used.
- Another issue is lighting. Some projectors have low resolution and the lights need to be turned off/dimmed or windows should be covered. Turning lights on and off a dozen times during a presentation can be very distracting. A small portable light at a speaker podium or an alternate presentation can be used.
- The text size for presentations is another issue: slide shows or other presentations that include text must be of a sufficient font size to be read from the back of the room.

Use of Videos/Videoconferencing/Teleconferencing in the Design and Delivery of Educational Materials

Videos are a useful adjunct to teaching because they reduce the time needed for one-on-one instruction (increasing their cost-effectiveness). Good-quality videos can be expensive to produce, although commercial products are available. Passive presentation of videos has limited value, but focused viewing in which the educator discusses the purpose of the video presentation prior to viewing and then is available for discussion after viewing can be very effective. Videos are also effective tools for demonstrating patient care techniques, such as wound care. Additionally, videos can be placed on course or learning management systems for anytime access. Providing focused questions for use during the video presentation helps increase retention by promoting active involvement. **Videoconferencing/Teleconferencing** allows for audio and visual collaboration at a distance and can be a valuable tool for education, providing access to experts without the transportation costs. In teleconferencing, students may be at multiple sites while interacting with each other and an instructor.

Design and Delivery of Reports

Many issues must be considered in the **design and delivery of reports,** such as the following:

- **Purpose**: The purpose of the report is primary and should be determined first. For example, the purpose may be to update recipients, gain support, indicate problems, or show progress.
- **Recipients**: Those who need to receive the report must be identified and grouped according to discipline or needs because different individuals or groups may need different reports, some that may be more complex and detailed than others.
- **Delivery mode**: This is the method of delivery, which may include a paper document, email, electronic document, spreadsheet, or PDF file.
- **Format**: The format may vary from detailed narratives to simplified graphs and illustrations or some combination. Whenever possible, templates should be used. Formatting should include such considerations as color, font, font size, and white space.
- **Size**: This refers primarily to the length (pages, kilobytes, or megabytes) of the report.
- **Frequency**: Reports may be issued at different frequencies, depending on the recipient and the purpose.

Medical Sciences

Body Planes and Anatomic Terms

Body planes include the following:

- **Sagittal/Lateral**: Vertical plane separating the right from the left.
- **Median/Midsagittal**: Sagittal plane at the midline (middle) separating the body into equal halves.
- **Coronal/Frontal**: Vertical plane separating the anterior (front) from the posterior (back).
- **Axial/Transverse**: Horizontal plane that separates the body into the superior (upper) and inferior (lower) parts.

A **cross section** is an axial/transverse (horizontal) cut through a tissue specimen or body structure, whereas a **longitudinal section** is a sagittal or coronal (vertical) cut.

Medial is toward the midline, whereas **lateral** is away from the midline and to the side. **Distal** is farthest from the point of reference, and **proximal** is closest. When describing an area of the patient's body, the description should be patient oriented, using phrases such as "patient's left" and "patient's right" to ensure accurate interpretation.

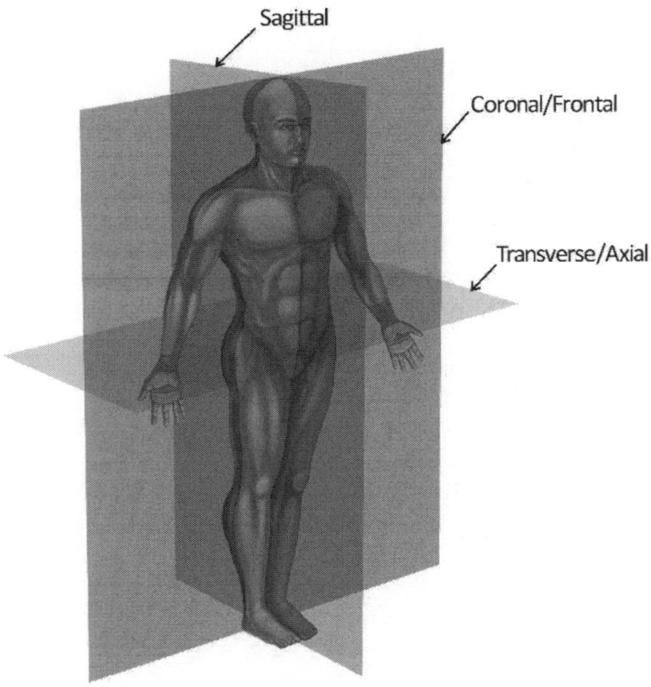

Abdominal Regions of the Body

Abdominal regions include the following:

- A: Right hypochondriac
- B: Epigastric (epi = on, above)
- C: Left hypochondriac
- D: Right lumbar
- E: Umbilical
- F: Left lumbar
- G: Right iliac
- H: Hypogastric (hypo = below, beneath, less than normal)
- I: Left iliac

The abdomen may also be divided into four quadrants (sections) with the umbilicus (navel) at the center: Right upper quadrant (RUQ), right lower quadrant (RLQ), left upper quadrant (LUQ), and left lower quadrant (LLQ).

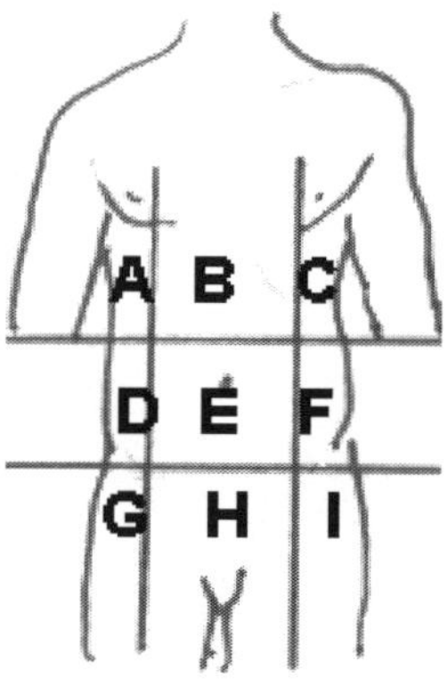

Homeostasis

Homeostasis is the tendency of an organism (such as the human body) to maintain stability in physiological states. The primary modes of maintaining homeostasis include the following:

- **Negative feedback loop** (counteracts a homeostatic change): Homeostasis is primarily controlled through negative feedback loops to maintain such things as temperature, hydration, glucose levels, and electrolyte levels. For example, in response to stress, the hypothalamus secretes corticotropin-releasing hormone, which stimulates the pituitary gland to release adrenocorticotropic hormone (ACTH), which activates the adrenal glands to produce increased cortisol. Cortisol, in turn, stimulates gluconeogenesis (the formation of glucose from noncarbohydrate sources) and elevates the blood glucose level to provide the energy needed to combat the stressor.
- **Positive feedback loop** (amplifies a system): For example, during childbirth, the fetal head pressing against the nerves in the cervix sends a stimulus to the brain, which in turn releases oxytocin, which causes uterine contractions, increasing pressure on the cervix and continuing the cycle of release of oxytocin.

Role of Insulin in Maintaining Glucose Levels and Providing Energy

About 2% of the pancreas has an endocrine function, and this part contains beta cells in the islets of Langerhans that produce **insulin** in response to chemical, hormonal, or neurological stimulus. When levels of glucose, amino acids (arginine and lysine), and gastrointestinal hormones (secretin, glucagon, gastrin, and cholecystokinin) increase, these increases trigger an increased release of a precursor of insulin, which converts into insulin in the liver. Although insulin is normally released continuously in small amounts, a bolus of insulin is produced in order to maintain homeostasis of glucose levels, which increase with the ingestion of food. Insulin levels are usually their highest about an hour after ingesting food. The function of insulin is to lower the level of blood glucose by moving it into the muscle, liver, and adipose (fat) cells, where it is used for energy. In the cells, the insulin metabolizes glucose, stores glucose in the form of glycogen, facilitates fat storage, and helps to transport amino acids into the cells. Insulin-dependent tissues (skeletal muscle and adipose tissues) have insulin receptors. In the liver, insulin facilitates the conversion of glucose to glycogen for storage.

Endocrine System and Hormones

Endocrine System and Hormones Produced	
Hypothalamus	Links the endocrine and nervous systems. Produces hormones that are stored in the posterior lobe of the pituitary gland and stimulates the pituitary to release hormones.
Pineal gland	Secretes melatonin and dimethyltryptamine, which control sleep cycles and dreaming.
Pituitary gland	The posterior lobe secretes oxytocin (uterine contractions/lactation) and vasopressin (aka antidiuretic hormone) (raises blood pressure, promotes water reabsorption). The anterior lobe secretes hormones that control cell growth (somatotropin) and body growth (growth hormone), and it controls thyroid release of hormones (thyrotropin), release of steroids from the adrenal glands (corticotropin), and reproductive functions (follicle-stimulating hormone and luteinizing hormone).
Thyroid gland	Secretes hormones that control protein production, basal metabolic rate, and oxygen consumption (T3, T4, and calcitonin).
Parathyroid glands	Secretes parathyroid hormone, which controls the use of calcium.
Adrenal glands	Produce cortisol (roles in metabolism), aldosterone (water and sodium levels), and androgens (male hormones).
Ovaries	Secrete female hormones (estrogen and progesterone).
Testes	Secrete androgens (testosterone).

Renal Excretory System

The **kidneys** are located on the right and left sides posterior to the peritoneal cavity and are responsible for the fluid balance and acid–base balance in the body. The cortex (body) is encased in a capsule. Inside the cortex are pyramids, papilla, major and minor calyces, and renal pelvis leading to the ureter that carries urine to the bladder. The nephron is the functional unit responsible for filtering the blood (about 1200 mL/min) and removing waste products. The nephron includes the following:

- **Glomerulus** (capillaries surrounded by Bowman's capsule): Fluids and solutes move from the blood across capillary membranes into Bowman's capsule, but plasma proteins and blood cells stay in the blood because they are too large.
- **Bowman's capsule**: Glomerular filtrate (similar to plasma) moves into the proximal convoluted tubule.
- **Proximal convoluted tubule**: Water and electrolytes are reabsorbed.
- **Loop of Henle**: Solutes, including glucose, are reabsorbed.

- **Distal convoluted tubule**: Sodium and water are reabsorbed according to the antidiuretic hormone (ADH) levels (from the pituitary gland) and aldosterone (from the adrenal cortex).
- **Collecting duct**: Carries urine into the calyces of the kidney for excretion.

GASTROINTESTINAL TRACT

Gastrointestinal Tract: Digestion	
Body Part	**Function**
Mouth	Chews, moistens, begins carbohydrate hydrolysis (breakdown of food by enzymes), creates a bolus of food. Connected to the esophagus by the pharynx.
Esophagus	Transports the bolus through the lower esophageal sphincter (which prevents backflow up the esophagus) to the stomach by peristalsis (wave-like contractions).
Stomach	Churns, secretes acids and enzymes, begins hydrolysis of proteins, creates chyme (a more fluid substance).
Small intestine (about 20 feet long)	**Duodenum**: Accepts chyme and digests food to prepare for absorption. **Jejunum**: Absorbs most nutrients from foods, including B_{12}. Accepts bile from the liver to digest fats and pancreatic enzymes from the pancreas to digest proteins, fats, and carbohydrates. **Ileum**: Contains the ileocecal sphincter that controls the flow of chyme into the large intestine.
Large intestine (about 5 feet long)	**Cecum**: Reabsorbs fluids and electrolytes. **Appendix**: Serves no function. **Ascending, transverse, descending**: Reabsorbs water, vitamin K, and electrolytes to form feces.
Rectum	Stores the feces.
Anus	Contains sphincters that control the expelling of feces.

DIABETES MELLITUS

CHILDREN

There has been a marked increase in **diabetes mellitus in children**, correlating with increasing obesity and lack of exercise. This is especially true for minority children. Until recent years, type 1 (insulin-dependent) diabetes was most common in children and type 2 was rare, but now 8%–45% of children presenting with diabetes have type 2 (insulin deficiency), although it may be difficult to determine the type with the initial diagnosis. Most cases are diagnosed during puberty when hormone changes affect insulin, but children as young as 4 have been diagnosed. Because obesity is a significant risk, health risk reduction efforts are aimed at improving diet and increasing exercise, but intervention aimed at the whole family is often more effective than tailoring diet and exercise just to the needs of one child. The family should work with a nutritionist. Screening with fasting blood sugar is normally done about every 2 years for those at risk or those presenting with symptoms.

TYPES 1 AND 2

Diabetes mellitus is the most common metabolic disorder in children, affecting about 1.5 million children and adolescents with 70%–85% with type 1 and the rest with type 2. More than 6% of adults have diabetes, but only two-thirds are diagnosed.

Type 1: Immune-mediated form with insufficient insulin production because of the destruction of pancreatic beta cells

Symptoms:

- Pronounced polyuria and polydipsia.
- Short onset.
- May be overweight or have recent weight loss.
- Ketoacidosis present on diagnosis.

Treatment:

- Insulin as needed to control blood sugar.
- Glucose monitoring 1-4 times daily.
- Diet with carbohydrate control.
- Exercise.

Type 2: Insulin-resistant form with defect in insulin secretion

Symptoms:

- Long onset.
- Obese with no weight loss or significant weight loss.
- Mild or absent polyuria and polydipsia.
- Ketoacidosis or glycosuria without ketonuria.
- Androgen-mediated problems such as hirsutism and acne (adolescents).
- Hypertension.

Treatment:

- Diet and exercise.
- Glucose monitoring.
- Oral medications.

HYPOTHYROIDISM

Hypothyroidism occurs when the thyroid produces inadequate levels of thyroid hormones. In about 95% of those with the disease, the abnormality is within the thyroid gland. If hypothyroidism is caused by failure of the pituitary or hypothalamus gland, it is referred to as central hypothyroidism. Normally, the hypothalamus releases thyrotropin-releasing hormone (TRH), triggering the pituitary gland to release thyroid-stimulating hormone (TSH), which in turn stimulates the thyroid to produce thyroid hormones. The thyroid absorbs iodine and then combines it with tyrosine to produce T3 (20%) and T4 (80%) thyroid hormones. These hormones are required by the body to convert oxygen and calories to energy. If more T3 hormone is needed, the body is able to convert T4 to T3 in other organs, such as in the hypothalamus. Anything that impairs this system at any level can result in hypothyroidism. This can include exposure to radiations, some drugs (lithium), overconsumption or underconsumption of dietary iodine, and surgical excision of the thyroid.

Malabsorption Disorders

Crohn's Disease/Regional Ileitis

Crohn's disease, also known as regional ileitis, manifests with inflammation of the gastrointestinal (GI) system. Inflammation is transmural (often leading to intestinal stenosis and fistulas), focal and discontinuous with aphthous ulcerations progressing to linear and irregular-shaped ulcerations. Granulomas may be present. Common sites of inflammation are the terminal ileum and cecum. This condition is usually chronic, but an acute flare-up may mimic appendicitis. Children may have delayed development and stunted growth, affecting their adult stature. There is a genetic component to the disease. Up to 75% of patients with Crohn's disease eventually require surgery, commonly an ileostomy, because of the severity of symptoms or complications such as bowel perforation. Signs and symptoms

- Perirectal abscess/fistula in advanced disease.
- Diarrhea usually presents with colonic disease. May have nocturnal bowel movements, watery stools, and rectal hemorrhage.
- Anemia may develop with chronic bleeding.
- Abdominal pain is most common in the lower right quadrant, usually indicating transmural inflammation; may include postprandial pain and cramping.
- Nausea and vomiting (usually related to strictures of the small intestine).
- Malabsorption.
- Fever, night sweats.

Celiac Disease, Lactose Intolerance, and Parasitic Diseases

Disorder	Pathology	Signs and symptoms	Treatment
Celiac disease	Autoimmune disorder with intolerance to gluten, which causes destruction of the surface epithelium of the small intestine.	Loss of weight. Diarrhea, bloating, steatorrhea (fatty stools), azotorrhea (nitrogenous wastes in stool/urine). Anemia. Vitamin/Iron deficiency (folate, B_{12}).	Gluten-free diet. Treatment for anemia as indicated.
Lactose intolerance	Deficiency of intestinal lactase causes increased lactose in intestine.	Diarrhea, cramping.	Oral lactase (Lactaid). Dairy-free diet.
Parasitic diseases (giardiasis, strongyloidiasis, coccidiosis)	Parasites live/multiply within the intestines, causing damage to the intestinal mucosa.	(Varies with parasitic agent.) Loss of weight. Diarrhea, steatorrhea.	Antiparasitic drugs as indicated for the specific parasite.

Obesity

Obesity increases the risk of coronary artery and heart disease, diabetes, and hypertension. Obesity limits mobility and stresses the cardiovascular and respiratory systems (reduces lung capacity), increasing the risk of respiratory infections, stroke, and heart attack. Fat deposits may invade the organs, such as the liver, impairing function. Obesity increases the risk of various types of cancer, including kidney, liver, and colorectal. Obesity is associated with gastroesophageal reflux disease and obstructive sleep apnea as well as joint disease and osteoarthritis. The body mass index (BMI) is a measurement that uses height and weight as an indicator of obesity/malnutrition, although this cannot be used alone to diagnose obesity. Tables are available to simplify calculations, but BMI can be calculated manually as follows:

$$BMI = \frac{Weight\ (kg)}{(Height\ (m))^2} = \frac{(Weight\ (lb)) \times 703}{(Height\ (in))^2}$$

Resulting scores for adults age 20 and over are interpreted according to this chart:

Below 18.5: Underweight
18.5-24.9: Normal weight
25.0-29.9: Overweight
30 and above: Obese

Effects of Pressure on the Human Body

Ambient air **pressure** at sea level is 1 atmosphere absolute (1 ATA), which equals 760 mm Hg/14.7 psi. The pressure decreases at higher altitudes and increases under water (diving). As the pressure increases, gas in the blood forms bubbles, which can result in ischemia, tissue injury, and collapse of the cardiovascular and neurological systems. **Intravascular/Arterial gas embolism** may occur with seizures and loss of consciousness, paralysis or peripheral weakness, and pneumothorax/pneumopericardium. **Decompression sickness** may occur within 24 hours of return and includes joint pain, hearing loss, vertigo, and neurological and respiratory impairment leading to complete collapse. At high altitude, oxygenation may be inadequate, leading to **acute mountain sickness**. Some may experience only shortness of breath, but others may develop **high-altitude cerebral edema** (HACE) with swelling of the brain tissue and increased intracranial pressure. The person may be confused, unable to walk, severely lethargic, and experience seizures and coma. Others may develop **high-altitude pulmonary edema** (HAPE) with fluid buildup in the lung, resulting in severe shortness of breath, cough, and cyanosis, leading to respiratory collapse. HACE and HAPE can lead to death if untreated and the person remains at high altitude.

Effects of Torque and Tension on the Human Body

Torque is a force that produces rotary motion (similar to a lever). Force increases the further it is from the axis (joint) of movement. When assessing torque, three forces are considered: (1) the force of the muscle, (2) the angle of the axis/joint, and (3) the length of the limb/muscle. Torque is involved in pushing and pulling, but it can lead to injury, so methods of reducing torque are important. The individual should mobilize other muscles rather than depending just on the joint and the attached ligaments and tissue.

Tension, meaning to stretch (Latin), is the force along the length of something, such as a muscle, used to exert pull. When muscles are tense, they stay partially contracted, leading to stress and pain, such as lower back pain. People may feel that their muscles are tight to the point that it restricts their activity. Muscle tension may be secondary to anxiety, which tends to tighten the muscles of the shoulders, neck, and head.

Effects of Movement and Elasticity on the Human Body

Movement involves the flexion and contraction of muscles and the support of the musculoskeletal system. Movement maintains muscle strength and elasticity, increases circulation and oxygenation of tissues as well as venous return, promotes peristalsis and digestion, strengthens the heart muscle and the lungs, strengthens the bones and prevents osteoporosis, prevents stasis and formation of blood clots, improves balance, and provides a sense of well-being. In addition, exercise reduces blood glucose levels and helps to control weight.

Elasticity is a function of muscles and tendons. When a muscle extends, the tendons and muscles stretch to accommodate movement, but when the muscle contracts, the muscle and tendons must shorten again in order to return to their resting state. Exercise, such as yoga and stretching, may improve elasticity, allowing the person to be more flexible. Inactivity or disorders that prevent adequate movement may impair elasticity, resulting in muscle contractions and weakness.

Musculoskeletal System

Bones

The **musculoskeletal system** includes 203 bones: long bones (femur in the thigh), short bones (carpal bones in the fingers), and flat bones (sternum). The outer hard shell of the bone is the cortex, and the inner porous area is the trabecular bone. The vertebrae lack the cortex layer. Long bones have three parts: The middle section is the diaphysis, followed by the metaphysis, and then the epiphysis (the bone ends). In growing children, an epiphyseal plate of cartilage separates the metaphyses and epiphyses, allowing bone growth. This closes in adults, but damage to this area in a child may impair bone growth. The middle part of the short bones contains yellow bone marrow (fatty tissue). Red bone marrow, which produces blood cells, is found in the middle of flat bones (pelvis, sternum, ribs, and scapula) and at the ends (epiphyses) of long bones. The skeletal system is connected by cartilage, tendons, and cartilage, and it is protected, supported, and allowed movement by about 700 soft-tissue muscles.

Muscles

Muscles are comprised of muscle fibers (elongated cells). Muscle tissue is contractile and elastic and allows movement of body parts by shortening and lengthening. There are three types of muscles in the human body:

- **Skeletal muscle**: These are voluntary muscles that are attached to the bones of the head, neck, arms, and legs and facilitate movement. The cells are threadlike—long and narrow—and have striations and many nuclei. Nerve stimulation causes muscle contraction, and the muscle relaxation occurs when the stimulation stops.
- **Smooth muscle**: These are involuntary muscles that make up the walls of blood vessels and hollow organs, such as the bladder. Smooth muscle cells are shorter than skeletal muscle cells, spindle-shaped with a single large nucleus, and lacking in striations. Smooth muscle contractions, for example, facilitate peristalsis.
- **Cardiac muscle**: These involuntary muscles are comprised of muscle cells that are found only in the heart and are branched and striated with a single nucleus. They are joined end to end by intercellular discs. Cardiac muscle pumps the blood through the heart and into the vessels.

Brain and Spine

The brain is protected by the skull and the meninges, three layers of lining: the dura mater, arachnoid mater, and the pia mater. The brain tissue is comprised of gray matter (neurons [nerve cells]) and white matter (covered nerve pathways that conduct messages). The main part of the brain is the cerebrum, which is composed of two hemispheres that contain the frontal parietal, temporal, and occipital lobes. The cerebrum controls higher brain functions, including thoughts, speech, vision, hearing, and actions. The cerebellum lies in the back of the brain below the cerebrum and controls equilibrium and coordination. The brain stem controls involuntary functions, such as respirations, heart rate, temperature control, and nerve transmission. The brain stem is continuous with the spinal cord, which is also protected by the meninges and by the vertebrae (cervical, thoracic, and lumbar). Cerebral spinal fluid circulates within the subarachnoid space of the brain and spinal cord.

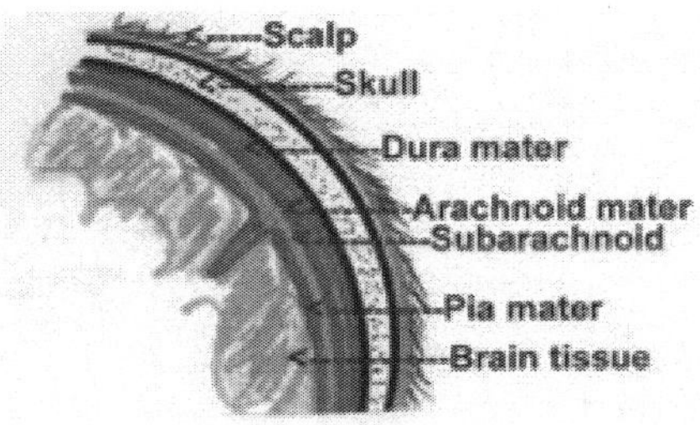

Neurological System

The **neurological (nervous) system** consists of the central nervous system (CNS) (brain, spinal cord, and nerves) and the peripheral nervous system (PNS) (sensory neurons, ganglia [nerve clusters], and nerves connecting to the CNS). The brain consists of the cerebrum (frontal, temporal, parietal, and occipital lobes), the cerebellum, and the brainstem, which is continuous with the spinal cord. The PNS is divided into the autonomic nervous system and the somatic nervous system. The autonomic nervous system controls the body's organs and maintains homeostasis (balance). Functions of the autonomic nervous system include heart rate and function, respiration, digestion, sexual arousal, and other systems. The somatic nervous system comprises cranial and spinal nerves that connect the CNS to the skeletal muscles and skin. The somatic nervous system is the voluntarily controlled component of the PNS, and it receives and responds to external sensory stimuli from the skin and sensory organs.

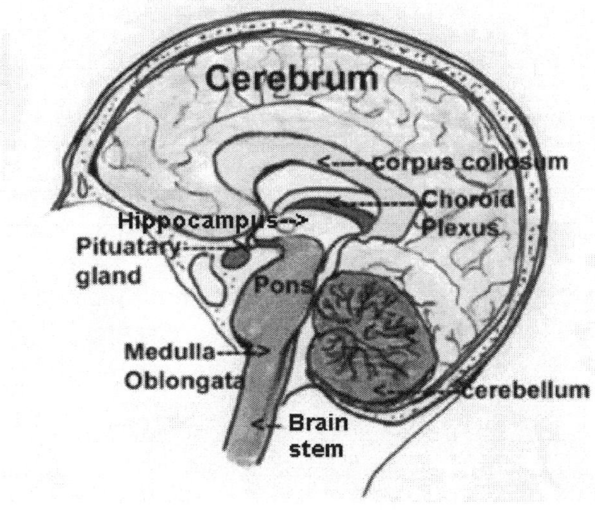

Circulatory System

Heart

The **circulatory system** is responsible for oxygenation of cells, perfusion (carrying of blood with oxygen, glucose, and nutrients to cells) and gas exchange (removing waste products such as carbon dioxide). The circulatory system serves as a blood reservoir (5 liters), maintains blood pH (7.35–7.45) through a buffer system, responds to infections, and facilitates coagulation (blood clotting). The **heart** is located between the lungs and under and to the left of the mediastinum (breastbone). The heart has four chambers, consisting of the upper (right atrium, left atrium) and lower (right ventricle and left ventricle). The myocardium (heart muscle) receives blood from two major coronary arteries and their branches. The inner lining of the heart is the endocardium, and the lining that surrounds the heart is the pericardium, which has a double inner serous membrane (visceral pericardium) and a fibrous outer layer (parietal pericardium). The **cardiac cycle** involves one complete heartbeat with systole (ventricular contraction) and diastole (relaxation). **Stroke volume** is the volume of blood ejected from the left ventricle in one cardiac cycle (about 60 to 70 mL), and **cardiac output** is the heart rate times the stroke volume.

Vessels and Blood Flow

The venous system includes veins, venules, and venous capillaries, and it brings blood back to the heart via the inferior and superior vena cava. The arterial system, including the coronary arteries, branches from the aorta after it leaves the heart and includes arteries, arterioles, and arterial capillaries. **Blood flow** proceeds as follows:

- Deoxygenated venous blood returns to the heart by the superior vena cava, inferior vena cava, and coronary sinus (bringing blood from the coronary arteries) into the right atrium, then through the tricuspid valve into the right ventricle.
- From the right ventricle, blood flows through the pulmonic (semilunar) valve into the pulmonary artery and to the lungs to exchange carbon dioxide for oxygen.
- Oxygenated blood flows from the lungs through the pulmonary veins into the left atrium and through the mitral (bicuspid) valve into the left ventricle.
- From the left ventricle, blood flows through the aortic valve and into the aorta, the coronary arteries, and the general circulation.

After blood flows through the valves, they close to prevent backflow. Both atria and both ventricles contract simultaneously.

Respiratory System

Control of Respirations

The brain's **respiratory center** in the medulla oblongata responds to the body's chemical and mechanical signals. The medulla oblongata contains chemoreceptors that respond to changes in the pH in the fluid surrounding it, and the carotids and aorta contain peripheral chemoreceptors that respond to decreases in oxygen and pH. If the blood becomes more acidotic, the medulla increases the respiratory rate and the tidal volume. If the blood becomes more alkalotic, the medulla does the opposite in order to maintain the blood pH within the normal range. Mechanical/Stretch receptors are located in the lungs, upper airways, chest wall, and diaphragm, helping to control respirations. The stretch receptors respond when the lungs inflate, and they send a message to the medulla via the vagus nerve to prevent overinflation and vice versa. In healthy individuals, increased carbon dioxide or a decrease in pH causes an increase in the respiratory rate whereas increased oxygen and pH decrease the respiratory rate. In conditions (such as chronic obstructive pulmonary disease [COPD]) in which carbon dioxide is chronically high, this mechanism is impaired.

Anatomy and Physiology

Air enters the **upper respiratory system** through the **nasal cavity** and/or mouth, where it is warmed and moistened by **nasal and oral mucosa** and passes through the **pharynx** (nasopharynx, oropharynx, laryngopharynx, hypopharynx, and soft palate/uvula) into the **lower respiratory system** and the **larynx** (voice box) into the **trachea** (windpipe). The **epiglottis** is a cartilage flap attached to the **thyroid cartilage** (above the cricoid cartilage), which closes over the larynx and glottis (vocal chords) when swallowing so food enters the esophagus. The trachea branches into two (right and left) **bronchi** (large tubes) that carry the air into the **lungs**. Each bronchus branches into smaller **bronchioles** (small tubes) and **alveoli** (small air sacs), which are connected to the ends of the bronchioles. The alveoli are covered with webs of tiny venous capillaries that deliver carbon dioxide and arterial capillaries that pick up oxygen. The muscles of respiration are the **diaphragm**, which is enervated by the **phrenic nerve**, and **intercostal muscles** (between the ribs), but **accessory muscles** in the neck and collarbone area may help during respiratory distress. The jawbones are the maxilla (upper) and mandible (lower).

Female Reproductive System

The **female reproductive system** includes the ovaries (produce eggs and estrogen), fallopian tubes (carry the eggs to the uterus), uterus (nourishes the fertilized egg, supports the placenta, and contracts for delivery), cervix (allows passage of menstrual fluid and the fetus), and vagina (expands to allow insertion of the penis, provides passage for menstrual fluids and fetus), the vulva and labia minora and labia majora (provide protection), and the clitoris (provides sensation) as well as the breasts (produce milk). Functions include ovulation, fertilization, menstruation, pregnancy, and lactation. Menarche (the onset of menses) is usually between 9 and 15, but it may occur earlier, and it should be considered as a possibility with younger girls. Menopause occurs at about age 50, usually following a time span of about 10 years of irregular periods during which the person may become pregnant. The normal menstrual cycle is 28 days, but it may be up to 45 days in adolescents. Problems may include abdominal or vaginal pain, vaginal bleeding or discharge, fever, nausea and vomiting, and dizziness.

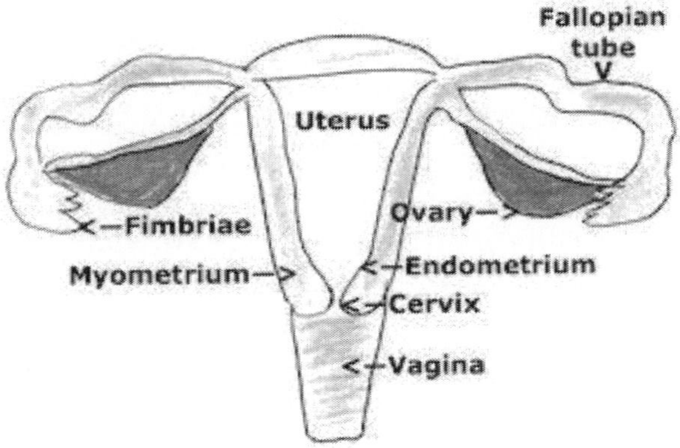

Male Reproductive System

The **male reproductive system** includes the following:

- **Scrotum**: Enclose and protect the testes, epididymis, and spermatic cord.
- **Testes/Testicles**: Primary reproductive organ, produce sperm and sex hormones (androgens, estrogen).
- **Epididymis**: Carries sperm from each testis to the vas deferens.
- **Vas deferens** (contained in the spermatic cord along with arteries, nerves, and veins): Ducts that carry sperm to the urethra by peristaltic action.
- **Seminal vesicle**: Secretes nutritive fluid into the semen.
- **Prostate**: Secretes alkaline prostatic fluid that aids in sperm survival in the acidic female reproductive system.
- **Urethra**: Carries urine and, during intercourse, carries semen during ejaculation.
- **Penis**: Functions in the excretion of urine and in the delivery of sperm, and it allows penetration of the partner by the erectile reflex.

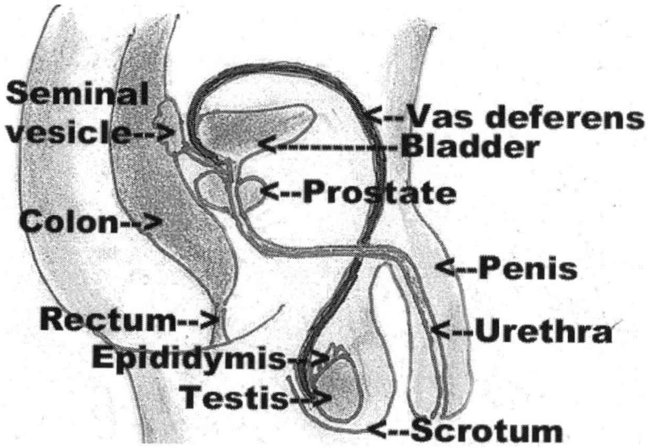

Pre-Embryonic Development Leading to Development of Germ Layers

During the **pre-embryonic stage of** development, cellular multiplication and cellular differentiation occur. During cellular multiplication, the morula (a ball of 12 to 16 cells) forms. When the morula enters the uterus, the intracellular fluid increases and a cavity forms within the morula. The inner mass of cells, the blastocyst, is surrounded by an outer layer that surrounds the cavity, the trophoblast. The trophoblast develops into the embryonic membrane called the chorion, and the blastocyst develops into the embryonic disc (a double layer of cells), from which the embryo will develop, and into the amnion, another embryonic membrane. About two weeks after conception, the mass of blastocyst cells differentiates into germ layers—the ectoderm, the mesoderm, and the endoderm—from which all organs and organ systems develop during the embryonic stage. The hematopoietic and lymphoreticular systems develop from the mesoderm. The first 8 weeks of gestation comprise the embryonic stage; the 9th week to delivery comprise the fetal stage.

Embryo Development

The **embryonic period** follows the germinal stage and implantation, and it begins in the third week after fertilization and lasts through week 8 of gestation, during which the organs are formed. Development of the organs begins at different points during the embryonic period and continue to develop throughout the period and (in most cases) into the fetal period. When the embryo reaches the fetal stage, it is approximately 2.5 cm in length.

Week	Beginning development
3	Neural tube that will form the nervous system, primitive tube that will form the heart and blood vessels, and the urinary tract.
4	Cardiovascular system and partitioning of the heart, eyes, diaphragm, respiratory system, intestines, limbs (buds), and genitalia.
5	Face, lips, mouth, tongue, and axial skeleton (vertebral cartilage).
6	Development continues.
7	Ears (internal structures).
8	Penis, labia, and clitoris.

Human Life Cycle

The **human life cycle** includes the following:

- **Prebirth**: The potential for life is present.
- **Birth**: Begins the cycle of life.

- **Infancy** (ages 0–3): Experience steady growth and exploration, learning from those providing care and becoming steadily more mobile and better able to communicate. Move from complete dependence to beginning stages of independence.
- **Early childhood/Preschool** (ages 3–6): Move past toddlerhood and begin to increase in stature and have improved mobility and communication skills, take an increasing interest in peers.
- **Middle childhood/School age** (ages 6–8): Develop imagination and begin to further explore the world and their place in the world, learn to read and play well with others.
- **Late childhood/School age** (ages 9–11): Begin to develop some sense of independence and have increased social skills and ability to solve problems.
- **Preadolescence and early adolescence** (ages 11–14): Time of transition in which hormonal changes take place and bodies go through changes, secondary sexual characteristics develop, and children may have anxiety about their bodies.
- **Adolescence**: (ages 15–17): Have strong identification with peers and experiment sexually, may have concerns about image and exhibit behavioral problems.
- **Late adolescence** (ages 18–21): Begin to take on adult roles, working, going to college, or engaging in high-risk behaviors.
- **Early adulthood** (ages 22–35): Begin to build family or relationships, settle into a vocation or profession and assume responsibilities such as home ownership.
- **Middle age** (ages 35–50): Begin to contemplate and evaluate their lives and value systems and the meaning of life.
- **Mature adulthood** (ages 50–80): May be satisfied or anxious, depending on circumstances and health, move from the world of work to retirement and experience a change in status.
- **Late adulthood** (ages 80+): May experience a decline in health and fear or accept death.
- **Death**: End of the cycle.

Emerging Technology Regarding Stem Cell Research

Stem cells are undifferentiated cells that can develop into any type of body cells. Types of stem cells include the following:

- **Embryonic**: These pluripotent cells (able to develop into any type of cell) are derived from 3-5-day-old embryos, and they are generally harvested during in vitro fertilization (IVF) procedures.
- **Adult (nonembryonic)**: These cells are derived from body organs/tissues such as bone marrow. These are generally used to treat the same type of tissue from which they are harvested.
- **Induced pluripotent**: Adult stem cells that have undergone a process that converts them to pluripotent cells. These cells may allow treatment of various diseases and transplants without rejection.
- **Umbilical cord blood**: These cells are harvested at birth and can be frozen and banked for later use, such as to treat leukemia and other blood disorders.
- **Amniotic fluid**: Stem cells can be harvested from amniotic fluid, although research is ongoing to determine possible uses.

Research is expanding the potential uses of stems cells: growing new tissues, replacing damaged or diseased tissue/organs, repairing organs, studying genetic defects, researching disease, and testing drugs.

Transplant Technology and Bioengineering

Transplant technology depends on bioengineering, which is the use of engineering in medicine and biology in order to develop innovative medical treatments such as cochlear implants and electronic prostheses. Transplant technology includes the following:

- **United Network for Organ Sharing (UNOS) database** (UNet) collects, stores, and analyzes data regarding transplantations and provides the patient waiting list and matching software to determine who receives donated organs.
- **Transport systems**, such as the Organ Care System (TransMedic), which keeps the organ, such as the heart, warm and functioning ("living transplant") and extends viability.
- **Heart-lung support** of donors with circulatory determination of death, using extracorporeal membrane oxygenation to maintain organ viability.
- **Normothermic perfusion** to maintain hydration and ventilation of donated lungs for up to 20 hours.
- **Artificial organs** are being developed in the laboratory.
- **3D printing** can print strips of tissue and some organs and is likely to expand transplant possibilities in the future. Artificial tracheas made with tissue scaffolds have been successfully transplanted.

History of Microbiology

The microscope was invented in the 1600s, and in 1665, Robert Hooke (1635–1703) published *Micrographia* after building an improved microscope that allowed him to observe microscopic fungi, fossils, and the cells of a cork tree. Later, Anton van Leeuwenhoek (1632–1723) used a microscope to observe sperm, red blood cells, protozoa, and bacteria, establishing the basis for bacteriology and refuting the idea of spontaneous generation. Francesco Redi (1626–1697) demonstrated that maggots developed from fly eggs and not decaying meat, and Lazzaro Spallanzani (1729–1799) demonstrated that boiling can destroy microbes. Louis Pasteur (1822–1895) developed a method of killing harmful bacteria (pasteurization) and the germ theory of disease, although his ideas were not initially accepted; however, germ theory was supported by Robert Koch (1843–1910) with research into anthrax bacteria. During the 1800s and 1900s, many different microorganisms were identified, and in 1928, Alexander Fleming (1881–1955) discovered that a mold (*Penicillium notatum*) had contaminated a petri dish of *Staphylococci* and prevented growth. The first patient, however, was not treated with penicillin until 1942. Microorganisms are now used in the development and manufacture of many pharmaceuticals.

Types of Microscopes

The **microscope** most commonly used is the **light microscope** (either monocular or binocular). This microscope uses external light or light from an internal filament that allows the light to pass upward through the specimen so that the specimen appears dark against the lighter background, although the light may be inverted, illuminating from the top, for such things as a culture in a liquid medium. **Phase contrast microscopes** that do not require staining of the specimen are used to assess cell growth, especially for organisms that are transparent with a standard light microscope. The **dark-field microscope** uses a special dark-field condenser that makes the specimen appear light against a dark background, useful for observing spirochetes. The **fluorescent microscope** uses an ultraviolet light for illumination. This microscope is used when fluorescent dye is attached to a specimen because the dye glows when exposed to ultraviolet light, which is useful for fluorescent antibody testing.

Techniques for Cultures Collection and Incubation Times

Cultures in which a sample is grown on a nutrient-rich media may be done with oxygen (aerobic) or without oxygen (anaerobic). After the organism is cultured, sensitivity tests are usually completed to determine which anti-infective agents are most successful in treating the particular pathogenic microorganism. A Gram stain is usually done initially, and then the culture is checked every 24 hours for colonization. Colonies are checked again with Gram stains and also transferred to a separate media for further observation and testing. Cultures are usually negative if there is no growth in 48–72 hours of incubation unless there is a very slow-growing bacterium or fungus, which may need 4–6 weeks before the final results are available. If antibiotics are begun prior to taking a sample for a culture, this can alter the results, making it very difficult to isolate the infective agent, so it's better to take a sample first and then begin antibiotics. **Swab cultures** are done by taking swabs of exudate or contaminated surfaces. The swab technique usually results in the smallest sample size, so the infective agent may not grow in the culture. It is also easy to contaminate the specimen with normal flora.

Processing and Planting Specimens Using Inoculating Agar and Broth

Processing and planting of specimens: Always maintain aseptic technique. To inoculate, use the following techniques:

- **Agar deep**: Insert the needle straight to the bottom and withdraw straight.
- **Agar plate**: Lift one side of the lid and slide the loop in horizontally, streaking the inoculum back and forth on the surface only. Reflame the loop after each third of the plate is streaked, reinoculate, turn the plate 90°, and continue until the entire plate (or three quadrants) is streaked. Invert the plate for incubation.
- **Agar slant**: Either insert the loop to the bottom of the tube and withdraw straight (for growth pattern) or in a back-and-forth manner (for increased growth).
- **Broth**: Swish the loop back and forth about the tube.

Once inoculation is complete, then the plate/tube is placed in the incubator with the temperature and duration to be determined by the type of medium and the type of organism. Note: Swab cultures are done by taking swabs of exudate or contaminated surfaces. The swab technique usually results in the smallest sample size, so the infective agent may not grow in the culture. It is also easy to contaminate the specimen with normal flora.

Infectious Process

The **infectious process** includes a pathogenic agent (e.g., bacteria, virus, or fungus), reservoir, portal of entry/exit (e.g., respiratory tract, eyes, gastrointestinal tract, skin, urogenital tract, or placenta), mode of transmission, and immune response:

- **Reservoirs** are places or substances in which a pathogenic microorganism, such as bacteria, normally occurs and multiplies, depending upon this place or substance for survival. A reservoir may include an animal, a plant, an inanimate surface area, soil, or water. Usually the reservoir provides sustenance to the microorganism without compromise and allows for transmission of the microorganism to a host.
- **Modes of transmission** include direct contact with infective material, an intermediate vehicle (inanimate carrier, such as a doorknob or food), or a vector (an animate carrier, such as an insect or animal).

- **Incubation periods** extend from the time a pathogenic microorganism invades a host until the first signs of tissue compromise or infection occur. If the host is a vector, it is the time from invasion until first transmission to other hosts occurs. Incubation periods vary considerably, from hours to years, depending upon the type of pathogenic microorganism as well as the type of host and the environment.

MODES OF INFECTION TRANSMISSION

Modes of infection transmission include the following:

- **Direct contact**: Direct touching, kissing (mononucleosis) and sexual intercourse (gonorrhea, syphilis, chlamydia, HIV). Vertical transmission involves mother to infant during pregnancy, delivery, or breastfeeding (HIV, hepatitis B, gonorrhea, herpes).
- **Indirect contact**: Contaminated fomite (inanimate object), such as a doorknob, syringe, or catheter, spreads infection (*Clostridioides difficile*).
- **Airborne**: Particles smaller than 5 μm inhaled from a cough, sneeze, or exhalation. Particles stay suspended in the air and travel large distances (TB, measles.)
- **Droplet**: Particles greater than 5 μm inhaled from a cough, sneeze, or exhalation are inhaled (influenza, mumps, meningitis, pertussis, pneumonia, rubella). Droplets travel less than 3 feet and do not stay suspended.
- **Vehicle**: Contact with contaminated water, air, or food (*Escherichia coli* diarrhea, cryptosporidiosis, hepatitis A).
- **Vector (mechanical)**: Contact with an animal/insect/device that carries infection from one host to another (such as a fly carrying bacteria from feces of an infected host to food [dysentery]).
- **Vector (biological)**: Infected biological vector (such as a tick or flea) transmits an infection directly to another host (Chagas disease, malaria, West Nile virus, Lyme disease).

ANTIMICROBIALS

Broad-spectrum **antibiotics** are useful against Gram-positive and Gram-negative bacteria. Medium-spectrum antibiotics are useful against Gram-positive bacteria and sometimes Gram-negative as well. Narrow-spectrum antibiotics are effective against a small range of bacteria. Antibiotics function primarily by killing the bacteria, by interfering with its biological functions (bactericidal), or by preventing reproduction (bacteriostatic).

- **Macrolides** - Narrow- to medium-spectrum antibiotics that prevent protein production.
- **Penicillins** - Medium-spectrum antibiotics are bacteriocidal and cause breakdown of the bacterial cell wall. Penicillin G is narrow spectrum.
- **Cephalosporins** - Medium-spectrum antibiotics effective against Gram-negative organisms; they are bacteriocidal and inhibit cell wall synthesis.
- **Polymyxins** - Narrow-spectrum antibiotics effective against Gram-negative organisms; they interfere with the bacterial cell membrane and are bactericidal.
- **Fluoroquinolones** - Broad-spectrum antibiotics that inhibit bacterial reproduction and repair of genetic material in the bacterial DNA.
- **Sulfonamides** - Medium-spectrum antibiotics with action against Gram-positive and many Gram-negative organisms as well as Plasmodium and Toxoplasma. Sulfa drugs interfere with folate synthesis and prevent cell division, so they are bacteriostatic.
- **Tetracyclines** - Broad-spectrum antibiotics that inhibit binding and synthesis in proteins.
- **Aminoglycosides** - Broad-spectrum antibiotics that are effective against Gram-negative bacteria and interfere with bacterial protein production and are bactericidal.

Human Pathogens

Viruses

Viruses (virions) are submicroscopic and are generally considered nonliving because they lack cell structures. Viruses consist of nucleic acid, single- or double-strand DNA and/or RNA (the genome), encapsulated in a protein coating called a capsid. Some have a lipid envelope about the capsid with glycoprotein spikes. The purpose of viruses is to reproduce, but they require a host cell with a protein receptor to which a virus must bind to penetrate the cell membrane. The viral genome carries encoding that allows it to use the cell to replicate in a lytic or lysogenic cycle. In the lytic cycle, the virus forces the cell to manufacture proteins and new genomes. After new viral particles form, the cell ruptures, releasing the viruses. In a lysogenic cycle, the virus integrates the DNA of the host, and as the cell replicates, the virus replicates with it. The virus remains dormant until it activates and begins a lytic cycle. Viruses that infect bacteria are bacteriophages (or phages).

Retroviruses

Retroviruses are a subcategory of viruses. Retroviruses must have three characteristics: a genome that contains ribonucleic acid (RNA), the enzyme reverse transcriptase, and a protein body surrounding by a protein envelope. Although some viruses contain DNA, retroviruses do not. After the virus enters the cell of a host, the reverse transcriptase uses the RNA genome to make DNA copies of the genome. Because genetic information was previously believed to transmit from DNA to RNA, this process was considered backward, "retro," thus the name retrovirus. After the DNA copy is made, it invades one of the host cell's chromosomes and becomes part of the genetic makeup of the cell. To date, two retroviruses are known to infect human hosts: HTLV-1, which causes adult T-cell leukemia, and human immunodeficiency virus (HIV). By invading T-helper lymphocyte cells, HIV attacks and disrupts the immune system that should detect and destroy pathogens.

Bacteria

Structure and Shape

Bacteria are critical for human survival, and most are benign, but some are pathogenic, leading to infection. Bacteria are ubiquitous, with about 10 times as many bacteria in the human body as there are human cells. Bacteria have simple prokaryote structures, with no membrane-encased nucleus or organelles but a tangle of looped DNA called a nucleoid. Bacteria also have plasmids, which are double strands of DNA outside of the nucleoid that allow for transmission from cell to cell or by attaching to viruses. Essentially, bacteria are able to trade genes, making them very adaptable. The cell membrane of most bacteria, except the Mollicutes (mycoplasmas), is surrounded by a cell wall, the composition of which varies. It's the composition of this cell wall that determines the Gram staining, either negative or positive. Bacteria have four different shapes:

- Cocci (round), occur in chains or clusters (*Staphylococci, Streptococci, Diplococci*).
- Spiral, includes spirillum (*Campylobacter* spp., *Helicobacter* spp.) and spirochetes (*Treponema pallidum, Borrelia* spp.).
- Bacilli (rods), occur singly, doubly, or in filaments.
- Incomplete spirals (*Vibrio* spp.).

Characteristics

Bacteria are often differentiated according to enzymes and genes that are submicroscopic. Their characteristics may vary:

- **Motility**: Some lack motility and others move by means of flagella or through creeping movements.
- **Environment**: Some bacteria are aerobic, requiring oxygen; others are anaerobic. Obligate anaerobes cannot survive in the presence of oxygen. Many are facultative anaerobes and prefer anaerobic conditions but can survive in either environment. Still other bacteria depend on other substances for survival, including sulfate, nitrite, and carbon dioxide.
- **Reproduction**: Bacteria reproduce through fission or by the production of spores. Some bacteria, primarily those found in water, soil, and human intestines, produce endospores, which seem to be able to survive indefinitely and are resistant to heat, light, solvents, and chemicals. Spores are usually activated by heat or age.
- **Nutrition**: Bacteria acquire food in different ways. Some (autotrophs) bacteria are able to manufacture their own food. Others (heterotrophs) gain nutrition from other organisms. Heterotrophs include those that cause disease.

Bacterial Reproduction and Gene Transfer

Bacterial reproduction is carried out asexually (there are no male or female bacteria):

- **Binary fission**: One cell splits into two identical (clone) daughter cells. This process can occur very rapidly.

Gene transfer processes do not create additional bacteria, but the bacteria are changed, essentially creating new bacteria, because of new genetic material (DNA):

- **Conjugation**: Bacteria join through an extension (pilus), and genetic material is inserted into the recipient bacterium. This new material is usually protective of the organism and may, for example, provide antibiotic resistance.
- **Transformation**: Bacteria absorb genetic material from the environment through their cell membranes. This usually occurs in response to some stressor, such as dehydration, and is dependent on the recipient.
- **Transduction**: Genetic material is carried by a bacterial virus (phage) from one bacterium to another. The phage attaches to the bacterium and injects the genetic material along with a phage enzyme, which breaks down the host DNA into smaller particles. The phage DNA is then replicated, and phage proteins are produced. Some bacterial DNA is incorporated, and when it is released, this infected bacterial DNA goes on to infect other cells and becomes incorporated into the recipient's DNA.

Fungi

Fungi were originally classified as plants, but they do not produce their own food through photosynthesis and must, like animals, get the food from another source. Fungi vary widely, from one-celled microorganisms to multicelled chains that are miles long. Fungi are used to make antibiotics, but they can also cause infection and disease. Two common classifications of fungi are molds (including mushrooms) and yeast. Fungi are not motile, but some produce spores, which can be inhaled. Some, such as the yeast *Candida albicans*, are part of the normal flora of the skin but can overgrow in an opportunistic infection. As microorganisms, fungal infections can invade the sinuses, the mouth, the respiratory system, and the vagina. Antibiotics may affect the balance between bacteria and yeast, causing infection. Fungal infections include histoplasmosis, blastomycosis, and coccidioidomycosis. Fungal infections, such as *Pneumocystis jirovecii* (formerly *P. carinii*) pose a serious problem for the immunocompromised. Antifungal drugs are available, but systemic fungal infections are difficult to treat.

Protozoa

Protozoa are single-cell microorganisms with a nucleus that live primarily off of bacteria. They share similarities to animals, but (except for Myxozoa) they are not, but they are also not plants. Many protozoa are free living and are ubiquitous in soil and water. They are often divided according to their method of locomotion: flagellates, amoeboids, sporozoans, and ciliates. Some protozoa are able to form protective cysts, which can survive outside the host, sometimes for long periods, before transmission to another host. Protozoa are parasites to humans and cause a wide range of infections. Enteric protozoa, such as *Giardia intestinalis* and *Entamoeba histolytica,* can cause severe diarrhea. Other diseases caused by protozoa include malaria, Chagas disease, babesiosis, toxoplasmosis, trichomonas infection, and amoebic dysentery. Protozoa take a huge toll of life, especially in developing countries, but some diseases, such as Chagas disease, are becoming more common in the United States as people emigrate from endemic areas of Latin America.

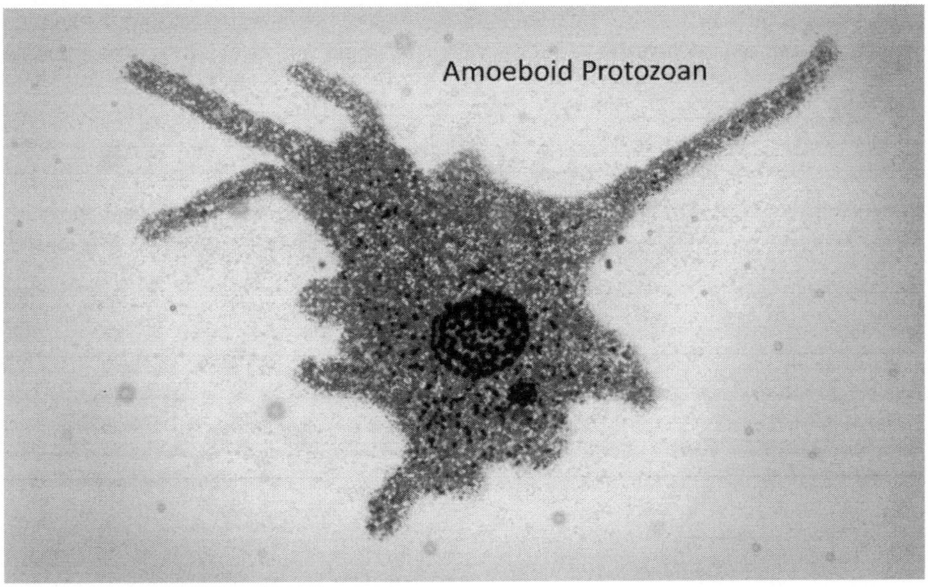

Normal Indigenous Flora

Characteristics

Normal flora gain access to the surface of the body by contact with the skin or the mucous membranes of the gastrointestinal, reproductive, or respiratory tracts. Normal flora are not usually found in internal organs, such as the brain or the blood. There are more than 200 organisms that are part of the normal flora (mostly bacteria), which vary according to genetics, age, sex, nutrition, environment, and other factors. Many bacteria, such as *Staphylococcus aureus,* are basically pathogenic and can cause opportunistic infections. The largest numbers of flora inhabit the intestinal tract. Intestinal bacteria, such as *Escherichia coli,* have an active role in digestion, and they prevent colonization of other pathogens, but they can also cause infection. Some types of flora are transient; others are permanent. Flora often has tissue tropism, a preference for some types of tissues. Some flora has surface components that allow it to bind with host cells in order to colonize. Others build bacterial biofilms, slime glue composed primarily of capsules, or use those built by other bacteria.

Benefits to the Host

The **normal flora** of the body is necessary and benefits the host in many ways, including the following:

- **Synthesis and secretion of vitamins**: Bacteria are an important source of vitamin K and vitamin B_{12}, which is secreted by enteric bacteria, such as *E. coli*.
- **Resistance to colonization**: The normal flora attaches to host cells, preventing competing bacteria from attaching and colonizing. They also compete for nutrition.
- **Inhibition or destruction of pathogens**: Bacterial flora may produce substances, such as fatty acids or bacteriocins, that destroy invading pathogens.
- **Development of tissue**: In response to normal flora, the walls of some structures, such as the cecum and some lymphatic tissue, thicken and strengthen.
- **Stimulation of antibodies**: Normal flora have antigenic properties that stimulate formation of "natural" antibodies in the host. These antibodies can cross react with the antigens of related pathogens as part of an immune response.

Species by Site

Site	Normal flora
Nose	Generally, Gram-positive bacteria, such as *Staphylococcus epidermidis*. Some people are nasal carriers of pathogenic bacteria, such as *Staphylococcus aureus* and beta-hemolytic streptococci.
Mouth	Numerous bacteria, including streptococci spp.
Throat	Similar to the mouth but also include staphylococci and *Neisseria*.
Skin	Generally Gram-positive bacteria, such as *S. epidermidis*, streptococci, and mycobacteria. Moist areas may carry yeasts, such as *Candida albicans*. Some may carry *S. aureus*.
Small intestine	Numerous bacteria, including enterobacteria, anaerobic bacteria, lactobacilli, and streptococci as well as the yeast *C. albicans*.
Large intestine	Numerous bacteria (primarily obligate anaerobes), including *Bacteroides*, *Escherichia coli*, clostridia, *Salmonella*, *Pseudomonas*, and streptococci.
Urethra	Similar to that found on the skin because it migrates from the skin to the urethra, especially *S. epidermidis* and diphtheroids.
Vagina	Varies according to age and maturity. Childhood and postmenopausal: *S. epidermidis*, *E. coli*, diphtheroids, streptococci. Puberty to menopause: diphtheroids, streptococci, staphylococci, multiple anaerobes, and *Lactobacillus acidophilus*.

Reemergence of Disease

MDR-TB and XDR-TB

Multidrug-resistant tuberculosis (MDR-TB) is resistant to at least two commonly used first-line drugs, isoniazid and rifampin, whereas **extensively drug-resistant tuberculosis (XDR-TB)** is also resistant to all fluoroquinolones and at least one of the three second-line drugs: amikacin, kanamycin, or capreomycin. XDR-TB emerged as a worldwide concern in 2005. In the United States, it is at present most commonly found in foreign-born patients but it also occurs in immunocompromised patients. Active TB requires treatment for extended periods of time, usually

18–24 months, with multiple drugs. Since the 1980s, there has been an increased need to use second-line drugs to combat infection. There are two primary causes for the increased resistance:

- failure to complete a course of treatment
- mismanaged treatment, including the incorrect medication, dosage, or duration of therapy.

People who have had TB previously are at increased risk and should be monitored carefully. Drug-resistant TB increasingly poses a risk for patients and staff in healthcare facilities.

Poliomyelitis

Poliomyelitis is a serious viral infection that can cause meningitis, paralysis, and death. Prior to the introduction of a vaccine in 1955, polio was responsible for >20,000 cases in the United States each year. There have been no cases of polio caused by the poliovirus since 1979 in the United States, but outbreaks still occur in some third-world countries (in Africa and the Middle East) especially those experiencing civil unrest/wars that interfere with vaccination programs, so continuing vaccinations in the United States is very important to maintain herd immunity because travelers may bring the poliovirus with them. Oral polio vaccine is no longer recommended in the United States because it carries a very slight risk of causing the disease (1:2.4 million). Children require four doses of injectable polio vaccine at 2 months, 4 months, 6–18 months, and a 4–6 years booster.

Malaria

Malaria is caused by *Plasmodium* spp. parasites and is transmitted through the bite of *Anopheles* spp. mosquitoes. The parasites invade the liver and destroy red blood cells, resulting in recurrent episodes of severe fever and chills. Malaria may be uncomplicated (fever, chills, and flu-like symptoms lasting up to 10 hours and recurring every other day) or severe, in which the parasite invades organs and can lead to death. During the 1950s and 1960s, malaria was almost eradicated through the extensive use of insecticide to control mosquito populations, but this was abandoned in the mid-1960s because of increasing drug and insecticide resistance. By the 1970s, the incidence had increased markedly. Although it is rare in the United States, malaria does occur, primarily resulting from travel to endemic areas and failure to take preventive measures (such as prophylaxis). Factors that contribute to reemergence include:

- drug resistance
- poor mosquito control
- increased immigration from endemic areas
- increased international travel
- positive environmental factors (global warming)

Mechanisms by Which Pathogens Become Drug Resistant

Pathogens may become **resistant** to antimicrobials through mutations or alterations in their DNA (through genetic transfer) that allow them to resist in various ways:

- Inactivate the drug.
- Alter the cell membrane to prevent uptake or inhibit uptake of the drug.
- Alter the target molecule of the drug.

Penicillin resistance, for example, occurs because bacteria mutated to produce beta-lactamase, which breaks down the antibiotic. Once a microorganism is resistant, it can continue to pass on this resistance to other microorganisms through genetic transfer. Resistance is associated with the use of antimicrobials, either overuse or improper use (such as stopping a prescription when symptoms subside). Clindamycin, a powerful antibiotic, tends to wipe out much of the normal flora of the intestines, allowing an overgrowth of *Clostridioides difficile,* which can cause severe infection and even death and is readily transmitted to others through spores, which are often resistant to antimicrobials.

MRSA

Methicillin-resistant *Staphylococcus aureus* (MRSA) was first identified in 1961 in Europe after the development and overuse of synthetic penicillins caused *S. aureus* to mutate into resistant strains. Since 1961, MRSA has infected millions of people worldwide. MRSA is resistant to methicillin and other beta-lactam antibiotics, such as amoxicillin and oxacillin, and sometimes other classes of antibiotics. *Staphylococcus* is able to form biofilms, which aids in resistance. **MRSA healthcare-associated infections** (HAIs) most commonly involve surgical sites, the urinary tract, bloodstream, and lungs (pneumonia). Because of increased awareness and better practices, MRSA HAIs decreased by 54% between 2004 and 2011 but still pose a threat to patients because of the severity of some infections and the risk of resistance to other drugs. **Community-acquired MRSA** most commonly results in skin infections, such as folliculitis, and it can easily spread to others when groups of people are in close contact with each other, such as in day cares, gyms, schools, and barracks.

MDROs and Vancomycin-Resistant *Enterococcus*

Multidrug-resistant organisms (MDROs): MDROs are those that have mutated and developed forms that are resistant to multiple antibiotics. Initially, resistance developed to one class of antibiotics, such as beta-lactams, which resulted in methicillin-resistant *Staphylococcus aureus* infections and penicillin-resistant *Streptococcus pneumoniae,* but bacteria continued to mutate, becoming resistant to more classes of antibiotics and severely limiting the antibiotic arsenal needed for treatment. Of current concern is extended-spectrum beta-lactamases (resistant to cephalosporins and monobactams) and multidrug-resistant tuberculosis (MDR-TB).

Vancomycin-resistant *Enterococcus*: Up until the 1980s, most enterococci responded to vancomycin, a strong antibiotic, but the increased use of antibiotics for all types of infections resulted in mutations that rendered some enterococci species vancomycin resistant, leaving few options for treatment of severe infection. There are currently six different forms (A–G) of vancomycin resistance. For example, the VanA form is resistant to vancomycin and teicoplanin (an alternative antibiotic for severe infections).

Cellular Processes

Cellular processes vary according to the type of cell and can include the following:

- **Motility**: Produces forces that result in movement (e.g., muscle cells).
- **Conductivity**: Electrical potential occurs in response to stimulus (e.g., nerve cells).
- **Absorption**: Nutrients are absorbed from the environment (all cells).
- **Secretion**: Creates new substances (proteins) from those absorbed and then secretes these proteins in response to signals (such as the release of hormones) (e.g., mucous cells).
- **Excretion**: Digestive enzymes in lysosomes break down nutrients and then excrete the residue as waste products (all cells).
- **Respiration**: Cells absorb oxygen, which transforms nutrients (through oxidation) into adenosine triphosphate (a form that can be used for energy) in the mitochondria (all cells).

- **Reproduction**: Cells may divide into daughter cells to replace dying cells, although not all cells can reproduce. For example, nerve cells are unable to reproduce.
- **Communication**: Cells communicate chemically through signaling, such as through the release of hormones that bind to receptor sites.

Homeostatic Disease Processes

Homeostatic disease processes occur when the body is unable to maintain the state of homeostasis, usually because of the inability of the body to maintain negative feedback, resulting in positive feedback loops that amplify the disease process. The organs most responsible for maintaining homeostasis are the brain (triggers production of hormones), liver (removes toxins and maintains metabolism of carbohydrates), and kidneys (maintain fluid and electrolyte balance). Hormonal disorders are homeostatic diseases because the body is unable to maintain the correct balance of hormones to meet the body's needs. Diseases that are commonly considered homeostatic include gout (increased levels of uric acid), diabetes (increased levels of glucose and inadequate production of insulin), dehydration (inadequate fluid balance), hypothyroidism (inadequate thyroid hormones), hyperthyroidism (excess thyroid hormones), and iron-deficiency anemia (decreased serum iron).

Risk Factors for Disease

Age, Gender, and Heredity

Risk factors for disease include the following:

- **Age**: One of the primary risk factors for disease (especially cardiovascular disease, osteoporosis, diabetes, neurodegeneration, and cancer). People tend to be less physically active as they age and often gain weight, putting increased stress on the body. Examples of changes that occur in all body systems as part of the aging process, making the body less able to fight disease, are as follows: the immune system is less efficient in the aged, vaccines are less effective, and healing is slower. Some mutation of cells occurs as part of the aging process, and this may accelerate over time, resulting in disease.
- **Gender**: Some diseases are more likely to occur in males than females, and vice versa, because of various factors, such as differences in body size and hormone production. Additionally, some added risk factors, such as smoking, may impact females more than males.
- **Heredity**: Some diseases are inherited outright (such as sickle cell disease) through abnormal genes, but other diseases may result from genes that increase risk (such as BRCA1). In some cases, multiple factors, including genes and lifestyle choices may determine whether a person develops disease (such as diabetes type 2).

Poverty

Poverty places patients at an increased risk of stress disorders and disease, especially if they are homeless. The following problems are common:

- Incomplete or no immunizations because of a lack of health care and regular well-baby or well-child visits.
- Frequent infections, such as respiratory infections or skin infections, because of a lack of adequate shelter, living in close quarters with others, and lack of adequate hygiene.
- Insufficient sleep, especially if people are sleeping in cars, on the ground, or in shelters.
- Nutritional deficiencies because of poor diet.
- Dental caries because of poor nutrition and lack of dental care or lack of toothbrushing supplies.

- Depression, common in all ages.
- Sexual abuse, pregnancies, and sexually transmitted diseases are frequent, especially with homeless teenagers.
- Injuries from a lack of safety equipment or the dangers of the street.

Global Environmental Factors

Many **global environmental factors** impact health:

- **Natural disasters**: Hurricanes, tornadoes, earthquakes, fires, and floods can have a profound effect on health. Some people may have direct injury (e.g., burns, traumatic injuries), whereas others may experience secondary effects from loss of shelter and economic hardship.
- **Climate extremes**: Severe heat waves in the summer increase the risk of heat stroke, especially in older adults. Many low-income older adults lack air-conditioning and are unable to access cooler environments because of physical disabilities. Severe cold in the winter poses risks of frostbite and death from cold exposure, especially for those who lose power, are homeless, or are unable to afford adequate heating.
- **Smog/Environmental contamination**: Exposure to air pollution increase rates of acute and chronic respiratory disorders. Environmental toxins in the soil, water, and plants may cause various disorders, including weakness, skin lesions/rashes, and cancers.

Alternative Lifestyle Choices

As young people become sexually active, most are attracted to members of the opposite sex, but others face **alternative lifestyle** choices:

- Gay and lesbian (homosexual) teenagers are attracted to members of their own sex, whereas bisexual teenagers are attracted to both sexes. Between 1% and 10% of teenagers identify themselves as homosexual, often feeling different from a very young age. These adolescents are at increased risk of violence, sexual abuse, depression, and harassment. They may not be accepted by their families or friends and sometimes become homeless. They are at risk for sexually transmitted diseases (STDs) and HIV and suffer from high rates of suicide.
- Some children are transgender, sometimes identifying from preschool age with the opposite gender and choosing to live in that role. They often suffer much prejudice because there is little understanding of transgender issues.

Intervention includes providing support and acceptance as well as practical assistance for housing, safe-sex instruction, counseling, and support groups.

Stages Involved in Pathogenesis/Disease

Pathogenesis is the cellular responses and other pathological events involved in the infectious process. A pathogenic organism must find a means of transmission from a reservoir to gain access to the host. Once entry is achieved, in order to grow and replicate, the microorganism must attach, through a mechanism called adherence, so that it can become established within the host. Some will then use adhesins to attach to a cell for the purpose of entering the cell. This can cause infection of just one type of cell or, in some cases, generalized infection. Microorganisms can cause localized infection, but some emit toxins that can cause disseminated or distant infection or cell damage.

Microorganisms produce a variety of chemicals, including toxins, to help them gain control. The invading microorganism must evade the immune system, which mounts a defense to protect the body. Once entrenched, the microorganism then transmits to a new host.

TRANSMISSION AND VIRULENCE

Transmission can often be evaded by the host if the skin is intact and the mucosa is healthy. Normal flora usually remains in balance unless disease or medications affect the immune system. Pathogenic microorganisms, however, have developed numerous strategies to invade a host. Some spores can withstand long periods in the environment and are resistant to heat and drying, some organisms thrive on the skin and can easily spread to wounds, some can survive well in contaminated fluids, and others thrive in conditions of poor hygiene. Incision, rashes, tubes, or traumas that compromise the integrity of the skin or mucous membranes facilitate transmission.

Virulence is the degree of pathogenicity, the ability to cause infection in the host. When comparing organisms, virulence is often evaluated in terms of the infectious/effective dose (ID50/ED50) that will likely cause infection in 50% of those exposed or the lethal dose (LD50) that will cause death in 50% of those that are exposed.

VIRULENCE FACTORS THAT ALLOW BACTERIA TO INVADE AND MULTIPLY IN A HOST

Virulence factors, which allow the microorganism to invade a host and multiply, vary from one microorganism to another, with some being much more virulent than others because of the following inherent characteristics:

- **Adherence**: Some bacteria are more readily able to adhere to mucosal surfaces, such as those that develop fimbriae that facilitate adherence, making them more able to colonize and multiply.
- **Invasiveness**: Some bacteria have chemical components on their surfaces, either on the plasmids or chromosomes, which facilitate invasion of host cells.
- **Structure**: Some bacteria are encapsulated, effectively protecting them from phagocytosis or destruction.
- **Toxins**: Many bacteria produce lipopolysaccharide, protein, or enzyme toxins (endotoxins and exotoxins) that are extremely poisonous to the host and can cause severe systemic reactions, acute infection, sepsis, shock, and death.
- **Iron-binding factors** (siderophores): Some bacteria are able to use the host's supply of iron to multiply and grow, competing with the host and facilitating infection.

STAGES OF PATHOGENESIS

The different **stages of pathogenesis** include the following:

1. **Exposure**: The pathogenic agent comes in contact with the host and enters through the portal of entry (such as by ingesting contaminated food products or water).
2. **Incubation**: The period between exposure and the time when the first symptoms appear. Incubation periods vary widely, and the incubation period for the same infection may vary from one individual to another depending on their general health and the effectiveness of their immune system. For example, the incubation period for the common cold may range from 2 to 7 days.
3. **Prodromal period**: Mild symptoms (e.g., headache, muscle aches, lethargy) that are the first symptoms of an infection and often precede more severe symptoms.
4. **Symptoms**: This is the acute stage in which the pathogen continues to invade the tissue, resulting in the most severe symptoms.

5. **Remission**: Period during which the infection may still be present but the symptoms have subsided. For example, patients treated for HIV may enter a period in which the retrovirus is not multiplying and the patient has no signs of infection, but HIV is still present in the body.
6. **Exacerbation**: An increase in the severity of an infection/disease, often following a remission.

Immunoglobulins

Immunoglobulins (Ig) are antibodies, soluble glycoproteins that serve as a defense against invasive bacteria, viruses, or parasites. The Y-shaped immunoglobulins identify foreign antigens and bind to them as part of the immune response. The ends of the Y structure contain paratopes that adhere to specific receptors, called epitopes, on antigens specific to a pathogen, signaling phagocytes to mobilize or directly destroying the pathogen. Producing immunoglobulins is the primary purpose of the antibody-mediated immune response (also called the humoral immune system). Immunoglobulins attached to B cells are bound by a membrane and called B-cell receptors and serve to activate these cells. Antibodies are found in the blood and other body fluids as well as in mucoid secretions. B cells produce plasma cells that in turn secrete Ig. Ig can bind to pathogens in mucus, preventing colonization and can also bind directly to toxins. Ig neutralizes viruses, but, if this is incomplete, as with HIV, the Ig increases infectivity.

Types

There are five different **types of immunoglobulins** (Ig) or antibodies (alpha, delta, epsilon, gamma, mu), with subtypes in some cases, based on their sequences of amino acids. Although these types are common to vertebrates, the base of the Y-structured immunoglobulin is specific to each animal:

- IgG has four subclasses and is the only Ig that is transferred placentally. It increases opsonization and phagocytosis, and it is the primary antibody-mediated immune response Ig.
- IgM has two subclasses and facilitates agglutination of microorganisms as well as fixing complement to lyse pathogens. IgM is part of the early cell-mediated immune response.
- IgA usually does not fix complement and is found in secretions of mucous membranes.
- IgD does not fix complement and is found on B cells, but its function is unclear.
- IgE binds to basophils and mast cells before antigens, triggering the release of histamine, so it is the cause of hypersensitive allergic responses. IgE also increases in helminth infection.

Complement Proteins in the Defense System of Bacteria

The complement system involves about 35 inactive proteins circulating in the blood and activating and "complementing" or assisting in the destruction of pathogens. When a complement protein encounters a pathogen, a "complement cascade," a series of biochemical reactions, occurs in which many protein complements coat microbes to disrupt the cell membrane, increasing susceptibility to phagocytosis. There are three pathways to activation:

- The classic complement cascade activates when the C1 (the first protein complement) encounters an antibody attached to an antigen–antibody complex and assists the antibody. Complement proteins attach in a cascade, one after the other, and they are able to puncture the cell membrane.

- Alternative complement cascade activates when a C3 complement protein directly attaches to a pathogen. It is useful for infections that do not involve antibodies.
- Mannan-binding lectin complement cascade activates when a C1q complement protein attaches to mannose and other sugars, allowing the protein to bind to many different pathogens.

Immune Host Defenses

Antibody-Mediated (Humoral) Immunity

Immune host defenses are more specific than innate and are directed against a specific pathogen or its by-products. This inducible defense system develops resistance and immunity. **Antibody-mediated (humoral) immunity** begins when a microorganism invades a host and carries antigenic substances, which can be components of the cell wall, structures such as fimbriae, toxins, or enzymes. When a macrophage encounters a pathogen, it phagocytizes and destroys it. Then the macrophage displays fragments of the antigen on its surface to activate T cells, which in turn activate B cells, which divide and form plasma cells, which release antibodies that are specific to the antigens. Antibodies are immunoglobulins, of which there are five types. The macrophage also forms memory cells, which become part of the permanent immune system. The antibodies bind to antigens, creating what is referred to as the antigen-antibody complex, and destroying the antigen, leading to destruction of the pathogen.

Cell-Mediated Immunity

Cell-mediated immunity is a delayed-type hypersensitivity response that activates cells rather than antibodies to fight pathogens. This same system is activated against transplants, causing rejection. After macrophages phagocytize antigens, proteins are encoded by major histocompatibility complex (MHC) so they can display antigenic fragments, alerting T-lymphocyte cells, which are coated with clusters of differentiation (CD), chemical molecules. The thymus releases cytotoxic T killer cells (CD8+) that can recognize the MHC-carrying foreign antigen, from bacteria, viruses, tumors, or transplanted tissue. In the activation phase, T cells with the correct receptors for the pathogen divide and multiply. In the effector phase, these cytotoxic T cells release lymphotoxins that destroy the pathogenic cells. T helper (TH) cells (CD4+) secrete lymphokines that stimulate both T cells and B cells to multiply. Suppressor T cells deactivate the immune response. Cell-mediated immunity is especially effective for viral, fungal, and protozoal infections as well as tumor cells and intracellular bacteria.

Effects on Disease

Air Pollution

Air pollution is primarily caused by the use of fossil fuels, such as oil, gas, natural gas, and coal, because these fuels release carbon monoxide, hydrocarbons, and other pollutants into the atmosphere when they are burned. Motor vehicles are the primary polluters, but industrial emissions from factories and manufacturing plants also are implicated because many depend on fossil fuels as well, and some release various chemicals used in or resulting from the manufacturing process. Air pollution can also result from agricultural chemicals (such as crop spraying) and household chemicals (such as fumigants). Air pollution can reduce visibility in some cases, but it may also be invisible, so people may be unaware that their air is polluted. Air pollution is considered as one of the causes of global warming. Air pollution can also have a serious impact on health by impairing lung function and resulting in an increased incidence of cancer and respiratory diseases, such as asthma and COPD.

Water Pollution

Water pollution occurs when pollutants flow into surface water sources, such as rivers, lakes, reservoirs, and oceans. Contamination of surface water can result from sewage, oil spills, industrial wastes, and chemical runoffs (fertilizers, weed killers). In areas with air pollution, surface water may become contaminated through atmospheric deposition (rain, snow). Drinking water, even from clean water sources, can become contaminated through erosion of lead pipes or lead solder used with other types of pipes that are part of the delivery system. Groundwater can also become polluted as pollutants, such as noxious chemicals from fertilizers and weed killers, are leached through the ground and enter underground water. Water pollution not only kills fish and wildlife, but it can also harm wetlands and coral reefs. Water pollution has been implicated in waterborne diseases (such as typhoid fever), neurological impairment, and cancer. Children exposed to polluted water may suffer developmental disorders and intellectual disabilities.

Trauma

Exposure to **trauma** (violence, bullying, assault, war, hurricanes, tornadoes, accidents) during a child's formative years may impair physical and emotional development and can result in severe mental health problems, such as depression. Many people exposed to severe trauma experience symptoms of post-traumatic stress disorder, which impairs their abilities to function, to work, and to interact with other people. Those exposed to trauma are more likely than others to engage in substance abuse, such as the use of drugs or alcohol, in order to self-medicate symptoms or to block out memories. Preventive measures, such as antibullying programs, alcohol education programs, better lighting, and improved traffic control, may help to reduce the incidences of trauma and the effects on disease. Additionally, identifying those affected by trauma and providing early intervention may help to prevent development or progression of disorders associated with trauma.

Hazardous Materials and Exposure

Hazardous materials are any that may cause harm (health or physical hazard) to humans or animals by themselves or through interaction with something else. Hazardous materials may be:

- **Chemical**: Include blister agents, blood agents, choking agents, nerve agents, asphyxiants, and irritants. These can enter the body through inhalation, absorption, ingestion, and injection.
- **Radiological**: Nuclear material, radioactive substances (alpha/beta particles).
- **Physical/Biological**: Infectious wastes, blood and other body fluids, biotoxins.

Almost any material or substance can be classified as hazardous depending on various factors, such as location, amount, and interactions. **Exposure** occurs when a person/animal comes in contact with the hazardous material, and **contamination** is the residue resulting from exposure. **Absorption** is the method by which hazardous material enters the bloodstream. Exposure and contamination may result in immediate (blistering, itching, pain) or delayed (nausea, vomiting, cancer, lung disease) responses.

Childhood Diseases

Varicella Zoster (Chicken Pox)

Varicella zoster (chicken pox) is a highly infectious communicable disease spread through touch and airborne particles. A rash develops 10 to 21 days after exposure, and the person is infective from 24 to 48 hours before the rash occurs until the blisters scab over. Initial symptoms include fever, poor appetite, headache, and rash. The initial rash is red and macular, but it rapidly progresses to papular and then vesicular with fluid-filled blisters, which become cloudy and then break, leaving scabs. The rash may be extremely pruritic. When a student has signs and symptoms of chicken pox, he or she should be immediately isolated from others, provided a face mask, and the parents/caregivers should be called to take the student home. Most who develop chicken pox were not vaccinated. Standard, contact, and airborne precautions are indicated. It is recommended that all children receive varicella vaccine. Two doses are needed: the first at 12–15 months and the second at 4–6 years (or at least 3 months after the first dose).

Rubeola (Measles) and Mumps

Rubeola (measles) is a viral disease characterized by fever and rash that can cause serious morbidity and death. It is highly infectious by droplets 4 days before and 4 days after the onset of rash and has an incubation period of 7–18 days. Symptoms include the following:

- Flu-like symptoms: cough, fever, runny nose.
- Red maculopapular rash.
- Koplik spots on mucous membranes.
- Complications include pneumonia, seizures, and severe neurological damage from encephalitis.

Vaccination (measles, mumps, rubella [MMR]) or previous infection provides immunity. The vaccine may be used as a prophylaxis for 72 hours after exposure, whereas Ig may provide protection if given within 6 days.

Mumps is a viral disease that causes fever and swollen parotid glands but can cause deafness, meningitis, and swelling of the testicles. Mumps is spread through contact with saliva or aerosolized droplets from someone who is infected. The incubation period is 2–3 weeks. Incidence has decreased since vaccinations have become routine. Symptoms include painful swelling of the glands on one or both sides of the face, fever, weakness, fatigue. Complications (rare) include orchitis, encephalitis, meningitis, ovarian inflammation, pancreatitis, and permanent hearing loss. Vaccination is per MMR.

Rubella and Mononucleosis

Rubella, also known as German measles, is a viral disease that can cause rash, fever, and arthritis, but the big danger is that it can cause a woman who is pregnant to miscarry or deliver a child with serious birth defects. Transmission is through airborne droplets. The incubation period is 2–3 weeks after exposure. Symptoms persist for 2–3 days and include fever ≤102º F, rhinitis, conjunctivitis, poor appetite, nausea, and inflamed lymph nodes behind the ears and at the back of the neck. A rash, red or pink and sometimes itchy, starts on the face and moves down the body with the face clearing of the rash as it progresses. Vaccination is per MMR.

Mononucleosis is an infectious disorder caused by the Epstein-Barr virus. It is spread through saliva and airborne droplets and occurs most commonly in teenagers and young adults. The incubation period is 4-6 weeks. Symptoms are usually similar to an upper respiratory infection or flu, with adults affected more than children, and the symptoms, which may persist for weeks, include the following: weakness, headaches, fever, persistent sore throat, enlarged lymph nodes in the neck and axillae, enlarged tonsils, generalized red macular rash, and enlarged spleen (which may rupture in rare cases).

Conjunctivitis and Pediculosis

Conjunctivitis, commonly referred to as "pink eye," is caused by viral or bacterial infection of the conjunctiva. Typical symptoms include red, itching eyes and complaints of "something in the eye." Watery or purulent (with bacterial infection) discharge may be evident. Conjunctivitis is highly contagious, and the infective agent is present in tears and is easily transmitted on the hands of students; however, states vary widely on whether students with conjunctivitis should be excluded from school, so the health educator must be aware of state and local policies. Applying cool compresses to the eye may help to relieve discomfort.

Pediculosis is infestation with lice, transmitted by direct contact with someone who is infested:

- Head lice (most common in children).
- Body lice (most common in transient populations/homeless). They feed on the body but live in clothing or bedding and are spread by sharing bedding, clothes, or towels.
- Pubic lice are spread by sexual contact or (rare) sharing clothes or bedding and may infest the genital area, eyebrows, eyelids, lower abdomen, and beard.

Symptoms include persistent itch (worse at night), irritation, excoriation, and sometimes secondary infections. Nits are usually evident in the hair. Treatment of choice is over-the-counter permethrin 1% (Nix).

Congenital Disorders

Down Syndrome (Trisomy 21)

Down syndrome (trisomy 21) is a congenital disease that occurs as a result of a trisomy (three copies) of chromosome 21 or 14/21 unbalanced translocation. There are many clinical manifestations:

- **Dysmorphism**: Small skull with flat occiput; inner epicanthal folds and an upward, outward slant to the eyes; saddle nose; protruding tongue; highly arched palate; short, thick neck; hypotonic musculature; lax joints; simian line on the palm; and broad, short stubby hands and feet.
- **Intellectual impairment**: May range from mildly to profoundly disabled.
- **Range of congenital anomalies**: Congenital heart disease, renal agenesis, duodenal atresia, Hirschsprung's disease, tracheoesophageal fistula, hip subluxation, and instability of cervical vertebrae 1 and 2.
- **Sensory deficits**: Hearing loss, strabismus, nystagmus, cataracts, conjunctivitis, and myopia.
- **Growth impairment**: Height and weight are reduced, and sexual development is delayed.

Pseudohypertrophic (Duchenne) Muscular Dystrophy

Pseudohypertrophic (Duchenne) muscular dystrophy is the most common and the most severe form. It is an X-linked disorder in about 50% of all cases with the rest being sporadic mutations, affecting males almost exclusively. An abnormal cytoskeletal protein (dystrophin) causes the sarcolemma (membrane) of the muscle to allow excess calcium, which in turn leads to muscle necrosis. Children typically have some delay in motor development, with difficulty walking and have evidence of muscle weakness by about age 3. Pseudohypertrophic refers to enlargement of muscles by fatty infiltration associated with muscular atrophy, which causes contractures and deformities of the joints. Abnormal bone development results in spinal and other skeletal deformities. The disease progresses rapidly, and most children are wheelchair bound by about 12 years of age. As the disease progresses, it involves the muscles of the diaphragm and other muscles needed for respiration. Mild to frank mental deficiency is common. Facial, oropharyngeal, and respiratory muscles weaken late in the disease. Cardiomegaly commonly occurs.

Sickle Cell Disease

Sickle cell disease is a recessive genetic disorder of chromosome 11, causing hemoglobin to be defective so that red blood cells (RBCs) are sickle shaped and inflexible, resulting in their accumulating in small vessels and causing painful blockage. Although normal RBCs survive 120 days, sickled cells may survive only 10–20 days, stressing the bone marrow that can't produce fast enough and resulting in severe anemia. There are five variations of sickle cell disease, with sickle cell anemia being the most severe. Different types of crises occur (aplastic, hemolytic, vaso-occlusive, and sequestration), which cause infarctions in organs, severe pain, damage to organs, and rapid enlargement of the liver and spleen. Complications include anemia, acute chest syndrome, congestive heart failure, strokes, delayed growth, infections, pulmonary hypertension, liver and kidney disorders, retinopathy, seizures, and osteonecrosis. Sickle cell disease occurs almost exclusively in African-Americans in the United States, with 8%–10% being carriers.

Review Video: Sickle Cell Disease
Visit mometrix.com/academy and enter code: 603869

Marfan Syndrome

Marfan syndrome is a genetic disorder of the connective tissue that may put athletes at risk. Connective tissue such as tendons, ligaments, heart valves, and blood vessels are often defective and weak. Depending upon the severity of the disorder, athletes diagnosed with this disorder may be restricted from team sports, especially contact sports that may result in chest trauma, or isometric exercises, such as weight lifting. Traits can include the following:

- Tall, thin stature with loose joints, with the long bones being disproportionately long.
- Scoliosis.
- Flat feet.
- Pectus carinatum (pigeon chest) or pectus excavatum (funnel chest).
- Long, narrow face with high arched roof of mouth and crowding of teeth.
- Dislocation of lenses of eyes and sometimes retinal detachment, myopia.
- Aortic dilatation (with risk of dissection).
- Cardiac valve disorders with heart murmur.
- Stretch marks.
- Abdominal/inguinal hernia.
- Sleep apnea (rare).

Spina Bifida and Myelomeningocele

The terms **spina bifida** and **myelomeningocele** are often used interchangeably, but there is a distinction. Spina bifida is a neural tube defect with an incomplete spinal cord and often missing vertebrae that allow the meninges and spinal cord to protrude through the opening. Neural tube defects are associated with paralysis/paresis of the legs, seizures, hydrocephalus, and lack of bowel/bladder control with the severity of symptoms depending on the degree of defect. There are five basic types:

- **Spina bifida**: Defect in which the vertebral column is not closed with varying degrees of herniation through the opening.
- **Spina bifida occulta**: Failure of the vertebral column to close, but no herniation through the opening, so the defect may not be obvious.
- **Spina bifida cystica**: Defect in closure with external sac-like protrusion with varying degrees of nerve involvement.

- **Meningocele**: Spina bifida cystica with the meningeal sac being filled with spinal fluid.
- **Myelomeningocele**: Spina bifida cystica with the meningeal sac containing spinal fluid and part of the spinal cord and nerves.

Clotting Disorders

Clotting disorders include the following:

- **Hemophilia** is an inherited disorder in which the person lacks adequate clotting factors, which results in bleeding with trauma, bruising, spontaneous hemorrhage (often in the joints) and epistaxis. There are three primary types: A (80%–90%), B, and C.
- **Disseminated intravascular coagulation (DIC)** (consumption coagulopathy) is a secondary disorder that is triggered by another factor, such as trauma, congenital heart disease, necrotizing enterocolitis, sepsis, and severe viral infections. DIC triggers coagulation (clotting) and hemorrhage through a complex series of events, with clotting and hemorrhage occurring simultaneously, putting the patient at risk of death.
- **Von Willebrand's disease** is a group of congenital bleeding disorders (inherited from either parent) affecting 1%–2% of the population, associated with deficiency or a lack of vW factor (vWF), a glycoprotein.

Public Health Issues

Public health issues include the following:

- **Asepsis**: Of primary concern is handwashing to prevent the spread of disease because many infections (and contamination of food products) are from contact. Medical asepsis is often concerned with maintaining a clean rather than a sterile environment.
- **Isolation**: Those with contagious diseases, such as meningitis and TB, must be maintained on isolation during the infectious stages in order to prevent the disease from spreading. Different types of isolation (contact, droplet, airborne) are indicated depending on how the pathogen is spread.
- **Immunization**: Immunization is critical to controlling infectious diseases. Between 80% and 95% of the population (varies according to the infectious agent) must be immunized in order to achieve herd immunity. Herd immunity thresholds are based on the number of unimmunized people that one infected person could infect. The higher this number, the greater the percentage of the population that must be vaccinated. There is recent concern because of the large number of parents who are refusing to vaccinate their children.
- **Quarantine**: Restriction of movement for those infected with a contagious disease that might spread to others, usually restricted to their homes or to one area until they can be decontaminated or cleared of infection.

Treatment Options for Disease

Treatment options for disease include the following:

- **Standard medical treatment**: This may include various types of testing and imaging and treatment with medications and surgery and/or some type of therapy (recreational, physical, occupational, speech, psychological, psychiatric).
- **Complementary/Alternative therapy**: This may include acupuncture, aromatherapy, music therapy, massage, meditation, relaxation, and self-hypnosis. These therapies may be used alone (such as meditation to reduce anxiety) or in conjunction with medical treatment (such as aromatherapy or acupuncture to relieve nausea that is caused by chemotherapy).

- **Traditional/Folk medicine**: Some cultural/ethnic groups (Navajo, Hmong, Chinese) may use traditional practices (cupping, coining) and/or healers as well as various herbal preparations as part of disease treatments.
- **Supportive care**: Treatment is provided to reduce symptoms and to provide comfort rather than for curative purposes, generally when patients are dying, have exhausted treatment options, or have opted to forego treatment.

PANDEMICS

A **pandemic** is a worldwide viral epidemic that causes serious respiratory illness and/or death in large populations of people. Pandemics can occur when a virus mutates, creating a new subtype that infects humans and spreads easily from person to person. The influenza of most concern recently has been avian flu, which primarily affects birds, but it has infected other animals, including humans, primarily those in contact with infected flocks. There are many subtypes of avian flu, and symptoms may range from typical influenza-like respiratory infections to severe pneumonia. Should a further mutation occur and a pandemic occur, the implications for health care are profound because of the potential number of infected patients overwhelming the medical system. According to the CDC, a mutated virus in a remote area can spread to major cities throughout the world within 36 hours. Epidemics/Pandemics may also be started as acts of terrorism. Organisms that pose a terrorist threat include Bacillus anthracis (anthrax), Clostridium botulinum (botulism), Yersinia pestis (pneumonic plague), and smallpox (variola virus). Zoonoses also pose a risk to humans (Ebola, Lassa, Marburg, yellow, Argentine, and Crimean-Congo) and are spread easily from person to person.

Occupational Knowledge

Stages Involved in the Aging Process

The **stages of aging** include the following:

- **Infancy (ages 0–1)**: The infant is almost completely dependent on adults for his or her needs. The child grows rapidly and begins to develop fine and gross motor skill as well as understanding of simple words. The infant begins to display some distinct personality traits.
- **Toddlerhood (ages 1–3)**: Growth slows but cognitive ability increases as the child begins to use words and shows beginning problem-solving skills. The toddler begins to enjoy playing side by side with others and has improved fine and gross motor skills. The toddler shows increasing independence and may react negatively if thwarted.
- **Early childhood (ages 3–6)**: The preschool years are characterized by steady physical growth, increased fine and gross motor skills, and increased visual acuity. The child begins to engage in associative play and interactions with other children. Language skills improve markedly. Personality traits of infancy persist and may be at odds with learning environments.
- **Middle childhood (ages 6–8)**: The child loses the primary teeth and begins to mature physically. The child relies on concrete experiences but improves at problem solving. The child begins to enjoy cooperating with others and team sports. The child's temperament remains relatively unchanged, but communication skills improve.
- **Late childhood (ages 8–12)**: Girls undergo a growth spurt at about age 9 and boys a year or so later with maturing of internal organs and lengthening of the long bones. The child understands the concept of conservation (matter remains unchanged when form changes) and continues to enjoy group activities and sports. The child may become interested in sexuality and gender differences.
- **Adolescence (ages 12–18)**: Sexual maturation occurs, and the adolescent is concerned with identity. The adolescent can reason abstractly and may begin to act independently and to rebel. Peer interactions are especially important. The adolescent may undergo a period of stress before developing a strong identity.
- **Early adulthood (ages 18–35)**: Physical and social changes emerge slowly as the adult makes choices about career and sets goals. The person may experiment with lifestyle and sexuality and expands social circles. Problem-solving skills improve and moral development continues.
- **Middle adulthood (ages 35–50)**: This is a period of relative stability and good health, although habits such as smoking may begin to cause impairment. The person has many obligations and responsibilities, including family and job, and may experience increased stress. Social relationships are often stable and rewarding.
- **Maturity (ages 50–80)**: The person experiences gradual physical decline and may have serious illnesses. Some may show cognitive decline and increased incidence of chronic and acute illnesses. The person may have an improved sense of well-being, self-confidence, and emotional stability.
- **Late adulthood (ages 80+)**: The person may have chronic illness and increased dependency on others, such as adult children. Cognition varies, with short-term memory loss being common. Many live alone or in assisted living.

Aging Process

Neurological Changes

There are many **neurological changes** associated with aging. Brain mass tends to decrease slightly with age, corresponding to loss of neurons (especially in the frontal lobes) and decreased cerebral blood flow. Short-term memory loss is most common, but mentation usually stays intact unless there is an underlying disorder, such as Alzheimer's or strokes. Scattered neurofibrillary tangles and plaques may be found in the brain, but there are fewer than with Alzheimer's. The effects of general anesthesia tend to be prolonged with a lower dosage requirement, and many elderly people have postoperative cognitive dysfunction, which may persist for weeks or months and may be permanent in some people. Postoperative delirium can occur with regional and general anesthesia. Peripheral nerve cells may degenerate, causing muscle atrophy. The threshold for sensory input may increase, and vibratory sensation may decrease. Autonomic changes cause reduced perspiration so that the core temperature is higher before sweating is induced.

Cardiovascular Changes

There are many **cardiovascular changes** associated with aging that may affect geriatric heart conditions. Patients may have existing heart disease, such as heart failure, coronary artery disease, or hypertension, that predisposes them to a decrease in arterial elasticity with increased blood pressure because the heart has to work harder to pump the blood. Enlargement of the heart, particularly left ventricular hypertrophy, is common. The resting and maximal heart rates may be reduced. Cardiac output reduces by about 1% every year after age 30, resulting in a prolonged circulation time, but it is usually sufficient for the individual's needs in everyday activities. However, exercise tolerance may decrease as the maximum heart rate falls and the heart cannot meet the exercise needs, resulting in tiredness and shortness of breath. Because the sympathetic nervous system is less efficient with age, the older individual may experience light-headedness if standing up quickly. Additionally, fat tends to accumulate about the heart and in the vessels (atherosclerosis) with age.

Pulmonary Changes

There are many **pulmonary changes** associated with aging. Typically, with age there is decreased pulmonary elasticity, decreases in alveolar surface area, and increases in chest wall rigidity, so the exchange of carbon dioxide and oxygen is impaired. Additionally, the decreased elasticity causes the small bronchioles to collapse during exhalation, trapping air in the alveoli and further impairing oxygen exchange. Overall strength is often decreased, so there is less ability to breathe deeply, and the cough reflex and ciliary action are decreased. Protective laryngeal reflexes are diminished, resulting in a greater chance of aspiration. The forced vital capacity (the maximal volume of air that a person can force out with one exhalation) peaks at age 21 and then tends to decline a little each year. The rib cage stiffens with age as the cartilage calcifies, impairing the ability of the rib cage to expand adequately during respirations. Although the pulmonary system may be able to generally meet the needs of the individual, the changes triggered by aging may result in decreased exercise tolerance with increased shortness of breath on exertion.

Integumentary (Skin) Changes

Age is an important consideration when evaluating the **skin** because the characteristics of the skin change as people age. An infant's skin is thinner than an adult's because, although the epidermis is developed, the dermis layer is only about 60% of that of an adult and continues to develop after birth. During adolescence, the hair follicles activate and the thickness of the dermis decreases about 20% and epidermal turnover time increases, so healing slows. As people continue to age, Langerhans cells decrease in number, making the skin more prone to cancer, and the inflammatory reactions decrease. The sweat glands, vascularity, and subcutaneous fat all decrease, interfering with thermoregulation and contributing to dryness and irritation of the skin. The epidermal-dermal junction flattens, resulting in skin that is prone to tearing. The elastin in the skin degrades with age and solar exposure. The thinning of the hypodermis can lead to pressure ulcers.

Cognitive Changes

Cognitive changes related to age vary among individuals but are usually not evident until after 70. Studies have shown that by age 81, about 60%–70% of people have a small decline in cognitive abilities. **Fluid intelligence** (information processing skills) tends to decline slightly with age, whereas **crystallized intelligence** (acquired knowledge and applied problem solving) is more likely to stay intact and may even improve. Older adults may have more difficulty in completing complex tasks that require the processing of new information. They may become more easily distracted and less able to focus their attention. Processing information and reacting may be slowed so that those older than 60 require more time to complete mental tasks even though their intellectual capability remains intact. Working memory declines, making it more difficult for older adults to complete mental processes that require keeping facts in memory (such as calculating costs and tips). Implicit memories (skills, reactions) usually remain intact, whereas explicit memories (facts, information) may decline. Older adults often have difficulty retrieving words (names of people or objects).

Issues Related to Aging

Nutrition

Older adults generally have lower calorie requirements because of lower levels of activity and decreased rates of metabolism, but they may require additional vitamins and minerals. Decreased appetite is common, resulting in weight loss and sometimes leading to malnutrition. Decreased appetite may be associated with a decreased sense of taste and smell, resulting in the desire for stronger seasonings. Additionally, food may be less appealing because the production of saliva and the perception of thirst decrease, resulting in a sensation of dry mouth. Digestion slows, including a decrease in the production of gastric acids and slower peristalsis (especially if the person is less active), so the older adult may feel full for longer periods. Some medications alter the taste of foods or cause nausea. Some disorders, such as stroke and Parkinson's disease, interfere with the person's ability to swallow and remain independent in eating.

Pharmacokinetics

There are many changes in the elderly that affect **pharmacokinetics**:

- **Absorption** slows because of increased gastric pH and slower emptying time, so medication may take effect more slowly, but excess medication may be absorbed.
- **Distribution** may alter because of decreased intracellular and extracellular water, reducing the distribution of water-soluble medications. Body fat increases (≤36% in men and ≤48% in women) between early adulthood and age 80, so that fat-soluble medications (e.g., benzodiazepines) accumulate in fat and the half-life is prolonged. Protein-binding alterations may change the half-life as well. Decreased cardiac output and systemic illness may impact distribution.
- **Metabolism** is affected by a decrease in liver size (25%–35%) and blood flow to the liver (≤40% by age 90). The enzymes necessary to break down medications are decreased. These changes can increase the half-life two to three times in some medications (benzodiazepines, diazepam, and alprazolam).
- **Elimination** of most drugs is through the kidneys, but renal function declines in about 65% of the elderly, so the half-life is extended, necessitating lower doses.

PHARMACODYNAMICS

There are many changes in the elderly that affect **pharmacodynamics**:

- **CNS changes** include changes in receptor sensitivity and in the numbers of receptor sites can result in increased side effects, delirium, and behavioral changes, especially with benzodiazepines, opioids, alcohol, antipsychotics, anticholinergics, and barbiturates.
- **Decreases in beta-adrenergic receptor function** may necessitate an increased dosage of some medications, such as β-blockers and the vasopressor isoproterenol (Isuprel).
- **Decreases in baroreceptor function** may affect the ability to increase vascular tone or cardiac output/heart rate in response to vasoactive medications, such as antihypertensives, resulting in orthostatic hypotension.
- **Impaired glucose counter-regulation** increases the risk of hypoglycemia for those on diabetes medications.

MEDICATION DOSAGE

There are many issues related to aging that can affect **medication dosage**:

- Adverse effects of drugs are two to three times more common in older adults than younger, often related to polypharmacy.
- Most drug trials are conducted on younger adults, so information is limited about correct dosage and effects on older adults.
- Some diseases (e.g., hypertension, heart failure, renal failure, and diabetes) are associated with drug intolerance, so alternative medications may be needed.
- Drug and nutrient interactions may impact nutrition by impairing the person's appetite. Interactions may also alter the pharmacokinetics of nutrients or drugs, interfering with absorption, distribution, metabolism, and elimination. Mixing drugs in tube feedings or giving them with food increases the risk of interactions, so medications should be taken with water unless contraindicated.

MI

Myocardial infarction (MI) occurs when there is an imbalance between the heart's demand for oxygen and the supply. An MI is part of the continuum of acute coronary syndrome and may occur after an episode of unstable angina caused by rupture of an atherosclerotic plaque and thrombosis (blood clot) associated with coronary artery spasm, but it may also result from vasoconstriction, acute blood loss, decreased oxygen, and ingestion of cocaine. Damage to the myocardium typically occurs in stages and in three zones: ischemia (impaired oxygenation, creating a zone of ischemia with viable cells), cellular injury in the zone of injury, and infarction with necrosis (death) of tissue in the zone of infarction. MI symptoms may vary considerably, with males having the more "classic" symptoms than females. Diabetic patients may have reduced sensation of pain because of neuropathy and may complain primarily of weakness. Elderly patients may also have neuropathic changes that reduce sensations of pain. Older adults have a higher incidence of pulmonary edema and complications such as left ventricular wall or papillary muscle rupture (1–4 days after MI). Symptoms include chest pain (66%), shortness of breath (20%–59%), neurological symptoms (anxiety, light-headedness, headache, visual abnormalities, slurred speech, and fear) (about 20%), palpitations, and hyper- or hypotension.

Myths Regarding Aging

Myths regarding aging include the following:

- **Weak and sick**: Some people assume that all older adults are weak and have illness. Although chronic disease is more common in older adults, many seniors function very well despite their disease and can remain controlled with treatment.
- **Stubborn, rigid, set in their ways**: Older adults are as varied as younger adults in their attitudes and belief systems.
- **Nonproductive**: Productivity is not measured only by work hours, although many older adults continue to work or do regular volunteer work. Older adults have a wealth of information and experience that they can share with others.
- **Asexual**: About 50% of adults >60 continue to enjoy sexual relationships.
- **Nursing home care**: In fact, only about 5% of those ≥65 reside in nursing homes and half of those are ≥85. Most older adults continue to live independently until an advanced age.
- **Inability to learn**: Older adults may process information a little slower, but, unless they have dementia or another condition that impairs learning, they are able to learn and master new material.

Cultural Responses to Aging

Cultural responses to aging vary widely:

- **Asian**: Older adults are often viewed positively and with respect. Families may not want an older adult to know if he/she is seriously ill or dying, and illness and disability may be viewed as shameful and something to keep hidden. Older adults expect to be cared for by their children, usually the eldest son.
- **Middle Eastern**: Older adults are viewed with respect and treated with honor. The oldest adult male in the family is often the one to make decisions for others. Because Middle Eastern cultures are almost exclusively patriarchal, females have little voice in decision making at any age. Older adults are cared for by their children, generally the eldest son.
- **Western**: Older adults tend to be viewed negatively and with less respect, but they are also generally considered to be more independent. Although many older adults live with their offspring, there is little cultural expectation for this.
- **Hispanic**: Older adults are respected and often have large extended families who care for them. In traditional families, the oldest male makes the decisions for the family. Older adults who are ill may expect to receive extra attention.

Effects of "Graying" of the Population on Twenty-First Century Health Care

Effects of the "**graying**" of the population on twenty-first century health care include the following:

- **Higher healthcare costs**: With most healthcare costs covering the costs of care for older adults, a larger percentage of the aging population is likely to dramatically increase costs for treatment and long-term care.
- **Greater need for healthcare providers**: The need for physicians, nurses, aides, and other healthcare providers will increase to keep up with the demand generated by a greater population of older adults.
- **Increased taxes**: Fewer people actively engaged in wage-earning means that those who are employed must assume a greater share of costs through higher taxes.
- **Lower percentage of workers**: With fewer workers in the job market, productivity is likely to decline, slowing economic growth.

- **Older adult services/activities**: Services and activities will increasingly be modified to meet the needs of older adults.
- **Increased immigration**: In order to meet the industrial demand for workers, immigration will need to be expanded to attract younger workers.
- **Low-cost housing**: Because many older adults have limited income, the need for low-cost housing will increase.

Social Services for Older Adults

Social services available to older adults include the following:

- **Adult protective services**: Identify abuse and neglect and provide protection for older adults.
- **Supplemental Security Income** (SSI): Supplemental income available by the Social Security Administration for those with low income.
- **Home health agencies**: Provide treatment to people in their home environments.
- **Senior centers**: Provide recreational opportunities for older adults and sometimes low-cost meals.
- **Transportation services**: Door-to-door services for the disabled and wheelchair-bound accommodating public transportation.
- **Meals-on-Wheels and other meal services**: Low-cost meals delivered (usually 5 days a week) to people's homes.
- **Medicaid**: Provides insurance coverage for health care for those with low income and may also pay for long-term care and home health aides.
- **Long-term care ombudsman**: Investigates complaints regarding care provided by long-term-care facilities.
- **Supplemental Nutrition Assistance Program** (SNAP): Provides food-purchasing assistance to allow those with low income to purchase food.
- **Caregiver services/respite**: Provides caregivers for the disabled and ill and respite services for family caregivers.
- **Legal aid**: Provides legal assistance at no or low cost.

Ethical Issues Regarding Older Adults

Ethical issues regarding older adults include the following:

- **Autonomy versus beneficence**: Although older adults have the right to self-determination, this must be balanced against the need to provide adequate and safe care. The cognitive ability and the ability of the older adult to make reasoned decisions must be considered. In some cases, a healthcare proxy must make decisions, but then this may pose another dilemma if family members, for example, are not in agreement.
- **Beneficence versus nonmaleficence**: Some treatments that are given for the good of the person (such as chemotherapy) may cause considerable harm to the person, so the benefits and the risks must be considered and balanced.
- **Restraints**: When and if to use restraints to prevent an older adult from being injured is an ethical concern. Restraints should be the least restrictive, used only as a last resort, and used for the shortest possible period.
- **End-of-life**: The desires of the older adult at the end-of-life stage should always be considered and respected as much as possible; however, sometimes what the person wants is counter to what is possible. For example, if a bedridden patient wants to die at home but there is no caregiver available, this may not be possible.

Psychological Effects of Aging

Grief, Mourning, and Bereavement

Grief is a normal response to loss, and older adults may face the loss of their spouse, family, income, status, health, mobility, home, and independence. **Mourning** is the public expression of grief, and **bereavement** is the time period of mourning. There are three primary types of grief:

- **Acute**: This occurs immediately in response to some type of loss and may be expressed as sadness, anger, fear, and anxiety.
- **Anticipatory**: This occurs when people fear a loss, such as the impending death of a spouse or transfer to a long-term-care facility.
- **Chronic grief**: This occurs when people are not able to comes to terms with loss, so grieving and mourning are prolonged, sometimes for years. People may develop anorexia, insomnia, panic attacks, self-destructive behaviors (alcohol and substance abuse), and contemplate or carry out suicide. Chronic grief poses a serious risk to people and should be treated as depression, with antidepressants, psychological evaluation, and counseling.

Kübler-Ross's Five Stages of Grief

Grief is a normal response to the death or severe illness/abnormality of a patient. How a person deals with grief is very personal, and each will grieve differently. Elisabeth Kübler-Ross identified **five stages of grief**, which can apply to patients and to family members. A person may not go through each stage but usually goes through two of the five stages:

Stage	Patient/Family	Appropriate Response
Denial	Resistive to information, stunned, immobile, detached, unable to respond appropriately.	Be patient and supportive and repeat information as needed.
Anger	Lashing out, overt hostility, self-blame, blaming others.	Do not respond in anger or take statements personally; remain calm and supportive, but be alert to risk of physical attack.
Bargaining	If—then thinking, demanding another opinion or expert, praying.	Avoid making any judgmental statements.
Depression	Tearful, crying, withdrawn, sad, isolated.	Encourage the expression of feelings, remain supportive, and assure the individual that these feelings are normal.
Acceptance	Resolution.	Listen patiently and remain supportive.

Nutrition Fact Labels

Nutrition facts labels are required by the Food and Drug Administration (FDA) for food sold in the United States and produced either in this country or in foreign countries in compliance with the Nutrition Labeling and Education Act. This label complies with current regulations, which will change slightly in 2020 and 2021 to make the calories more prominent and provide more nutritional information. Some foods and drinks are exempt from the labeling requirement: fish, raw fruits, raw vegetables, coffee, and tea. Any food that makes a nutritional claim ("gluten free") must be labeled. Some types of businesses (small businesses with less than $50,000 food sales or less than $500,000 total sales) and low-volume food products (less than 100,000 units) are also exempt. Students should be especially aware of the total calories, the serving size, and the differences in caloric value among fats, carbohydrates, and proteins.

Diet and Nutrition

Adults

According to *Dietary Guidelines for Americans, 2015–2020*, people should maintain a balanced caloric intake and eat more nutrient-dense foods and fluids. **Diet and nutrition** recommendations include the following:

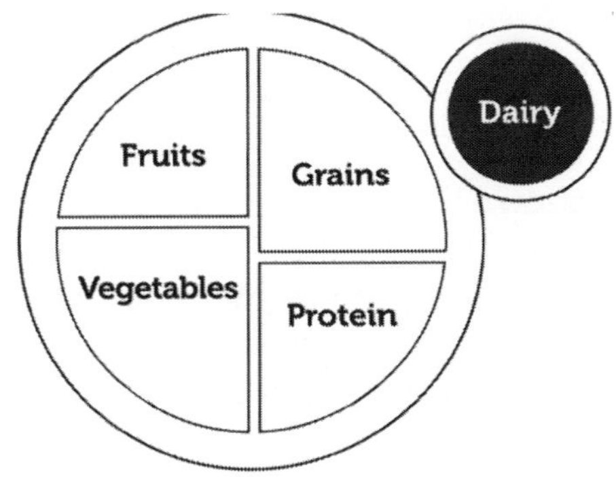

- Sodium: $<2,300$ mg/day and 1,500 mg/day for those ≥ 51 years or African-American or with existing cardiovascular or renal disease or diabetes.
- Saturated fat: $<10\%$ of calories.
- Dietary cholesterol: <300 mg/day.
- Alcohol: ≤ 1 drink daily for women and ≤ 2 for men.
- Eat more fruits and dark-green, red, and orange vegetables.
- Replace half of refined grains with whole grain.
- Use lower fat milk products.
- Eat a variety of high-protein foods, including seafood, beans, and nuts.
- Replace solid fats with oils.
- Limit trans fatty acids, solid fats, sugar, and refined grains.

Pregnant women are advised to choose foods high in heme iron and vitamin C and take 400 mcg of synthetic folic acid daily. Breastfeeding women should eat 8–12 ounces of seafood per week but limit white tuna to 6 ounces and avoid tilefish, shark, swordfish, and king mackerel. People ≥ 50 should include food or supplements with vitamin B_{12}.

Children and Adolescents

Children and adolescents need well-balanced diets with a variety of different foods, especially fruits and vegetables. The nutritional needs of the child should be met through diet rather than supplements. The plate recommendations for children are similar to those of adults. The need for protein increases during childhood and adolescence to promote growth. Whereas a child needs approximately 19 g of protein daily, the preteen needs 34 g and the adolescent needs 46–52 g, equal to about 10%–30% of total calories. Carbohydrates should be limited to 130 g or 45%–65% of total calories, and fats to 25%–35% of total calories with saturated fats limited to less than 10%. Carbohydrates should include fruits and vegetables and whole grains, which are high in fiber, but simple carbohydrates, such as sugar and foods made with white flour, should be limited. The growing child generally needs three meals and at least two snacks daily.

Nutritional Needs During Chemotherapy

There are numerous **chemotherapy** drugs, so the effects on nutrition may vary somewhat, but most result in anorexia, nausea and vomiting, changes in taste, mouth sores/inflammation, diarrhea and/or constipation, putting people at risk for weight loss, malnutrition, and cachexia. People receiving chemotherapy need a well-balanced diet with adequate protein and plentiful water to help remove by-products. People usually do best with frequent small meals and bland foods. Cold and cool foods are usually tolerated better than hot foods (because heat increases food odor). People generally avoid high-fat foods, which may exacerbate nausea, but they may need to supplement diet by adding eggs to foods and drinks or drinking diet supplements, such as Ensure or Boost, to add protein and calories to diet. If tolerated, increasing fat may help to prevent weight loss. Cold foods, such as milk shakes, may be soothing to the mouth if it is sore.

Nutritional Needs During Radiation Therapy

Radiation therapy can have differing localized effects on nutritional status depending on the administration site:

- Head and neck: Mouth sores (stomatitis), dry mouth, altered sense of taste, esophagitis, and tooth loss.
- Throat and midchest: Nausea, dysphagia, esophageal strictures.
- Abdomen/Pelvis: Nausea, vomiting, diarrhea, bowel constriction/obstruction, bleeding, and malabsorption.

People are likely to develop some degree of malnutrition (weight loss of >5% from baseline) over the course of treatment and may need to take diet supplements, such as Ensure or Boost. Dietary alterations depend on the symptoms. Those with stomatitis may be unable to tolerate solid foods or hot foods but may tolerate enriched milkshakes. Those with bowel problems (diarrhea, constipation) may benefit from added fiber if their fluid intake is adequate. Adequate protein is important to help to heal damaged tissues.

Role of Culture in Nutritional Preferences

Culture has an important role in nutritional preferences, although what may be true for the culture as a whole may not be true for the individual. Common cultural preferences include the following:

- **African-Americans**: Diet is high in total fat (fried meats/foods), sodium, and sugar and low in fruits and vegetables.
- **American** (in general): Diet is high in calories but low in fruits, vegetables, healthy oils, and dairy food.
- **Asian**: Vary according to culture, but all tend to include less red meat and protein than Western diets and more plant-based foods, but they are high in carbohydrates, especially because of rice and noodle intake.
- **Mexican/Latino**: High fat, sodium, and carbohydrate diet because rice, beans, and corn products (such as tortillas) are commonly included in meals, but the traditional diet also includes ample fruits and vegetables.
- **Mediterranean/Middle Eastern**: These diets are similar with an emphasis on olive oil, fish, fruits, legumes, and vegetables with smaller amounts of red meats, sugars, and dairy foods.

Nutritional Assessment

Nutritional assessment is based on numerous observations:

- **Food diary**: A record of food intake (including snacks) for a set number of days (usually 3 to 7) is a good beginning place for assessment.
- **Height, weight, and BMI**: These measurements help to determine if the person is over- or underweight, and this is often a reflection of diet.
- Physical assessments of **malnutrition** and **vitamin/mineral deficiency**:
  - Hair: dry and brittle or thinning.
  - Skin: poor turgor, bruising, tears, pressure areas, ulcerations, abrasions, or other compromises.
  - Mouth: dry mucous membranes. Lips may have cheilosis, cracking at the corners, or they may be scaly (riboflavin deficiency). Gums may be swollen or bleeding, and teeth may be loose or needing care. The tongue may be inflamed, dry, or cracked, or it may have sores.

  - Nails may become brittle. Spoon-shaped nails or a pale nail bed indicates low iron.
- **Health history**: This may provide information that may affect nutritional status, such as the presence of malabsorption syndromes.
- **Cultural background**: Helps to identify possible food choices and dietary habits.

Eating Disorders

Anorexia Nervosa

Anorexia nervosa is an eating disorder characterized by the following:

- Refusal to maintain a minimal normal body weight.
- Extreme fear of becoming fat.
- Disturbed perception of body weight or shape.
- Denial of low body weight and a high priority placed on weight or body shape.

Anorexia nervosa may be restrictive without binging and purging, or it may include binging and purging. Anorexia nervosa is usually chronic and requires a lifetime of monitoring. Patients with anorexia nervosa exhibit many mental health symptoms and commonly have comorbidity with depression and dysthymia. They may be irritable, have sleep disturbances, lack of interest in sex, and withdrawal from social interactions. They will be obsessed with the thought of food and may also have other obsessive-compulsive tendencies that may or may not involve food. They are at high risk for suicide. Characteristic physical findings (emaciation, osteoporosis, hair loss, cardiac dysfunction) result from malnutrition and starvation.

Bulimia Nervosa

Bulimia nervosa is an eating disorder in which the individual eats more than normal within a 2-hour period and carries out repetitive behaviors in order to control weight, such as excessive use of laxatives, diuretics, and exercise. Individuals with bulimia often engage in self-induced vomiting. Some may restrict eating and then binge and purge. Weight is often within normal range, but other symptoms include chipped teeth, dental caries, mouth sores, amenorrhea (occurs in about 50%), and heart and gastrointestinal disorders. Some may exhibit Russell's sign (callouses and scarring on the hand from using the hand to induce vomiting). The cause of bulimia nervosa is unclear, although people often have other mental health problems and low self-esteem. Criteria include repetitive cycles of binge eating; use of inappropriate behaviors to prevent weight gain, such as induced vomiting; overuse of laxatives, diuretics, or enemas; excessive exercise or fasting; and binge eating along with inappropriate behaviors to prevent weight gain at least one time per week for at least 3 months.

Therapeutic Diets

Weight Control, Diabetes, Hypertension, Lactose Sensitivity/Intolerance, and Gluten Intolerance/Celiac Disease

Therapeutic Diet Guidelines	
Weight Loss	Diets vary: low carbohydrate, low fat, and/or low calorie. Most include more whole grains, vegetables, and fruit and less refined sugar and flour.
Diabetes Mellitus	People eat three meals daily and sometimes two small snacks, but calories and portion sizes are usually limited. People avoid sugar and high-carbohydrate foods and eat food high in fiber, lean meats/fish, vegetables, and limited amounts of fruit.
Hypertension	The DASH diet (2,100 calories) is plant-focused and high in vegetables, fruits, and nuts and with limited fat, lean meats, and sweets/sugar.

Lactose Intolerance	Diet is free of milk products (cheese, milk) because the patient lacks the enzyme necessary to metabolize milk. Some patients may take lactase tablets in order to tolerate milk products.
Gluten Intolerance/ Celiac Disease	Gluten is a protein found in wheat, rye, and barley, so patients must avoid all products containing these grains, including pastas, breads, and pastries. Gluten is commonly found in many prepared foods and seasonings (chicken broth, salad dressings, soy sauce, frozen foods), which must also be avoided.

OBESITY

Obesity in children and teenagers is increasing with 16%–33% being classified as overweight. Although there is no clear agreement about weight standards for children, excess weight is having a profound effect on children's health. However, helping the child to lose weight can be difficult:

- Dieting is best approached as a healthier change in eating habits for the whole family so that the child does not eat differently from others.
- No more than 30% of nutrition should be fats.
- Carbohydrates should be complex rather than simple sugars, decreasing consumption of white flour and sugar.
- Healthy snacks, such as fruit, air-popped popcorn, and nonfat yogurt, should be provided. And high-calorie snacks (chips, candy) should not being available.
- The child should eat three meals daily, served adequate but not with large portions, and children should not be forced to clean their plate.
- Television viewing or other sedentary activities should be progressively limited over time, and exercise activities should be encouraged.

FOOD ADDITIVES AND FOOD ALLERGIES

Food additives are substances that are added to food products. Food additives may be chemicals used as preservatives, flavor enhancers (monosodium glutamate), dyes (to add color), and, in some cases, vitamins or minerals in order to prevent deficiencies. For example, vitamin D is routinely added to milk products and iodine is added to salt. **Allergic reactions** are a response of the body's immune system to an antigen (substance), such as peanuts, shellfish, or food additives. The body produces antibodies (immunoglobulins, such as IgE or non-IgE) that can identify and try to neutralize or destroy antigens. Allergic responses may be mild (local rash, redness, itching, swelling, congestion), moderate (generalized itching, difficulty breathing), or severe (life-threatening anaphylaxis). With **anaphylaxis**, an antigen triggers release of substances that affect the skin, cardiopulmonary, and GI systems. Histamine causes initial redness and swelling by inducing vasodilation. In some cases, initial reactions may be mild, but subsequent contact can cause severe life-threatening response. Symptoms include a sudden onset of weakness, dizziness, and confusion; tachycardia; generalized swelling; itching; severe low blood pressure leading to shock; airway obstruction; nausea and vomiting; hives; diarrhea; seizures; coma; and death.

VITAMINS AND VITAMIN SUPPLEMENTS

Vitamins are essential for growth and development because the body is unable to manufacture most of them. Vitamins are organic compounds composed of carbon, oxygen, hydrogen, nitrogen, and other elements, and they are used for cellular biochemical reactions. Vitamins are individual molecules that are required in small amounts. Although they do not provide energy directly, they are required to metabolize energy. Vitamins often have more than one form, so natural and synthetic vitamins may differ somewhat and may be absorbed differently. For example, synthetic folic acid is absorbed better than natural folate. Because vitamins are organic, they are susceptible to destruction. Some vitamins, for example, are susceptible to light and others to heat and can be destroyed by exposure. Many vitamins serve as coenzymes, which activate enzymes (proteins in cells). Some vitamins (C, E, beta-carotene) serve as antioxidants, protecting cells from oxidation.

Fat-Soluble and Water-Soluble Vitamins

Fat-soluble vitamins (A, D, E, and K) are found in the fat/oil parts of food and are transported in fat droplets (chylomicrons) after being absorbed into the lymphatic system from the intestines. They enter the blood attached to protein carriers because blood is watery and cannot absorb the vitamins. Fat-soluble vitamins are stored as fat in adipose tissue and the liver. Because they are stored, excess amounts of some vitamins (A and D) may become toxic, and they do not have to be consumed daily because the body can access those stores. **Water-soluble vitamins**, on the other hand, are absorbed directly into the bloodstream and are transported freely through the blood and cells. They are not stored except for small amounts in cells but are excreted in the urine. Most, except for vitamin B_6, are not toxic if taken in large amounts, but they must be consumed daily since they are not stored. Water-soluble vitamins include thiamine (vitamin B_1), riboflavin (vitamin B_2), niacin (vitamin B_3), vitamin B_6, folate, vitamin B_{12}, pantothenic acid, biotin, and vitamin C.

Dietary Deficiencies

Although poor nutritional intake can result in many different **dietary deficiencies**, some are more common in infants and children:

- **Calcium**: Calcium is essential for the growth and development of bones, but children, especially teenagers, are increasingly substituting fruit juice and sodas for milk. This can cause fractures and osteomalacia with eventual osteoporosis as an adult. Recommended daily intake for adolescents is 1,500 mg.
- **Folic acid**: Intake is often low among teenagers, resulting in high rates of congenital abnormalities if they get pregnant. Cereals and breads are fortified with folic acid to combat this.
- **Iron**: Newborns deplete their maternally supplied iron by about 4 months and may become anemic if breast-fed without supplementary rice cereal. Formula is iron fortified. Teenage girls are also often iron deficient because of menses and poor dietary intake.
- **Vitamin D**: Deficiencies are on the rise because of the judicious use of sunscreen and protecting children from all sun exposure. Breast-fed infants may need vitamin D supplements.

Herbal Remedies and Dietary Supplements

There are literally thousands of **herbal remedies and dietary supplements** and myriad claims of success in treating or preventing disease despite there being very little scientific evidence to support most claims. Many doctors recommend one daily multivitamin to ensure adequate vitamin intake and fish oil concentrate to reduce cholesterol, but patients often take high doses of herbal remedies and dietary supplements. This poses many problems. High doses of some vitamins can cause toxicity:

- Vitamin A: Headaches, loss of hair, liver damage, bone disorders, and birth defects.
- Vitamin C: Diarrhea and gastrointestinal upset.
- Vitamin D: Kidney stones, muscle weakness, and bleeding.
- Vitamin E: Inhibits action of vitamin K.
- Niacin: Liver damage, gastric ulcers, and increased serum glucose.
- Vitamin B_6: Neurological damage.

Herbal remedies often contain small amounts of agents found in drugs, so they can cause drug reactions and interactions. Also, patients often fail to inform their physicians when they are using alternative treatments.

Relationship Between Nutrition and World Health

Disparities in nutrition have a profound effect on **world health**. People in developed countries generally have access to nutritional foods and a wide range of meats, fruits, and vegetables, and the poor are often eligible for assistance through food stamps, welfare, or other programs. However, in developing countries, there may be no safety net, and drought, famine and war may destroy crops and the means of food production. Entire populations may be at risk of starvation and malnutrition because they are too poor to purchase food or because there is simply no food available. Small children and the elderly are often the most vulnerable and the first to die. Malnutrition increases risk of other diseases. At the other end of the spectrum is the increasing trend toward obesity in developing countries, especially in urban areas where people are more affluent, leading to increases in cancer, diabetes mellitus, hypertension, and heart disease.

Impact of Government Services and Regulatory Agencies on Nutrition

Government services and regulatory agencies have an impact on nutrition in many different ways:

- **Food and Drug Administration** (FDA): Regulates food products (other than those regulated by FSIS).
- **Food Safety and Inspection Service** (FSIS): Regulates meat, poultry, and egg products.
- **Centers for Disease Control and Prevention** (CDC): Collects data, disseminates information, and provides control efforts for foodborne diseases.
- **Women, Infants, and Children** (WIC): Provides supplemental food and education to low-income women and children under five.
- **Supplemental Nutrition Assistance Program** (SNAP): Provides food-purchasing assistance to allow low-income people to purchase food.
- **United States Department of Agriculture/HHS**: Produce the *Dietary Guidelines for Americans* every 5 years, providing diet and nutrition guidance for all ages.
- **Supplemental Security Income** (SSI): Supplemental income for those with low income, enabling them to buy additional food.
- **National School Lunch Program/ School Breakfast Program**: Provides nutritional school breakfasts and lunches for children who qualify because of low income.

Macrobiotic Diets

A **macrobiotic diet,** based on Zen Buddhism and the Asian concept of yin–yang, uses diet as a means to achieve balance and is usually individualized for the person, depending on what is available in the area. Common foods that are restricted or forbidden include meat (other than occasional seafood) and other animal fats or products, spinach, avocados, beets, eggs, poultry, dairy products, simple sugars, and all artificially produced foods. Nightshade vegetables (tomatoes, eggplants, potatoes, and peppers) are generally avoided or used very sparingly. The diet is usually very high in grains, such as brown rice (about 50% of total), vegetables, and beans. Sea vegetables, such as seaweed, are encouraged. People are advised to eat regular meals but to chew their food thoroughly and to pay attention to the body's need for food. Additionally, cooking in electric ovens is generally avoided, and wood and glass cooking utensils are recommended.

Antioxidant Diets

As body cells burn oxygen, they produce free radicals (uncharged molecules without paired electrons). Other factors that may produce free radicals in the body include smoking, ultraviolet radiation, food metabolism, and air pollution. Free radicals can oxidize and damage or destroy cells, and **antioxidants** inhibit oxidation and render the free radicals harmless. An antioxidant diet aims to reduce free radicals and maintain the health of body cells by eating a diet full of antioxidants. Foods that are high in antioxidants include fruits, vegetables, and plant-based food products. Primary antioxidants include the following:

- **Vitamin C**: Found in vegetables (e.g., broccoli, brussels sprouts) and fruits (e.g., citrus, strawberries, papayas, tomatoes) and works to destroy free radicals within the cells because it is water soluble.
- **Vitamin E**: Found in vegetable oils, seeds, nuts, and green leafy vegetables. Works to destroy free radicals in fat cells because it is fat soluble.
- **Beta-carotene** (converts to vitamin A, which is fat soluble): Found in red-yellow-orange fruits and vegetables.

PDR

The ***Physicians' Desk Reference*** (*PDR*), which is issued each year, contains a wealth of information about drugs, and it is an invaluable resource for information about adverse effects, correct dosage, and administration. The *PDR* contains reference lists of telephone numbers for the FDA (such as medical product reporting programs), for poison control centers, and drug information centers. The product information guide provides colored pictures of medications in actual size to help to identify unlabeled medications. Manufacturers provide information about the drugs that matches the package inserts, which are required by the FDA to provide indications, effects, dosages, routes, methods, frequency and duration of administration, and any warnings, hazards, contraindications, side effects, and precautions. The *PDR* is available in a print edition and also an online version (PDR.net) and includes a mobile version with safety alerts.

Instructions for Drug Administration

Instructions for drug administration may include the following:

- **Take medication with food or milk**: In some cases, food helps promote the absorption of the medication (such as calcium carbonate). In other cases, taking medications on an empty stomach increases the risk of nausea and vomiting and stomach irritation (steroids). Some medications may be necessary to promote digestion (digestive enzymes).
- **Avoid specific foods and drinks** within 2 or more hours of medication: Some food products affect the absorption and action of drugs.
- **Take medication on an empty stomach**: Food may interfere with the absorption of the medication (thyroid hormones).
- **Frequency/Spacing**: Medications are spaced according to their half-life and peak of action. To maintain a stable blood level of a drug, some drugs may need to be spaced over 24 hours. Most drugs, however, are spaced during daytime hours (between 8 a.m. and 8 p.m.).

Common Medication Classifications and Modes of Action

Medication	Classifications and Modes of Action
Antibiotics	There are seven classes of antibiotics, all targeting different types of bacteria. The mode of action varies: Some kill bacteria by impairing the cell membrane; others interfere with cell metabolism, leading to death of the cell.
Antihypertensives	Some decrease blood pressure by affecting the CNS or the sympathetic nervous system. Others are vasodilators that allow vessels to expand and reduce pressure. Diuretics (water pills) reduce pressure by removing excess fluid.
Hypoglycemics (Diabetes)	Oral medications help the body metabolize carbohydrates (sugars/starches), decrease production of glucose (sugar) by the liver, or stimulate the pancreas to produce more insulin. Insulins (given by injection) replace natural insulin that the pancreas can no longer produce to metabolize carbohydrates.
Selective Serotonin Reuptake Inhibitors (SSRIs)	Antidepressants, such as Prozac, increase the level of serotonin (a neurotransmitter) to decrease depression.
Statins	Statins (such as Lipitor) inhibit production of cholesterol in the liver and lower blood cholesterol levels.
Vasodilators	May be smooth muscle relaxants that dilate arteries or veins or both. Calcium channel blockers primarily dilate arteries. Angiotensin-converting enzymes limit the production of peripheral vasoconstricting angiotensin. Alpha-adrenergic blockers block receptors in the arteries and veins, resulting in vasodilation. Used for hypertension and heart failure.
Antidysrhythmics	Act on the conduction system of the heart to control heart rate and rhythm with many different drugs available depending on the type of dysrhythmia.
Diuretics	Loop diuretics (furosemide, bumetanide) and thiazide diuretics (chlorothiazide) inhibit reabsorption of sodium and chloride and increase excretion of other electrolytes, including potassium. Potassium-sparing diuretics inhibit reabsorption of sodium but do not reduce potassium levels. Thiazide diuretics are the first-line drugs for hypertension. Loop diuretics are used for heart failure with peripheral or pulmonary edema.

Pharmacokinetics

Pharmacokinetics relates to the effects that the body has on a drug, and pharmacodynamics relates to the effects that a drug has on the body. Both must be considered to ensure adequate dosing to achieve the optimal response from medications. With all drugs, there is an intake (dose) and a response. Elements of pharmacokinetics include the following:

- The **route of administration**, the absorption, the dosage, the frequency of administration, the distribution, and the serum levels achieved over time.
- The drug's **rate of clearance** (elimination) and doses needed to ensure therapeutic benefit must be considered. Most drugs are cleared through the kidneys, with water-soluble compounds excreted more readily than lipid-soluble compounds.

- The **volume of distribution** (dose per plasma) determines the rate at which the drug passes into tissue. Drug distribution depends on the degree of protein binding and ion trapping that takes place.
- **Elimination half-time** is the time needed to reduce plasma concentrations to 50% during elimination. Usually the equivalent of five half-times is needed to completely eliminate a drug. Five half-times are also needed to achieve steady-state plasma concentrations if giving doses intermittently.
- **Context-sensitive half-time,** in contrast, is the time needed to reach a specific amount of decrease (50%, 60%) after stopping administration of a drug.
- **Recovery time** is the length of time it takes for plasma levels to decrease to the point that the drug loses effect. This is affected by the plasma concentration.
- **Effect-site equilibrium** is the time between the administration of a drug and the clinical effect (the point at which the drug reaches the appropriate receptors), and it must be considered when determining the dose, time, and frequency of pharmacological agents.
- **Bioavailability,** the degree to which a drug is available to the tissues after administration, may vary, depending upon the degree of metabolism that takes place before the drug reaches its site of action.

Pharmacodynamics

Pharmacodynamics relates to biological effects (therapeutic or adverse) of drug administration over time on the body. Drug transport, absorption, means of elimination, and half-life must all be considered when determining effects. Responses may include continuous responses, such as blood pressure variations, or dichotomous responses, in which an event either occurs or does not (such as death). Information from pharmacodynamics provides feedback to modify medication dosage (pharmacokinetics). Drugs provide biological effects primarily by interacting with receptor sites (specific protein molecules) in the cell membrane. Receptors include voltage-sensitive ion channels (sodium, chloride, potassium, and calcium channels), ligand-gated ion channels, and transmembrane receptors. Agonist drugs exert effects after binding with a receptor, whereas antagonist drugs bind with a receptor but have no effects, so they can block agonists from binding. The total number of receptors may vary, upregulating or downregulating in response to stimuli (such as drug administration). Dose–response curves show the relationship between the amount of drug given and the resultant plasma concentration and biological effects.

Pharmacology

Drug Interactions

Drug interactions occur when one drug interferes with the activity of another in either the pharmacodynamics or pharmacokinetics:

- With **pharmacodynamic interaction**, both drugs may interact at receptor sites causing a change that results in an adverse effect or that interferes with a positive effect.
- With **pharmacokinetic interaction**, the ability of the drug to be absorbed and cleared is altered, so there may be delayed effects, changes in effects, or toxicity. Interactions may include problems in many areas. Absorption may be increased or (more commonly) decreased, usually related to the effects within the gastrointestinal system. The distribution of drugs may be affected, often because of changes in protein binding. Metabolism may be altered, often causing changes in drug concentration. Biotransformation of the drug must take place, usually in the liver and gastrointestinal system, but drug interactions can impair this process. Clearance interactions may interfere with the body's ability to eliminate a drug, usually resulting in increased concentration of the drug.

Food and Drug Interactions

Food and drug interactions can impact the drug's effect on the body:

Drug	Caution
ACE inhibitors (captopril and moexipril)	Avoid potassium supplements or foods high in potassium (e.g., bananas, oranges, and leafy green vegetables).
Antibiotics (quinolones and tetracyclines)	Avoid milk products. Avoid vitamins and minerals containing iron, and avoid caffeine.
Anticoagulants	Avoid foods high in vitamin K (e.g., broccoli, spinach, brussels sprouts, cauliflower, kale). Avoid vitamin E supplements.
Antifungals	Avoid milk products and alcohol.
Antihistamines, antidepressants, antianxiety drugs	Avoid alcohol. Avoid grapefruit juice (buspirone, sertraline).
Beta blocker (propranolol), nitrates, narcotics, nonsteroidal anti-inflammatory drugs (NSAIDs)	Avoid alcohol.
Bronchodilators, histamine blockers	Avoid caffeine and alcohol.
Carbamazepine, cyclosporine and tacrolimus, HIV medications, statins	Avoid grapefruit juice
Diuretics, potassium-sparing	Avoid food high in potassium.
Monoamine oxidase inhibitors	Avoid alcohol and nonalcoholic substitutes for beer or wine, foods high in tyramine (e.g., organ meats, cured meats, caviar, cheese products, avocados, bananas, raisins, soy, fava beans), and products containing caffeine (e.g., tea, cola, chocolate, coffee).

Commonly Administered and Assisted Medications

Medication	Dose/Route/Use	Side effects/Interactions
Aspirin	Orally, 325 mg chew and swallow for fast action when a person is having a heart attack (chest pain, left arm pain, shortness of breath).	Avoid with signs of stroke or gastrointestinal bleeding. Decreases clotting time and may increase risk of bleeding.
Glucose	Orally for hypoglycemia related to insulin reaction in diabetics. May be in liquid or tablet form or may substitute a glass of orange juice or candy if no other glucose is available.	Minimal unless hyperglycemic. Should reverse the symptoms of hypoglycemia rapidly.
Oxygen	Inhaled, usually 2–6 liters but varies according to protocol. Administered for breathing difficulties and suspected heart attack if available.	Minimal, although oxygen toxicity can occur with high doses for prolonged periods of time.

Bronchodilators (albuterol, levalbuterol)	Inhaled, usually two puffs of a handheld inhaler. Dosage varies according to medication. For bronchospasm, wheezing, typically for those having an asthma attack.	Adverse effects: tachycardia, dizziness, nervousness, tremor, headache, rhinitis, increased cough.
Epinephrine (EpiPen)	Autoinjector, 0.3 mg 1:1,000 for ≥66 lb. 0.15 mg 1:2,000 for 33–66 lb. for severe allergic reaction/anaphylaxis.	Avoid using with antihistamines, thyroid hormones, and alpha blockers. Adverse effects: drowsiness, headache, palpitations, nervousness, tremors.
Nitroglycerine	Sublingually for angina (chest pain), 0.3–0.6 mg, repeated every 5 minutes up to three times.	Avoid with acute heart attack. Adverse effects: headache, flushing, dizziness, orthostatic hypotension, palpitations. Interactions: avoid with erectile dysfunction drugs (sildenafil, tadalafil, vardenafil).

Adverse Drug Reactions

Adverse drug reactions may vary from mild temporary symptoms (drowsiness) to severe anaphylaxis, so patients should be advised to report any new symptoms or changes in condition when starting a new medication. Common adverse reactions include the following:

- **GI disturbances**: Nausea and vomiting, distension, constipation, and diarrhea common with many drugs, such as antibiotics.
- **CNS effects**: Drowsiness and confusion, especially common in older adults taking antianxiety and antidepressant medications.
- **Cardiovascular effects**: Hypotension or hypertension. Older adults often experience much lower blood pressure in response to antihypertensive drugs than younger adults.
- **Dermatologic effects**: Itching, dry skin, and rash are common and may result from allergic response to many drugs, including antibiotics.
- **Hematologic effects**: Some drugs (antibiotics, nonsteroidal anti-inflammatory drugs [NSAIDs], levodopa) may cause hemolytic anemia, and others (chemotherapeutic drugs, NSAIDs) may result in thrombocytopenia, iron-deficiency anemia, and leukopenia.
- **Anaphylaxis**: This systemic reaction may result from a severe allergic response to almost any type of drug, but it is most common with penicillin, morphine, contrast dye, aspirin, and latex exposure.

Adverse Reactions to Drugs Common to Children

Adverse reactions to some drugs are common in children:

- Adrenocorticoids may cause numerous adverse effects including delayed maturation and growth suppression.
- Aspirin may cause Reye's syndrome in children with viral infections, so fevers should be treated with acetaminophen or ibuprofen.
- Indomethacin can result in kidney failure or intestinal perforation.
- Phenytoin can result in changes in appearance of the face with coarsening of features and thickening of the skull.
- Loop diuretics, such as furosemide (Lasix) may cause increased calcium levels in the kidneys (nephrocalcinosis).

- Phenothiazines can cause extrapyramidal reactions, such as intermittent or prolonged muscular contractions.
- Phenobarbital may cause hyperactive behavior in some children and may impair cognitive development.
- Sodium valproate/valproic acid can cause severe hepatotoxicity and liver failure, particularly in children younger than age 2.
- Tetracycline can result in yellowish discoloration of the permanent teeth.

Overdose Symptoms of Commonly Used Drugs

Drug	Overdose Symptoms
Acetaminophen (Tylenol)	Toxicity occurs with dosage >140 mg/kg in one dose or >7.5g in 24 hours: (Initial symptom) Minor gastrointestinal upset. (Days 2–3) Hepatotoxicity (liver damage) with RUQ pain. (Days 3–4) Hepatic failure with metabolic acidosis, coagulopathy, kidney failure, encephalopathy, nausea, vomiting, and possible death. (Days 5–12) Recovery period (survivors).
NSAIDs/ Salicylates	Toxicity (4–48 hours after ingestion) includes headache, nausea, abdominal pain, tinnitus (ringing in the ears), diaphoresis, hypertension, fluid in the lungs, alterations in mental status, cardiac dysrhythmias, seizures, and respiratory arrest.
Dextromethorphan (cough syrup/cold medications)	Mild: restlessness and euphoria and signs of intoxication. Moderate: slurred speech, lack of coordination, memory loss, hallucinations, and "stoned" appearance. Severe: altered state of consciousness, impaired vision, hearing, emotional detachment, inability to comprehend spoken words, leading to hallucinations, delusions, tachycardia, temporary blindness, and respiratory arrest. Some exhibit violent or psychotic behavior.
Cardiac	**Digitalis (digoxin) toxicity** may cause (initially) increasing fatigue, lethargy, depression, and nausea halo vision, and vomiting progressing to sudden changes in the heart rhythm, such as regular or irregular rhythm, palpitations, heart block, tachycardia, and later bradycardia.
Psychiatric	**Benzodiazepine toxicity** may result from accidental or intentional overdose with such drugs as Xanax and Valium. Indications are often nonspecific neurological changes: lethargy, dizziness, alterations in consciousness, and ataxia. Respiratory depression and hypotension are rare complications. Prehospital: Supportive care. Mild **lithium toxicity** (Eskalith, Lithobid) can include severe vomiting and diarrhea, increased muscle tremors and twitching, lethargy, body aches, ataxia, ringing in the ears, blurry vision, vertigo, or hyperactive deep tendon reflexes. More severe symptoms can include elevated temperature, low urine output, hypotension, heart abnormalities, decreased level of consciousness, seizures, coma, or death.

Pediatric Pharmacology

There are many **pediatric pharmacology** concerns. Pediatric doses are calculated according to the child's weight in kilograms, but other factors may affect the dosage. Weight is estimated by age (although the actual weight is safer):

- 50th percentile weight (kg) = (age × 2) + 9.

Only pediatric medications should be prescribed if possible. Adult pills, for example, should not be cut for use for a child because even small variations in dosage may have adverse effects. Dosage should always be checked. Drug therapy in children may sometimes require adult dosages due to children's increased ability to quickly metabolize the medications. Children may also exhibit unusual responses or side effects to drugs compared to adults and should be very closely evaluated and frequently assessed.

Routes of Drug Administration

Routes of drug administration include the following:

- **Oral**: Most drugs, including pills, tablets, capsules, and liquids, are taken orally with water and with or without food (depending on the drug). Enteric (hard) coated pills and tablets are absorbed in the small intestine, whereas most other drugs are at least partially absorbed in the stomach.
- **Sublingual/Buccal**: Dissolvable wafers are administered under the tongue or in the side of the cheek. This route provides rapid absorption into the bloodstream.
- **Parenteral**: Injectable drugs may be administered by intramuscular (IM), subcutaneous (SQ), or intravascular (IV) routes. IV drugs enter the bloodstream immediately, IM next, and SQ last.
- **Topical**: Ointments, creams, and gels are applied to the skin.
- **Rectal**: Some drugs in suppository or liquid form (enema preparations) are administered per the rectum.
- **Vaginal**: Creams, gels, and suppositories may be administered vaginally.

Generic and Brand-Name Drugs

All drugs have a **chemical name** that indicates their chemical properties, a **generic name** provided by the United States Adopted Names Council, and a **brand name** provided by the manufacturer. For example, the chemical name for a common drug is *N*-acetyl-*para*-aminophenol. The generic name is acetaminophen, and the most common brand name is Tylenol. The endings of generic names often indicate the type of drug:

- -cillin: Penicillin-type antibiotic (penicillin, amoxicillin).
- -prazole: Proton-pump inhibitor (omeprazole, pantoprazole, rabeprazole).
- -olol: beta-adrenergic blocker (metoprolol, atenolol, nadolol).

Brand names may have no obvious connection to the generic name. Although the active ingredient in a generic drug and the brand name drug is the same, the fillers used to make the drug may be different; and in some cases, this may affect absorption or other qualities of the drug. Generic drugs are almost always less expensive than brand-name drugs.

Importance of Sample Size in Clinical Trials

Sample size (number of participants) is an important factor in clinical trials in order to produce meaningful results. If the sample size is too small, researchers may be unable to detect a clinical significance. If the sample is too large, then the costs may be prohibitive and, again, it may skew the results. When calculating sample size, numerous formulas are used, depending on the type of trial and the structure of the research, and in most cases the sample size should be calculated by an experienced statistician. Additionally, it's important to include the potential dropout rate in calculations. Another factor to consider is whether both arms of a study (control and study group) should have the same sample size. The researcher should base the sample size in part of the expected outcomes. If a wide variability in outcomes is expected, then the sample size must be larger. If consistently positive or negative outcomes are anticipated, a smaller sample size is needed.

FDA Approval and Clinical Trials

A manufacturer must submit data and information about a new drug to the **Food and Drug Administration** (FDA) and gain approval prior to beginning clinical trials. Before a drug can be administered to humans, preclinical research must include *in vitro* (test tube) and/or *in vivo* (in a living body, often an animal) testing to ensure that the drug is unlikely to cause harm. **Clinical trials** involve four phases:

- **Phase I**: 20–100 volunteers or patients with the target disorder take the drug, usually for several months to determine the drug's safety and the correct dosage. 70% advance to phase II.
- **Phase II**: Several hundred volunteers with the target disorder take the drug. This phase may last for several months to 2 years to determine the drug's effectiveness and adverse effects. About 33% advance to phase III.
- **Phase III**: A few hundred to 300 volunteers with the target disorder receive the drug for 1–4 years to determine the drug's effectiveness and adverse effects. About 25%–30% advance to phase IV.
- **Phase IV**: Several thousand volunteers with the target disorder take the drug to ensure its continued effectiveness and safety prior to final approval by the FDA and marketing of the drug.

Alternative Medicine

Ayurveda is a traditional Indian method of healing that focuses on balancing the mind, body, and spirit to prevent or cure illness. Practitioners believe that when the *prana* (life force) and *dosha* (basic metabolism) are out of balance, the person becomes ill. Although people may still use Western medicines, they may also want their child to follow Ayurvedic traditions through the use of herbs, diet, special breathing exercises, and yoga. Because some herbs contain active ingredients found in medications, the healthcare provider should ask about herbal supplements or dietary restrictions (often vegan).

People who practice **homeopathy** believe that healing must occur from the inside and that they can use small doses of plants or minerals to promote healing by causing similar symptoms to the ones being treated. Homeopathy prescribes specific substances for different diseases, depending on the person's physical and emotional condition. The treatment usually does not include active ingredients found in medications, so the treatments rarely interfere with other medical treatment, although some people choose to use homeopathic treatment rather than traditional medication, and this can put the person at risk.

Acupuncture is an integral part of traditional Chinese medicine that involves balancing qi (vital energy) through inserting tiny needles into specific sites referred to as acupoints based on 12 major meridian pathways. Needles are usually left in place for 30 to 60 minutes. Specific acupoints are used to treat different organs or areas of the body. Acupuncture is especially effective for pain control and relief of nausea and vomiting after radiation or chemotherapy, although people use it for many different disorders. In some cases, electrical stimulation is added to the needles to enhance the effect. Some practitioners also use moxibustion, a process that warms the needles after insertion to increase blood flow and energy.

Traditional Chinese medicine (TCM) has some similarities to Ayurveda. TCM is concerned with balancing the vital energy (qi) of the body through diet, meditation, herbs, acupressure and acupuncture, and exercise such as Tai Chi. Because TCM relies on the use of herbs, the health provider should ascertain which herbs are being used.

Aromatherapy uses essential oils derived from plant extracts. These oils are applied topically to the skin, heated and inhaled, or sprayed in the environment. Practitioners believe that aromatherapy can be used to treat and prevent disease, but it is usually used as an adjunct, and by itself is rarely harmful, although healing claims are dubious.

Music therapy involves listening to music (often classical, but any music that the person likes is acceptable). Music therapy is most often used to reduce anxiety. It can also be used as part of visualization or meditation to help the person slow breathing and focus attention. Music is sometimes used as part of an exercise program to help the person pace the exercises. In this case, faster music may be used.

Chiropractic therapy is commonly used to relieve muscle pain. Practitioners use various manipulations of muscles and joints to relieve discomfort and pressure on nerves. Practitioners believe that aligning the spine is critical to maintenance of health, and people may receive routine "adjustments" for months or years. Chiropractic therapy has not been proven effective for treatment of disease.

Therapeutic touch is a type of energy therapy in which the practitioner places the hands on the person's body to redirect energy and promote health. It is used to reduce stress and relieve discomfort.

Magnetic therapy involves applying magnets to various parts of the body to redirect energy. Magnetic therapy is used primarily to increase circulation and relieve pain. In some cases, people may use special magnet pads on their beds or chairs so that they have prolonged treatment.

Massage therapy is commonly used in sports and may be used before activities, at breaks during activities, and after the activity is completed. Many types of massage are used in sports, and some massage therapists specialize in sports massage, but all practitioners who work with athletes of any age should know the basic techniques of sports massage because it is used to treat and to prevent injuries. Sports massage is based primarily on Swedish massage, although the massage may be deeper and targeted toward a particular injury, and other types of massage may be incorporated into a sports massage program. Massage of an injured area is delayed for the first 48–72 hours to prevent further injury to tissues. Different techniques include compression (deep massage), effleurage (soft massage with oil), friction, petrissage (with or across the muscles to stretch them), tapotement (quick, rhythmic tapping), vibration, and trigger point (applying pressure with a finger or thumb).

Use of Technology

Database Search with Boolean Logic

Literature research requires comprehensive evaluation of current (≤5 years) and/or historical information. Most literature research begins with an Internet search of databases, which provide listings of books, journals, and other materials on specific topics. Databases vary in content, and many contain only a reference listing with or without an abstract, so once the listing is obtained, the researcher must do a further search (publisher, library, etc.) to locate the material. Some databases require a subscription, but access is often available through educational or healthcare institutions.

In order to search effectively, the researcher should begin by writing a brief explanation of the research to help identify possible keywords and synonyms to use as search words:

- Truncations: "finan*" provides all words that begin with those letters, such as "finance," "financial," and "financed."
- Wildcards: "m?n" or "m*n" provides "man" and "men."
- Boolean logic (AND, OR, NOT):
  - Wound OR Infect* OR ulcer
  - Wound OR ulcer AND povidone-iodine
  - Wound AND povidone-iodine NOT antibiotic NOT antimicrobial.

SQL Database Search

Structured query language (SQL) is a fourth-generation programming language (4GL) that differs from a 3GL, such as Java, in that SQL uses syntax similar to human language to access, manipulate, and retrieve data from relational database management systems, which store data in tables. The American National Standards Institute (ANSI) and the International Organization for Standardization have adopted SQL as a standard; however, because the language is complex, many vendors do not use the complete standard, and this limits portability between vendors without modifications. Despite many available versions, ANSI standards require that basic commands (UPDATE, DELETE, SELECT, etc.) be supported. Language elements of SQL include the following:

- Clauses: From, where, group by, having, and order by.
- Expressions: Produce scales and tables.
- Predicates: Three-valued logic (null, true, false) and Boolean truth values.
- Queries: The most commonly used SQL operation, require a SELECT statement.
- Statements: Includes the semicolon (to terminate a statement).

Search Using the PICOT Format

The **PICOT** format is one method of developing appropriate questions to use in searching quantitative research. This method helps clarify the question and necessary information and to identify key words used in searching.

P	Patient/ Population	List important characteristics: 35-year-old male with low back pain.
I	Intervention/ Indicator	Explain the desired intervention under consideration: Acupuncture.
C	Comparison/ Control	List other possible interventions or alternatives: Surgery.
O	Outcome	Provide the desired measurable outcomes: Decreased pain levels (from 6–7 to 1–2) and increased mobility.
T	Time	Time frame (if appropriate).

This format is then used to formulate a question:

- In a 35-year-old male with low back pain, how does acupuncture, compared with surgery, affect pain levels and mobility?

Based on this question, then the search may be conducted with the following (including synonyms): (Back pain or sciatica) and (acupuncture or surgery) and (pain management or pain-free or pain control).

Psychological Factors Affecting Health and Wellness

Hardiness	Hardiness is the ability to survive stress without developing illness. Components include commitment (involvement in activities), control (ability to make effective and appropriate decisions), and challenge (ability to see change as positive rather than negative). Hardiness relates to resilience in the face of stress and the ability to experience growth from stress. Hardiness is more of a factor in cultures that value individuality (Western culture) than in cultures focused on the group.
Self-efficacy	Self-efficacy is the belief that behavior affects events in life. Clients with high feelings of self-efficacy tend to be motivated and set high goals and are able to turn to others for help when needed and cope with stress. Clients with low feelings of self-efficacy set low goals and experience self-doubt, anxiety, and depression.
Resilience	Resilience is a healthy and adequate response to stress, including protecting one's mental health. Clients with low resilience become overwhelmed by stressful events, such as illness, and are unable to cope, whereas those with high resilience can cope with the same situations without developing stress.
Resourcefulness	Resourcefulness is the ability to use problem-solving skills and to cope with stressful situations, including health-seeking behaviors, self-care, and taking action.
Spirituality	Spirituality is belief about the meaning of life and a higher power, such as God, Allah, or Buddha. Spiritual beliefs often help people cope with illness and stress. Hope and faith are important factors in psychiatric rehabilitation. Many 12-step programs focus on spirituality.

Pathophysiology of the Nervous System

The **nervous system** comprises the brain and spinal cord (CNS) and nerves (peripheral nervous system). The brain is comprised of gray matter (neurons) and white matter (neuronal axons). The neurons are the primary cells of the nervous system. Other cells include astrocytes, oligodendrocytes, and microglia. Pathology can occur at any part of the neuron: axonal deterioration, deterioration of the myelin sheath (as in multiple sclerosis), and impaired transmission of impulses at the axonal terminals. The meninges and the brain may become infected. The brain may swell from infection or trauma, resulting in compression of brain tissue. The spinal cord may be injured, resulting in weakness or paralysis. The brain may be injured secondary to other disorders: Thiamine deficiency may cause damage to neurons, and hepatic encephalopathy may damage astrocytes.

Physiologic Response to Stress and Anxiety

Parasympathetic Nervous System

The **physiologic response to stress and anxiety** occurs on a continuum from mild to severe. These responses are not controllable by the person experiencing these feelings and are mediated through the immune and autonomic nervous systems. The sympathetic nervous system turns on the physiologic response to stress and anxiety and readies the body to react. Under stress, the hypothalamus acts to stimulate the pituitary gland to secrete a hormone, which leads to increased cortisol levels. This increased production may lead to elevated availability of glucose for heightened cellular metabolism. In some individuals, the **parasympathetic nervous system** can dominate during stress. The associated symptoms often have the opposite effect of what is seen with the sympathetic nervous system in control. Cardiovascular responses can include decreased blood pressure and heart rate, feelings of faintness, or actual fainting. There can also be an increased need to urinate along with feelings of abdominal pain, nausea, and diarrhea.

Sympathetic Nervous System (Cardiovascular and Respiratory Systems)

The **sympathetic nervous system** releases epinephrine in response to stress and anxiety. This affects the cardiovascular and respiratory systems by revving up their normal responses and readying the body to respond to a threat. In the cardiovascular system, the heart rate and blood pressure increase with associated feelings of palpitations. Blood is shunted away from nonvital organs, such as the stomach, intestines, and kidneys, resulting in decreased peristalsis and urinary output. There is increased blood flow to necessary muscle groups to encourage a quick response time. Blood coagulation time increases. In the respiratory system, there is an increase in the rate of respirations and a decrease in the depth; therefore, breathing becomes rapid and shallow and is associated with feelings of shortness of breath.

Sympathetic Nervous System (Gastrointestinal, Neuromuscular, and Integumentary Systems)

In response to stress, the **sympathetic nervous system** usually leads to a decrease in blood flow in the gastrointestinal (GI) tract. This decreases appetite and movement of the intestinal tract. The neuromuscular system is charged up and ready to respond. The reflex time is increased, and there can be some twitching or shaking of muscles. The need for sleep is greatly reduced, leading to periods of insomnia. The facial expression may be tense and anxious, and the client may actually pace about. The client may have uncontrolled muscle movements, restlessness, fast speech, avoidance, or startle easily. The integumentary system also responds. The skin may become flushed or itchy, and there is an increase in sweat gland production. These reactions can lead to ineffective interpersonal communication or social withdrawal. Cognitive functioning can also be affected by stress and anxiety. The client might appear distracted or unable to concentrate, forgetful, and confused or may make errors in judgment not normally seen. The client may also experience flashbacks or have frightening hallucinations.

Depression

Depression is a depressed mood, profound and constant sense of hopelessness and despair, or loss of interest in all or almost all activities for a period of at least 2 weeks. Family history of depression is a major risk factor. Developmental hormone changes at puberty or hormone disruption from disease can also contribute to depression. Depression is associated with neurotransmitter dysregulation, especially serotonin and norepinephrine. Major depression can be mild, moderate, or severe, and it is characterized by a combination of symptoms that interfere with the ability to work, study, sleep, eat, and enjoy once-pleasurable activities. Criteria include at least five of the following (including the first two):

- Depressed mood most of the day.
- Diminished interest in most or all activities that were previously enjoyable.
- Significant weight gain or loss without dieting.
- Insomnia or hypersomnia.
- Persistent pessimism.
- Constant fatigue.
- Feelings of worthlessness.
- Reduced ability to focus on tasks.
- Recurring thoughts of death or suicide.

Paranoia

Paranoia, an intense irrational suspicion of others that is not founded in reality, is not a diagnosis in itself but is a symptom associated with other diagnoses, such as schizophrenia, bipolar disorder, and delusional disorder. Indications of paranoia include feelings of intense mistrust and suspicion that can lead the person to feeling anger and fear. The person may become very vigilant, expecting the worst from others, being very sensitive to criticism (real or imagined), and believing that others are lying or have hidden motives. Some paranoid concerns may be projections or may be associated with events in the person's life. The person may become increasingly delusional because of feelings of persecution, often believing in bizarre conspiracy theories. The cause of paranoia is not clear, but it may be related to a genetic predisposition, alterations in brain chemistry, trauma, or some combination of various factors. Identifying and treating (medications, therapy) the underlying cause is essential in controlling paranoid thoughts.

Schizophrenia

Schizophrenia is a thought disorder that causes psychotic episodes and distortion of reality and the inability to determine the line between fantasy and reality. The onset may be acute or more insidious, but onset usually occurs in early adulthood. Schizophrenia appears to be caused by combined genetic and environmental factors. Schizophrenia is actually a related group of psychiatric illnesses that include subtypes: paranoid, disorganized, catatonic, undifferentiated, and residual. Symptoms may vary widely but include **positive** symptoms, such as delusions (false beliefs) and hallucinations (seeing or hearing something that is not present), and **negative** symptoms, such as flat affect, lack of motivation, and inability to function normally in society. Comorbidities, such as obsessive-compulsive disorder and depression, are common as well as substance abuse and suicidal tendencies. In older adults, psychosis often reduces, but some cognitive impairment is common during all ages and is a persistent problem with chronic schizophrenia.

Anger, Aggression, and Violence

Psychological aspects of increased **anger, aggression, and violence** can be associated with uncontrollable instinctual urges or as a result of the person's particular life experiences. Exposure to violence, altered mother/child bonding, altered socialization skills, or reinforcement of aggressive behavior by achievement of a goal can all lead to increased utilization of aggression and violence. Overexposure to violence through the media, entertainment, or the immediate environment can possibly lead to a desensitization of aggression and violence and lead to maladaptive behavioral responses. During an assessment, the background history of an individual can reveal many different predictors of future maladaptive responses associated with aggression and violence. The history may reveal violent behaviors and rage responses, increasing irritability, or loss of control. Some examples of maladaptive background behaviors include cruelty to animals or children, setting fires or other destruction of property, drug or alcohol abuse, self-directed violence such as cuts or burns on the arms, or juvenile delinquency. Many of these behaviors are evident during childhood.

Five-Phase Aggression Cycle

Triggering	The person responds to a triggering event with anger or hostility. He or she may exhibit anxiety, restlessness, and muscle tension. Other signs include rapid breathing, perspiration, a loud angry voice, and pacing.

Escalation	The person's responses show movement toward lack of control. His or her face flushes, and he or she becomes increasingly agitated, demanding, and threatening, often swearing, clenching fists, and making threatening gestures. The person is unable to think clearly or resolve problems.
Crisis	The person loses emotional and physical control. He or she throws objects, hits, kicks, spits, bites, scratches, screams, shrieks, and cannot communicate clearly.
Recovery	The person regains control. The voice lowers, muscle tension relaxes, and he or she is able to communicate more rationally.
Postcrisis	The person may attempt reconciliation and may feel remorse, apologize, cry, or become quiet or withdrawn. He or she can respond appropriately.

Behavior Modification Options

Behavior modification is a type of systematic therapy that works toward the goal of replacing maladaptive behaviors with positive behaviors. This type of therapy can be used with individuals, groups, or entire communities. There are three types of behavioral modification:

- **Operant conditioning** uses positive reinforcement directed toward the desired behaviors. By using positive reinforcement, the participant will want to repeat the good behaviors to gain the reward, creating a new pattern. Operant conditioning can be effective with eating disorders, smoking cessation, or addictions.
- **Desensitization** in which clients are increasingly exposed to those things that cause them stress (such as phobias) so that they can overcome their fears.
- **Aversion therapy** applies a negative consequence to an action (such as using medications to induce vomiting after drinking alcohol) to create negative associations with the action in order to modify behavior.

CBT

Cognitive-behavioral therapy (CBT) focuses on the impact that thoughts have on behavior and feelings and encourages the individual to use the power of rational thought to alter perceptions and behavior. This approach to counseling is usually a short-term solution, and it lasts about 12–20 sessions, with the first sessions to obtain a history, middle sessions to focus on problems, and the last sessions to review and reinforce. Individuals are assigned "homework" during the sessions to practice new ways of thinking and to develop new coping strategies. The therapist helps the individual identify goals and then find ways to achieve those goals. CBT acknowledges that all problems cannot be resolved, but one can deal differently with problems. The therapist asks many questions to determine the individual's areas of concern and encourages the individual to question his/her own motivations and needs. CBT is goal-centered, so each counseling session is structured toward a particular goal, such as coping techniques. CBT centers on the concept of unlearning previous behaviors and learning new ones, questioning behaviors, and doing homework. Different approaches to CBT include Beck's cognitive therapy, rational emotive behavior therapy, and dialectical behavior therapy.

FFT

Functional Family Therapy (FFT) is designed for adolescents (11–17) with antisocial behavior. FFT uses principles of family systems theory and cognitive behavior therapy and provides intervention and prevention services. Although the therapy has changed somewhat over the past 30 years, current FTT usually includes three phases:

- **Engagement/Motivation**: The therapist works with the family to identify maladaptive beliefs in order to increase expectations for change, reduce negativity and blaming, and increase respect for differences. Goals are to reduce dropout rates and establish alliances.
- **Behavior change**: The therapist guides the parents in using behavioral interventions to improve family functioning, parenting, and conflict management skill. Goals are to prevent delinquent behavior and build better communication and interpersonal skills.
- **Generalization**: The family learns to use new skills to influence the systems in which they are involved, such as school, church, and juvenile justice system. Community resources are mobilized to prevent relapse.

HRT

Habit reversal therapy (HRT), a form of CBT, is used to help people with tic disorders and for those with impulse control disorders, such as trichotillomania (hair pulling). Many steps are involved:

Awareness	The patient must pay attention because behaviors are often unconscious. This often involves keeping a detailed log of the behavior, including the time; duration; activity during the episode; and the patient's emotional state before, during, and after the activity.
Identification of Triggers	The log and patient interviews help to identify triggers to help patients understand when they are at risk of the behavior and how to use stimulus control to prevent the behavior or to avoid triggers.
Assessment	The patient begins to identify those feelings (negative or positive) associated with the behavior and the reason for it.
Competitive Response	The patient carries out another action to compete with the urge to carry out the behavior, thereby preventing it.
Assessment of Rationalizations	The patient must confront the rationalizations used to allow the behavior to continue.
Mindfulness	The patient learns that it's not necessary to give in to the urge to carry out the behavior because urges often are of short duration.

Self-Help and Prevention Services Available for Substance Abuse Problems

Self-Help and Prevention Services for Substance Abuse	
Alcoholics Anonymous (AA)	A 12-step program of men and women who share their experiences, strength, and hope with each other in order to solve their common problem of alcoholism and help others to recover.
Narcotics Anonymous (NA)	NA developed from AA to serve those with drug addictions.
Cocaine Anonymous (CA)	CA developed in Los Angeles in 1982 to address the special needs of those addicted to cocaine.
Secular Organization for Sobriety (SOS)	This group is designed for individuals with an agnostic view of spirituality because many do not feel comfortable with the spiritual aspects of traditional 12-step programs.
Al-Anon, Nar-Anon, and Alateen	These organizations offer support to family members, loved ones, and significant others living with or otherwise involved with an individual afflicted with substance abuse issues.
Adult Children of Alcoholics (ACoA)	ACoA offers support for individuals who grew up with alcoholic parent(s) or in dysfunctional homes and who suffer the effects of their experiences.

Treatment Options for Mental Health Disorders

Treatment Option	Description
Medications	First-generation (typical) antipsychotic medications, such as haloperidol (Haldol), perphenazine and amitriptyline (Etrafon), and fluphenazine (Prolixin). Second-generation (atypical) antipsychotic medications, such as clozapine (Clozaril), aripiprazole (Abilify), and olanzapine (Zyprexa). Antidepressants: Commonly used SSRIs including sertraline (Zoloft) and fluoxetine (Prozac) treat depression.
Illness management techniques	Individual: Clients are taught about their disease and treatments and learn signs to help them monitor their disease and avoid relapses. Family education: Helps families access support systems and solve problems.
Therapy/Skill training	CBT: Helps clients learn to test the reality of their perceptions (such as persistent hearing of voices). Rehabilitation: Social and vocational training. Integrated substance abuse/other diagnosis treatment: Programs specifically designed for clients with dual diagnoses tend to be more successful in helping those with substance abuse. Self-help and support groups: Social support and networking
Hospitalization	For those who pose a threat to themselves or others.

Cultural Views on Physical and Mental Illness

Many cultures have specific traditional beliefs regarding the **source and meaning** of illnesses. For instance, some cultures may believe that illness is the result of an imbalance between a person's body and spirit or that it is a punishment for actions taken earlier in life. **Mental illnesses** are particularly subject to these types of beliefs. Even in cultures where beliefs are not primarily based on superstition, mental illness frequently has a stigma attached to it. Many Eastern cultures value conformity to social norms and emotional control, and mental illness directly interferes with a person's ability to achieve these things. In Western cultures, mental illness is still often misunderstood and stigmatized, seen by many as a sign of a weak mind or simply a lack of willpower on the part of those affected.

It is important to recognize that the client's **cultural background** may significantly impact how the client receives a diagnosis of mental illness and what information, support, and resources they will require. Beliefs held by the **client's family**, regardless of whether they are shared by the client, can directly affect the client. If the client has a strong negative reaction to a psychiatric diagnosis, the source of the distress should be explored and addressed appropriately.

Socioeconomic Factors That Affect Mental Health

Socioeconomic factors that affect mental health include the following:

- **Poverty/Income inequality**: Can lead to stress and frustration and may prevent people from obtaining adequate treatment to deal with psychological issues. May lead to hunger and inadequate housing/homelessness, furthering mental health issues and increasing the risk of general health problems and injury.
- **Childhood abuse/neglect**: May impair growth and development and result in feelings of inadequacy, fear, and anger.
- **Lack of adequate education**: Often results in poverty and an inability to find employment or low-paying employment with little chance of advancement or options. People may develop anger and resentment toward others and may turn to substance abuse. Having parents with little education may impact the type of exposure that individuals have in formative years. For example, they may have little exposure to books or magazines and may have little assistance with homework or little encouragement to study.
- **Bullying/Prejudice**: Unfair treatment by others may result in increasing depression and impaired self-esteem. Some may respond through aggressive behavior and violence.

Substance Abuse Rehabilitation Centers

Substance abuse rehabilitation centers may vary in the programs that they offer, and some provide outpatient services whereas others provide inpatient. Common program components include the following:

- Medical supervision, especially during withdrawal.
- Individual therapy.
- Group therapy.
- 12-step programs.
- Opioid substitution therapies (methadone and buprenorphine).

Methadone and buprenorphine may be used in order to prevent withdrawal symptoms that often drive the user to seek drugs again when trying to quit. Because these medications are long acting and have a slow onset, the person doesn't experience the "high" associated with other drugs, allowing the person to stop drug-seeking behavior and improve his/her life. Some long-term inpatient programs require that people stay for a specified period of time, such as 6 to 12 months, although many require a minimum of only 30 days. Treatment may be very structured and may include resocialization therapies and employment training. Most programs are voluntary, although some people, such as those arrested for drunk driving, may be required by the legal system to attend.

EMERGING TRENDS IN ADDICTION TREATMENT

Emerging trends in the treatment of addiction include the following:

- Accepting relapses as part of the process of recovery rather than expecting total abstinence.
- Participating in intensive residential rehabilitation programs for a minimum of 30 days rather than relying on only outpatient support.
- Focusing on lifestyle changes for long-term solutions to the client's problems.
- Identifying and treating dual diagnoses rather than focusing solely on addiction.
- Encouraging family participation in development of the treatment plan.
- Providing follow-up services (AA, AN, support groups, telephone contact).
- Using prescription medications (methadone, Suboxone) to help wean clients from illegal drugs.
- Providing programs for specialized populations (lesbian, gay, bisexual, transgender, adolescents, older adults, ethnic groups).
- Focusing on client autonomy.
- Applying evidence-based research to practice.
- Applying principles of distributive justice to access to care.
- Increasing insurance/Medicare/Medicaid coverage for rehabilitation services.
- Carrying out multiple types of assessments (client-oriented, goal attainment, values, functional, environmental).
- Disclosing the professional relationship at the onset of treatment.

INTERVENTION AND TREATMENTS FOR SUBSTANCE ABUSE

Interventions and treatments for substance abuse include the following:

- **Drug rehabilitation**: Addicted and alcoholic substance abusers may require inpatient or outpatient treatment in a drug rehabilitation center. Many programs are covered by insurance, although some may be prohibitively expensive for some students and others may have waiting lists.
- **Smoking cessation programs**: These include support groups, online programs, and nicotine replacement (such as patches).
- **Counseling**: Substance abusers often have unresolved problems that require professional intervention, so referral for counseling is often indicated.
- **Detoxification**: This should be carried out under medical supervision because of the potential for life-threatening complications. Adolescents should not attempt detoxification by themselves or under the supervision of friends.
- **Medications**: Methadone or buprenorphine may be used for maintenance after detoxification for drug addicts. Naloxone is administered in emergent conditions for opioid overdose.

PROVIDING ANTICIPATORY GUIDANCE REGARDING HEALTH AND WELLNESS

CHILDREN/FAMILIES

Providing anticipatory guidance to **children/families** is an important role for the health provider, who is guided by knowledge about risk factors and growth and development. As the child moves from one stage of development to another, the health provider should provide information to both the child and parents about what to expect in terms of development, both physically and emotionally as well as how to minimize risk factors. Guidance may be related to many different areas of concern:

- Diet and nutrition, especially for those children at risk for obesity or eating disorders.
- Safety measures, including information about common types of childhood injuries.
- Sexual development and normal related changes and behaviors.
- Sports activities and exercise that is age appropriate.
- General growth and development.
- Academic progress and advice about testing and intervention for learning disabilities.
- Peer influence.
- Drug and alcohol abuse.

EARLY ADOLESCENCE

Children during **early adolescence** (ages 11–14) are undergoing many changes in their bodies and emotions. Relationships with family and peers may begin to change, and children may be very self-conscious and concerned about whether they are normal. **Anticipatory guidance** helps the child to navigate changes in his/her life and to negotiate changes in relationships as the child seeks more autonomy:

- **Physical changes**: Outline what the child should expect in terms of bodily changes, such as development of secondary sexual characteristics, including normal variations, and height and weight changes.
- **Cognitive changes**: Allow the child to express changes in thought patterns and awareness and discuss how that relates to developing maturity and stress the importance of maintaining academic responsibilities.
- **Sociobehavioral changes**: Ask the child about peer groups and pressures at school and discuss methods to avoid gangs, tobacco, drugs, alcohol, and abusive relationship.

MIDDLE ADOLESCENCE

Middle adolescence (ages 15–17) is a time of conflict for many young people as they strive to establish an identity separate from their parents and at the same time fit in and find acceptance with their peers. For many, this is the most difficult time of adolescence, and the healthcare provider should provide anticipatory guidance to the adolescent through this time, even if the adolescent appears uninterested. Adolescents want respect and often respond when treated with respect. Encouraging the adolescent to discuss issues is more productive than providing direct guidance:

- **Physical changes**: Discuss the responsibilities that come with sexual maturity, including abstinence or birth control. Discuss breast and testicular self-examinations.
- **Cognitive changes**: Discuss future goals, including life plans and academic plans, providing guidance in relation to steps that the adolescent needs to take in order to meet those goals.
- **Sociobehavioral changes**: Discuss relationships and risk-taking behavior while focusing on means to increase safety.

HEALTH PROMOTION AND DISEASE PREVENTION

The goal of **health promotion** of assisting people to maintain or achieve a high level of health and function is central to health education. Health promotion involves teaching and encouraging people to make changes in their lifestyles, such as with diet and exercise. Health promotion activities can be done whenever the opportunity arises. Preventing illness involves more specific protection of people from illness or threats to their health or well-being. There are three types of prevention activities:

- **Primary**: Specific preventive interventions, such as immunizations, use of safety glasses, fluoridation of water, and changing habits (e.g., smoking, drinking, and diet) to prevent disease.
- **Secondary**: Screening to identify risks or disease (e.g., STDs, diabetes, and hypertension) so preventive measures can be started to prevent progression of disease.
- **Tertiary**: Interventions to promote recovery and prevent disabilities, such as turning patients to prevent pressure sores and enrolling patients in rehabilitation programs.

Maslow's Hierarchy of Needs

According to Maslow's hierarchy of needs, life-threatening needs and safety needs take priority over others, and the needs at one level must generally be met before an individual can progress to the next level.

1	Physiological (basic needs to sustain life, namely, oxygen, food, fluids, and sleep)	The basic needs take precedence over all needs and must be dealt with first before individuals can focus on other needs.
2	Safety and security (physiological and psychological threats)	Once the basic needs are met, individuals become concerned about safety, including freedom from fear, job security, war, and disasters. Children respond more intensely to threats than adults.
3	Love/Belonging (support, caring, and intimacy)	Individuals tend to avoid isolation and loneliness and have a need for family, intimacy, or membership in a group where they feel that they belong.
4	Self-esteem (sense of worth, respect, and independence)	To have confidence, individuals need to develop self-esteem and receive the respect of others.
5	Self-actualization	Individuals choose a path in life that leads to fulfillment and contentment.

Warning Signs and Developmental Concerns

School-Age Years (Ages 6–12)

During the ages of **6–12,** routine health assessments should be done at ages 6, 8, 10, 11, and 12 to determine if there are developmental delays or problems, which may include the following:

- **6 years**: Peer problems, depression, cruelty to animals, poor academic progress, speech problems, lack of fine motor skills, and inability to catch a ball or state their age.
- **8 years**: No close friends, depression, cruelty to animals, interest in fires, very poor academic progress with inability to do math, read, or write adequately and poor coordination.
- **10 years**: No team sports and poor choices in peers (gangs); failure to follow rules; cruelty to animals and interest in fires; depression; failure to understand causal relationships; poor academic progress in reading, writing, math, and penmanship; and problems throwing or catching.
- **12 years**: Continuation of problems at 10 years with increasing risk-taking behaviors (drinking, drugs, sex) and continued poor academic progress in reading, following directions, doing homework, and organization.

Early Adolescence (Ages 11–14)

Early adolescence, ages **11–14,** is a transitional time for children as their hormones and their bodies go through changes. Children mature at varying rates, so there are wide differences. Emotions may be labile, and the child may feel isolated and confused at times, trying to find an identity. Peers take on more influence, and the child may challenge the values of the family. Children may have much anxiety about their bodies and sexuality as secondary sexual characteristics develop. Developmental concerns include the following:

- Delayed maturation.
- Short stature (female).
- Spinal curvature (females).
- Poor dental status (caries, malocclusion).
- Chronic illnesses such as diabetes.
- Lack of adequate physical activity.
- Poor nutrition, anorexia.
- Concerns about sexual identity.
- Negative self-image.
- Depression.
- Lack of close friends, fighting, or violent episodes.
- Poor academic progress with truancy and failure to complete assignments.
- Lack of impulse control.
- Obesity.

Middle Adolescence (Ages 15–17)

In middle adolescence, ages **15–17,** most body changes have occurred, and there is less concern about this but more concern about the image they are projecting to others. Girls may worry about weight and boys about muscle development. Teenagers are interested in sexuality, and many begin sexual experimentation. There is strong identification with peer groups, including codes of dress and behavior, often putting them at odds with family. Developmental concerns include the following:

- Spinal curvature (females) and short stature (males).
- Lack of testicular maturation/persistent gynecomastia.
- Acne.
- Anorexia, obesity.
- Sexual experimentation, multiple partners, and unprotected sex.
- Sexual identification concerns.
- Depression, poor self-image.
- Lack of adequate exercise, poor nutrition, and poor dental health.
- Chronic diseases.
- Experimentation with drugs and alcohol and problems with authority figures.
- Lack of peer group identification, gang association.
- Poor academic progress, failing classes, truancy, attention deficits and disruptive class behavior, poor judgment and impulse control.

Late Adolescence (Ages 18–21)

Late adolescence, **ages 18–21,** is the time when adolescents begin to take on more adult roles and responsibilities, entering the world of work or going to college. Most have come to terms with their sexuality and have a more mature understanding of people's motivations. Some young people will continue to engage in high-risk behaviors. Many of the problems associated with middle adolescence may continue if unresolved, interfering with the transition to adulthood. Developmental concerns include the following:

- Failure to take on adult roles, no life goals or future plans.
- Low self-esteem.
- Lack of intimate relationships, sexual identification concerns.
- Gang association.
- Continued identification with peer group or dependence on parents.
- High-risk sexual behavior: multiple partners and unprotected sex.
- Poor academic progress or ability.
- Psychosomatic complaints, depression.
- Lack of impulse control.
- Poor nutrition, obesity, anorexia.
- Poor dental health.
- Chronic disease.
- Lack of exercise.

Relationship Among Nutrition, Disease, and Quality of Life

Good **nutrition** is essential for the growth and development of children and adolescents and the prevention of chronic disease. Children and adolescents whose nutrition is inadequate or who are hungry because of an actual lack of food have difficulty concentrating and poor academic performance and are less resistant to communicable diseases because their immune systems are impaired. They may feel chronically fatigued and anxious and may develop health disorders, such as scurvy (a lack of vitamin C), based on vitamin deficiencies, or anemia, based on inadequate iron intake. On the other hand, children who overeat and are obese markedly increase their risk of chronic diseases, such as cardiovascular disease, osteoporosis, and diabetes mellitus. In addition, children who are obese are often socially isolated and bullied, causing some to become withdrawn and depressed and others to become angry and aggressive. Obesity in children is associated with a diet high in fat and carbohydrates (candy, snacks, pastries, and sodas) and a lack of adequate exercise.

Suicide Prevention Strategies

Strategies for preventing suicide include the following:

- Gain knowledge about the warning signs of suicide, such as talking about committing suicide, being preoccupied with death, having self-hatred, being depressed, and withdrawing.
- Speak up if someone shows warning signs, show concern, and ask the person about thoughts of and plans for suicide, but avoid arguing, promising confidentiality, or giving advice.
- Respond quickly with those at high risk, especially those with a specific lethal plan or means of committing suicide, by asking directly about plans and taking the person at high risk to a crisis center or emergency department. Risk is high anytime a person is able to articulate a lethal plan, such as using a gun, taking an overdose, or cutting wrists, even if the person promises not to carry out the plan.
- Help the person to obtain professional help and set up a safety plan.

Maintaining Good Mental and Emotional Health

Strategies for **maintaining good mental and emotional health** include the following:

- Keep physically active, such as with a regular exercise program.
- Get adequate sleep and nutrition.
- Practice relaxation techniques, such as meditating, to help deal with stress.
- Develop a support system of friends and family members.
- Engage with others, making time to do things with friends, families, and coworkers.
- Develop hobbies or activities of interest, such as photography, painting, sports, or music.
- Get a pet, such as a dog or cat, that interacts and requires attention.
- Avoid excessive use of alcohol (a depressant), and avoid illicit drugs.
- Maintain a healthy work/school/life balance to avoid overwork and burnout.
- Deal with problems when they arise rather than letting them build.
- Develop strategies for dealing with stress, such as keeping a journal or talking with a friend.
- Engage in volunteer activities in the community.
- Explore spirituality, religion, or belief systems.

Supporting People in Making Positive Health Choices

Strategies and skills for **supporting people** in making positive health choices include the following:

- **Establishing a trusting relationship**: People are more likely to be receptive if the person has already established an open and honest relationship.
- **Preparing with research**: If supporting someone's decision making, it's important to be armed with factual information about the issues, such as the effects smoking on the individual and others, as well as information about the resources available, such as the availability of smoking cessation programs.
- **Picking the right time**: The best time to influence people is when they are alone, relaxed, and not stressed or impaired in some way. For example, talking to someone who is drunk about not drinking is probably pointless.
- **Using "I" messages**: Stressing the personal effects of someone else's choices is more effective than focusing on the other person: "I'm concerned when I see you eating so much fast food."
- **Discussing alternatives, advantages, and disadvantages**: All sides of an issue as well as the different choices that may be made should be part of the discussion.

Use and Abuse of Alcohol, Tobacco, and Other Legal and Illegal Drugs

Prevention strategies for the use and abuse of alcohol, tobacco, and other legal and illegal drugs include the following:

- Enlist the parents/caregivers/family members: Provide information about the signs of use and abuse of alcohol, tobacco, and drugs and guidelines about how to talk to others about these issues as well as lists of community and Internet resources.
- Promote self-esteem: Identify and recognize individual's talents and skills and encourage them to develop their talents.
- Develop critical thinking skills: Focus on problem solving and values in class discussions and assignments.
- Educate regarding risks: Include facts, dangers, and laws related to drug and alcohol use. (However, education alone without skills training has not proven to be effective.)

- Provide skills training: Focus on specific skills, such as assertiveness, refusal methods, and methods of withstanding peer pressure.
- Provide alternatives: Engage young people in activities such as sports, music, and computer clubs. Provide afterschool programs/activities for high school students.

ORGAN DONATION

People of any age can **donate organs and/or tissue**, including the following:

- Organs.
- Stem cells.
- Blood/platelets.
- Tissue.
- Whole body.

There are different types of donations:

- Whole body: Usually, organs cannot be donated separately and the body is donated intact.
- Living donor (one kidney, one lobe of liver, one lobe of lung, part of intestine, blood, stem cells).
- Donation after cardiac or brain death: Solid organs must be transplanted between 6–72 hours after removal, although tissues can be frozen and banked.

Tissues and organs are screened for diseases that may infect the recipient. People who are HIV positive are restricted from donating. People may indicate that they wish to be organ donors, but family members often must make the decision after a person dies. The request for donor organs should be made with sensitivity, and no one should be coerced into approving donation.

CONSCIENTIOUS OBJECTION AND RELIGIOUS BELIEFS

Conscientious objection is objecting to or refusing to participate in an activity or treatment based on religious or moral grounds. In health care, conscientious objection most often relates to refusal of different types of treatment. Religious beliefs that may affect medical care include the following:

- **Christian Scientists**: Believe that prayer is the first treatment for sickness or disease. Although the religion leaves participation in regular medical treatments up to the individual, many choose to have no medications or treatments. This can pose real challenges when parents have the power to make decisions regarding a child's care.
- **Jehovah's Witnesses**: Have traditionally shunned transfusions and blood products as part of their religious belief. However, they can receive fractionated blood cells, thus allowing hemoglobin-based blood substitutes.
    - Acceptable: Fractions from red cells, white cells, platelets, and plasma
    - Not acceptable: Whole blood – red cells, white cells, platelets, plasma
- **12-Step group followers**: People with a history of addiction may be very reluctant on moral grounds to accept pain medication because of the fear of addiction.

Issues Related to Access to Health Care

Access to health care is very uneven with access limited by many different factors:

- **Poverty and lack of insurance**: Many cannot afford to pay for health care and may be unaware of programs available for those with low income.
- **Immigration status**: Illegal immigrants are ineligible for most programs intended for low-income residents. Additionally, people may be fearful of immigration authorities and avoid seeking medical help.
- **Lack of availability of medical care**: Some areas may lack physicians, clinics, and hospitals, especially rural areas. In other cases, the available hours of care may be during usual work hours so that people are unable to make appointments.
- **Transportation**: Some lack transportation (motor vehicles, public transportation) to healthcare facilities.
- **Lack of education**: People may have low health literacy and lack of awareness of health risks or may be unaware of rights and responsibilities.
- **Language barriers**: Non-English speakers may have a difficult time accessing health care and understanding directions.

Risk Factors for Unhealthy Behavior

Peer Pressure

Peer pressure is pressure to conform to the behavior or ideals of a group that is approximately the same age and social class. Most adolescents are introduced to drugs and alcohol by peers, and peer pressure to participate in high-risk behavior, such as substance abuse, is very strong because the adolescent wants to be accepted as part of the group. Groups that use drugs or alcohol tend to view others as abnormal, not themselves, so adolescents that refuse to participate may find themselves ostracized. Thus, although an adolescent may be aware of the dangers of drugs and alcohol and doesn't want to participate in their use, he or she may feel compelled to do so. Assertiveness training and refusal skills can help the adolescent to deal with peer pressure, but the reality is that he or she may need to align with a different group of peers in order to make good decisions about avoiding substance abuse.

Teasing and Bullying

Teasing is good natured and harmless only when the person being teased is in on the joke and is not threatened in any way by the teasing. In most cases, however, there is an element of aggression in teasing with the person doing the teasing exercising control over the one being teased and doing it to make the other person uncomfortable or to draw attention to the person's weakness. Teasing is often used to establish dominance and has a negative impact on interpersonal and social relationships because others tend to shun those who appear weak, in case they also become targets. Teasing is often one aspect of **bullying**, which involves unwanted aggressive behavior, such as name calling, pushing, shoving, hitting, making threats, humiliating, and intimidating. Bullying can profoundly affect the victim's self-esteem and result in social withdrawal and depression. The victim is often reluctant to admit being bullied to family, authorities, or friends because of shame and fear of retaliation.

Harassment and Discrimination

Although sexual harassment is the most common type of **harassment**, people may also experience harassment based on a wide range of issues, including political beliefs, criminal history, social status, income, occupation, gender identification, sexual orientation, age, ethnicity, religion, disability, and appearance. Harassment involves aggressive actions or words of intimidation toward another because of who or what the person is. Harassment is often an element in bullying, stereotyping, and discrimination, and the line can be hard to draw.

Discrimination involves unfair or prejudicial treatment, such as refusing to allow an ethnic minority to participate in a club that is open to all other students or giving a gay student a low grade because of disapproval of his lifestyle. Discrimination often limits the interpersonal and social opportunities available to people and tends to isolate them from others while fostering resentment and anger.

High-Risk Sexual Behavior

High-risk sexual behavior in teenagers is often coupled with other health-risk behaviors, such as drinking and drug use, and teenagers are having sex at younger ages. About 47% of high school seniors have had sex, with many beginning as young as 10–12 years of age. Risk factors include poverty, single-family homes, lack of supervision, and siblings or peers who are sexually active. Those who have sex before age 15 are especially vulnerable, often having multiple partners and unprotected sex, leading to STDs and pregnancy. They are emotionally vulnerable and often can't deal effectively with relationships. *Intervention* should begin early with age-appropriate, honest sex education. Abstinence education, while the ideal, has not been successful in changing the sexual behavior of teenagers, with studies showing that many of those signing pledges to remain virgins are already sexually active. Teenagers who are sexually active should be advised regarding the use of condoms, birth control, and protection from STDs in a nonjudgmental manner.

Alcohol Use

Alcohol is a significant problem in adolescence and even in younger children. It is the most commonly abused substance. Studies have shown that about 32% of young people drink and 20% are binge drinkers. Although alcohol can impair development of almost all body systems in a growing child, it is of particular concern for the effects on the neurological system and liver. Additionally, because alcohol interferes with impulse control, adolescents who drink are often involved in violence, abuse, and at-risk sexual behavior. Drinking should be expected if a child has memory problems, changes in behavior, poor academic progress, emotional lability, and physical changes, such as slurring of speech, general lethargy, or lack of coordination. Intervention includes teaching children from about age 9 about the dangers of drinking, identifying those who are drinking, identifying underlying problems, and providing programs to help teenagers stop drinking, such as counseling or Alcoholics Anonymous.

Drug Use

Drug use continues to be a serious problem for children and teenagers, with some starting as young as age 9 or 10, using a wide variety of drugs, including marijuana, crack, prescription drugs, cocaine, inhalants (such as glue and lighter fluid), hallucinogens, and steroids. Risk factors include aggressive behavior, poor social skills, and poor academic progress coupled with a lack of parental supervision, poverty, and availability of drugs. Small children are often reacting to circumstances within the family, whereas teenagers are responding to peer pressure from outside the family. Studies have shown that early intervention to teach children better self-control and coping skills is often more effective than trying to change behavior patterns that are established, so family-based programs often show positive results. Teenagers may need help with basic academic skills and social skills to improve communication. Methods of resisting drugs must be provided and reinforced. Drug recovery programs can be helpful but are often too expensive or not available for those who need them.

Tobacco Use

The CDC conducts the Youth Risk Behavior Surveillance System to determine health-risk behaviors that contribute to significant morbidity in adolescents. **Tobacco**, often thought of as an adult issue, is also a cause of concern for children and teenagers. Tobacco use is one of the leading preventable causes of death in the United States, but about 70% of children have tried smoking before high school, often beginning by age 12, putting themselves at risk for heart and lung disease as adults. Additionally, many teenagers use chewing tobacco or cigars (which can cause mouth cancer) or they vape (which can lead to tooth and gum damage and can lead to the smoking of tobacco). Those most at risk are males in low-income families with parents who smoke. Male adolescents may smoke to be rebellious, but females often smoke to lose weight. Other factors include the desire to be part of a group, a lack of supervision, and the accessibility of tobacco. Intervention includes identifying those smoking, providing information about the dangers of smoking beginning with children at about 9 years old, and providing programs to help teenagers quit smoking.

Child Abuse and Reporting

About 5 million cases of suspected **child abuse** are reported in the United States each year. In accordance with the Child Abuse Prevention and Treatment and Adoption Act Amendments (1996) and the Model Child Protection Act, Texas has instituted mandatory reporting of child abuse. The health educator in Texas is a mandatory reporter and must report suspected abuse within 48 hours:

- Child abuse or neglect that places the child at risk of harm (physical or emotional), death, or exploitation.
- Sexual abuse including rape, molestation, prostitution, incest, or engaging in any type of sexually explicit behavior.

Texas does not require proof of abuse prior to reporting, only suspicion based on observations and reasonable cause. Regardless, there is criminal and civil liability (class B misdemeanor) involved if child abuse is not reported, and Texas provides immunity for reporters. Reports are confidential. Thus, the best course is to report even suspicions to the Texas Department of Family and Protective Services or to a law enforcement agency.

Signs of Physical Abuse in Children

Children rarely admit to being abused and, in fact, typically deny it and attempt to protect the abusing parent. Therefore, the healthcare provider must often rely on physical and behavioral signs to determine if there is cause to suspect **abuse**:

- **Behavioral indicators**: The child may be overly compliant or fearful with obvious changes in demeanor when a parent/caregiver is present. Some children act out with aggression toward other children or animals. Children may become depressed or suicidal or present with sleeping or eating disorders. Behaviors may become increasingly self-destructive as the child ages.
- **Physical indicators**: The type, location, and extent of injuries can raise the suspicion of abuse. Head and facial injuries and bruising are common, as are bite or burn marks. There may be handprints or grab marks and unusual bruising, such as across the buttocks. Any bruising, swelling, or tearing of the genital area and the identification of STDs are also causes for concern.

Signs of Neglect and Lack of Supervised Care in Children

Although some children may not be physically or sexually abused, they may suffer from profound **neglect or lack of supervision** that places them at risk. Indicators include the following:

- Appearing dirty and unkempt, sometimes with infestations of lice, and wearing ill-fitting, torn clothing and shoes.
- Being tired and sleepy during the daytime.
- Having excessive medical or dental problems, such as extensive dental caries.
- Missing appointments and not receiving proper immunizations.
- Being underweight for their current stage of development.

Neglect can be difficult to assess, especially if the health educator is teaching a homeless or very disadvantaged population. Home visits may be needed to ascertain if there is adequate food, clothing, or supervision, and this is beyond the scope of care provided by the health educator. Thus, suspicions should be reported to child protective services so that social workers can arrange a follow-up assessment of the home environment.

Health Promotion

Exercise Needs at Different Ages

Daily **exercise** is an important component of good health practices but should be age-appropriate, and some health conditions may pose restrictions. Toddlers and young children usually get exercise by running and playing and do not need organized activities, but others benefit from planned exercise:

- **4–5-year-olds** may participate in dancing, skating, and other supervised activities but may lack coordination and judgment about safety.
- **6–12-year-olds** are still growing and muscles are short, so they do best with noncompetitive sports, such as bicycling and swimming, until about age 10. Team sports should be supervised to ensure that children are not straining their muscles. Weight lifting may be done starting at age 11 to build strength. Gymnastics may begin, but children should be monitored for eating disorders.
- **12–18-year-olds** can participate in any sports activity unless limited by illness or disability. Exercise should be done at least three times weekly for 30 minutes.
- **Adults** should exercise at least 30 minutes daily or 150 minutes/week.

Resiliency and Asset Development

Resiliency is the ability to cope with risk factors, such as poverty, and to remain emotionally healthy. One of the current trends is to aid students in developing resiliency by providing a safe and supportive environment. Promoting resiliency also includes identifying problems early and taking steps to deal with them before they become ingrained as well as proving aid for severe or long-term problems. Holding students to high expectations and supporting them in attaining goals helps to build self-confidence and coping skills.

Asset development focuses on identifying and developing the assets that children and adolescents need in order to become physically and emotionally healthy. Traits that indicate good development include good grades, good health, diverse friends, leadership roles, avoidance of risk-taking behaviors, and the ability to delay gratification and deal with adversity. Children and adolescents need external assets (support, empowerment, boundaries, expectations, and meaningful activities) as well as internal assets (positive values, positive self-identity, social awareness and competency, and interest in and commitment to learning).

Evaluation of Information and Products Related to Health Care

Evaluation of information and products related to traditional and alternative health care includes the following:

- **The source**: Determine if the information is provided by a credible source, such as a professional organization (.org), an educational institution (.edu), or a government site (.gov) as opposed to a commercial site (.com) or a juried journal as opposed to the popular press.
- **Evidence**: Assess whether the information/product is supported by evidence, such as research studies, and the size of the studies, number of participants, and format. Additionally, check dates to ensure that the material is not outdated.
- **Warning signs**: Be aware that a lack of information about the publisher or author is a red flag. Anything that is advertised as a "miracle cure" is likely not, and if an advertisement suggests that there is a medical conspiracy to prevent access to information or products, this is almost always a warning sign. Watch for poor spelling and grammar because this information is often derived from unregulated foreign sources.

Technology Used in Health Care

X-Rays

X-rays are used for diagnosis and evaluation of treatment and to determine correct placement of medical devices. X-rays pass more readily through soft tissue than dense tissue, so dense tissue, which has less radiation exposure, appears as white against the darker background of soft tissue. Therefore, X-rays are most commonly used for the evaluation of bones, such as for fractures or dislocations. They may also be used for soft tissue when a disease or disorder alters the density of the tissue, such as with pneumonia in the lungs or gallstones, kidney stones, or tumors (although small tumors may go undetected). Different types of tissue have different color gradations. For example, organs with a high fluid content (stomach, liver) appear gray whereas muscles appear slightly darker. Spaces filled with air (such as the lungs) appear very dark. X-rays may be used with contrast medium as well to take images of the cardiovascular or GI systems.

CT, MRI, and Ultrasound

Computed tomography (CT) involves scanning tissue in successive layers through a narrow-beam X-ray, providing a cross-sectional view. CTs can demonstrate differences in soft-tissue density. CT scans may be done with fluoroscopy or contrast material, such as iodine dye, to evaluate for infections, tumors, or other abnormalities. CT scans can differentiate between cellulitis and the formation of abscesses better than a routine X-ray.

Magnetic resonance imaging (MRI) uses magnetic fields and radiofrequency signals to create a cross-sectional view, and the images are more detailed than with CT. MRI may be done with or without contrast material. MRI uses radio waves and magnetic fields to create images of internal structures, providing information about infections, tumors, or other abnormalities that may not be obvious with X-rays, CT scans, or ultrasounds. MRIs are more expensive than X-rays, CTs, or ultrasounds, so they are often done after other testing has been inconclusive.

Ultrasound uses ultrasonic sound waves transmitted by a transducer, which picks up reflected sound waves that a computer converts to electronic images. Ultrasound can show fluid accumulation, the movement of blood through the organs, masses, malformations (congenital abnormalities), changes in the size of the organs or other structures, and obstructions.

ECG and Echocardiogram

An **electrocardiogram** (ECG) is used to create a graphic record of the heart's electrical activity. The 12-lead ECG is usually used, but a 15-lead ECG may be used to diagnose right ventricular and posterior left ventricular infarction. An 18-lead ECG may be used to diagnose myocardial ischemia. Continuous ECGs may be used to monitor those at high risk for dysrhythmias.

An **echocardiogram** is a form of ultrasound used to determine the size, shape, and movement of cardiac structures. High-frequency sound waves are transmitted into the heart by a handheld transducer held against the chest wall; however, images tend to be poor because of interference caused by tissue and bone. A more effective method is the **transesophageal echocardiogram** in which a small transducer is fed through the mouth and down the esophagus, allowing the transducer to be closer to the heart.

Student Opportunities to Observe Therapeutic and Diagnostic Procedures and Preprocedural Preparations

Students face some restrictions in **observing** therapeutic and diagnostic procedures and preprocedural preparations, but some programs are available, such as through colleges and universities. Most programs require that students be 16 years or older. For example, the University of Texas has programs specifically for high school students who want to observe for 2- to 4-month periods. The students may observe but may not provide any direct patient care or any hands-on activities or data collection. In Texas, age 18 is the prerequisite for training to be a certified nurse assistant (CNA), so this precludes most high school students. Some hospitals allow adolescents 15 years and older to serve as volunteers, although their roles are limited. Individual physicians and clinics may also permit some observations if patients agree. Some high school programs, such as those at magnet schools, have agreements with medical centers that allow those who are interested in the health professions to observe and participate in some activities.

Monitoring Health Status

Physical Growth and Development During School-Age Years (6–12)

During the school years **(ages 6–12)** children go through many changes:

- **Dental**: Children lose deciduous teeth and begin acquiring permanent teeth.
- **Height and weight**: These should progress slowly and steadily, gaining an average of 2 inches each year, beginning at about 45 inches at 6 and 59 inches at 12. Weight usually doubles during this time from 46 pounds at 6 to 88 pounds at 12. Boys and girls are similar in size, but by 12, some girls will be undergoing pubertal changes and may gain height and weight over boys.
- **Proportions**: The body becomes slimmer and better proportioned with an increase in muscle mass and a decrease in fat. In relation to height, head circumference decreases, leg length increases, and waist circumference decreases. Facial characteristics change.
- **Body systems**: Systems mature with respirations and heart rate decreasing. Bladder capacity is usually better in girls than boys. Muscles strengthen and bones begin to ossify. Physical variation increases with age.

Screening for Scoliosis

Scoliosis is the lateral curvature ≥11° of the spine, usually occurring (in 2%–3% of adolescents) during the period between ages 10 and 15 when the child goes through a growth spurt, so screening should be done at least twice during this period. Scoliosis is more common in girls than boys. Screening includes the following:

- The child stands upright, and the shoulders, waist, and hips are assessed.
- Adams forward bending test, in which the child bends over at the waist (as in toe touching) and the screener observes the hips to determine if there is a difference in height.
- Scoliometer measures the curvature of the spine in the thoracic and lumbar area when the child bends over.
- Moiré topography uses a grating positioned near the child so it casts shadows that show contour lines.
- X-rays confirm positive screenings.

Positive findings may include one shoulder being lower than another, an uneven waistline, prominence of shoulder blade(s), one hip higher than another, or lateral leaning when upright.

Vital Signs

Children's **vital signs** vary considerably according to age, height, and weight:

- **Heart rate** (at rest): Preschool and school-age children to age 10 have heart rates of 70 to 100, and older children and adolescents have normal heart rates of 55 to 90.
- **Respiratory rate**: Respiratory rate averages about 21 by age 6, and it is 16–19 thereafter.
- **Temperature**: The typical "normal" temperature of 37°C (98.6°F) is reached at 5 years, but it usually continues to decline to a normal of 36.6°C (97.8°F) by age 13.

The proper cuff size is necessary for accurate blood pressure readings in children. BP slowly increases with age, so the average for a boy at 6 is 96/57 and for a girl 96/57. By age 15, BP is becoming closer to adult level with 114/65 for boys and 111/67 for girls. **Blood pressure** (to estimate):

- Systolic (ages 1 to 7): Add age in years to 90.
- Systolic (ages 8 to 18): Multiply age in years × 2 and add to 83.
- Diastolic (ages 1 to 5 years): 56.
- Diastolic (ages 6 to 18 years): Add age in years to 52.

Safely Moving, Lifting, and Transporting Patients

Generally, patients (such as students) can only be **transported** with parental/guardian permission; however, in the case of emergency or serious illness, patients can be transported to the nearest emergency department for treatment, but an attempt should be made to contact parents or guardians. A 9-1-1 call should be placed, and the patient should be transported by ambulance. Patients should not be moved unless absolutely necessary; and if he or she is severely injured, precautions for head and neck injuries should be used. If the patient must be moved and lifted, at least three people (one on each side and one carrying the feet) should participate. However, if the patient is in danger (such as from a fire) and must be moved rapidly, one person may move the patient by squatting down, placing arms under the patient's shoulders and axillae and dragging, using the back muscles. The patient should be moved onto a stretcher, if possible, secured, and transported with at least two carriers. Emergency incidents that may require transport include hemorrhage, penetrating wounds, respiratory distress, distended and rigid abdomen, and amputations. Only in the gravest of situations (multiple casualties, no 9-1-1 response) should a student be transported in school vehicles.

Blanket Drag, Clothing Drag, and Arm Drag

Emergency moves may be needed if the person is in immediate danger from fire, explosives, or other hazards; if the person requires life-saving treatment (such as CPR); or if the person is in water, such as a pond or lake. Emergency moves include the following:

- **Blanket drag**: Log roll the person onto a blanket, package the person, and grasp the blanket near the person's head while in a squatting position with the back straight and drag the person. If there are two rescuers, the other should be positioned at the foot and push.
- **Clothing drag**: Squat down by the person's head, securely grasp the clothing near the person's neck, and drag the person.
- **Arm drag**: Squat down by the person's head. Fold the person's arms across the chest. Grasp him or her under the arms, wrapping the arms about the torso and grasping the wrists to stabilize the arms. Drag the person.

Urgent moves, such as with altered mental status, shock, or breathing difficulties, should also be done as quickly as possible.

Accuracy in Documentation

There are many requirements regarding **written communication and documentation,** including accuracy: Regardless of format, recording should always include any change in a person's condition, any treatments, other interventions, responses, and any complaints. Health providers should avoid subjective descriptions (especially negative terms, which could be used to establish bias), such as tired, angry, confused, bored, rude, happy, and euphoric. Instead, more objective descriptions, such as "Yawning two to three times a minute," should be used. People can be quoted directly, "I shouldn't have to wait for to see the counselor when I need to!" If errors are made in documenting, for example, charting another person's information in the record, the error cannot be erased, whited-out, or otherwise made illegible. The error must be indicated by drawing a line through the text and writing "Error."

Assessing Hygiene

Assessing hygiene may be carried out by administering a self-assessment test that asks about such things as how frequently people bathe, brush their teeth, wash their hair, and change their clothes and whether they use body products, such as soap, shampoo, and deodorant. This should be followed by a discussion about norms and expectations. Assessment may also be carried out through observation. Indications of poor hygiene include dirty and stained clothing, greasy limp hair, obvious dirt on the skin, dirty fingernails and elbows, body odor, and bad breath. Addressing hygiene issues directly can be more difficult because not all students are receptive. Asking a person about his or her understanding of hygiene practices, discussing problems associated with poor hygiene (bad breath, dental caries, infections), and providing information (videos, pamphlets) may provide some guidance. Some people, such as students, may have no access to washing machines or showers, and (if possible) facilities at the school may be made available to these students.

ADLs

Activities of daily living (ADLs) are those activities that are essential for an individual to be independent in personal care. ADLs include the ability to:

- Eat, using usual or modified utensils.
- Bathe in a tub or shower.
- Dress, putting on and taking off all necessary clothing and shoes.
- Toilet, including using the toilet, commode, and/or urinal.

- Transfer, getting in and out of bed, chairs, automobiles.
- Groom, washing and combing hair, brushing teeth, trimming nails.
- Walk, getting from place to place independently or with assistive devices.

ADLs are usually mastered by most people during the first few years of life, and people often are able to continue to manage ADLs even with some degree of cognitive impairment. Skills needed to carry out ADLs include cognitive, motor (balance, movement, strength) and perceptual. ADLs are assessed when determining the degree of independence that a person has and when deciding on the types of assistance the person may need to continue to live, work, or study.

Rehabilitative Care

Rehabilitative care is provided in order to return an individual with some type of impairment to maximal functioning, even though the level of function may be less than prior to disability. Rehabilitative care may include the following:

- Occupational therapy: Focuses on helping clients manage activities of daily living, such as dressing, bathing, and preparing food.
- Rehabilitation therapy: Devises methods to assist clients to return to normal physical, mental, and emotional functioning.
- Physical therapy: Uses special equipment and exercises to help people regain or maintain body strength and physical function.
- Recreational therapy: Uses recreational activities to improve people's sense of well-being and physical functioning.
- Psychological care: Provides research, testing and assessment, and therapy for psychological or behavioral disorders.
- Physician care: Orders treatment protocols.
- Nursing care: Provide medications and treatments and monitor general health.
- Speech therapy: Provides exercises and strategies to help people recover speech, improve communication, and improve the ability to drink, chew, and swallow safely.

Protection of Human Subjects

The Food and Drug Administration, Code of Federal Regulations, Title 21, Volume 1, regulates **protection of human subjects** and states that any researcher involving patients in research must obtain informed consent, in language understandable to the patient or the patient's agent. The elements of this informed consent must include an explanation of the research, the purpose, and the expected duration, as well as a description of any potential risks. Potential benefits and possible alternative treatments must be described. Any compensation to be provided must be outlined. The extent of confidentiality should be clarified. Contact information should be provided in the event the patient/family has questions. The patient must be informed that participation is voluntary and that he/she can discontinue participation at any time and without penalty. Informed consent must be documented by a signed, written agreement.

Presentation of Data

The **presentation of evidence** is an important element of collaboration. The presentation should be tailored to the audience, using appropriate language, and the discussion should include the following:

- **Overview**: An explanation of the type of research and evidence, the outcomes, and the potential for integrating the results of this research into current practice.
- **Validity**: A discussion of the manner in which the research was conducted, the type of research format, and an explanation of how the research exhibits external validity.
- **Reliability**: The outcomes of the research should be completely explored, including effectiveness and any problems encountered.
- **Applicability**: The possible benefits to applying the research to practice must be clearly outlined, including a discussion of how the research population aligns with the target population as well as how feasible (and cost-effective) implementation would be.

Importance of Communication in Collection and Dissemination of Healthcare Data

There are many ways to communicate **evidence-based healthcare data** about policies, procedures, products, or technology to internal and external stakeholders:

- Presentations to administration and those in positions of leadership, such as the board of directors, team leaders, managers, to garner support for incorporating findings into practice.
- Inservice training/education that focuses on results of research and explains applicability.
- Print distribution in the form of flyers or newsletters that outline the research findings.
- Electronic newsletters or training modules that present the research findings.
- Discussions with intra- and interdisciplinary team members about the research and ways in which to apply those to the practice of care.
- Presentations to community agencies and community members about benefits to the population.
- Dashboards to report ongoing findings and progress.
- Media notices: Sending information to local newspapers, magazines, TV, and radio and giving interviews about evidence-based findings.

Diffusion of Innovations

The adoption of new ideas and how they spread is referred to as the **diffusion of innovations**. According to Rogers (2003), innovations spread by stages through an organization and innovations may be continued if accepted and supported by outcomes or may be rejected. The five stages involved in the diffusion of innovations include the following:

- **Knowing**: Staff must be exposed to an intervention and understand how it functions. Information may be sought or discovered in various ways, such as journal articles and conference presentations.
- **Persuading**: Steps must be taken to engage and interest staff members and to communicate openly about the innovation in order for them to develop positive attitudes.
- **Decision making**: The innovation may be adopted as is, adapted to meet organization needs, or rejected.

- **Implementing**: The innovation is put into practice with support of key stakeholders, requiring change in behavior. The innovation must be evaluated and modified if necessary.
- **Confirming**: A final decision, based on evaluation, must be made whether to continue the innovation or discontinue it.

Collection and Dissemination of Healthcare Data Through Technology

Technology, in terms of equipment and software applications, is developing at a rapid pace, with new technology available almost weekly. When **evaluating and applying technology to support innovation,** a selection committee should include members with expertise in technology as well as clinical staff or others who will use the technology. There are many steps that should be carried out during evaluation and selection:

- Evaluate existing resources and technology.
- Identify areas in which new or upgraded technology may benefit innovation.
- Prioritize.
- Research available technology to determine which technology is most appropriate.
- Identify human resources for implementation.
- Estimate training needs in terms of time and costs.
- Estimate ongoing costs based on life expectancy of technology and need for upgrades.
- Conduct a cost–benefit analysis.
- Project return on investment in terms of financial returns and healthcare benefits.

HIPAA and the Privacy Rule

HIPAA regulations are designed to protect the rights of individuals regarding the privacy of their health information. Healthcare providers must not release any information or documentation about a patient's condition or treatment without consent because the individual has the right to determine who has access to his or her personal information. Personal information about the patient is considered protected health information, and it consists of any identifying or personal information about the patient, such as health history, condition, or treatments in any form, and any documentation, including electronic, verbal, or written. Personal information can be shared with a spouse, legal guardians, parents, those with durable power of attorney for the patient, and those involved in the care of the patient, such as physicians, without a specific release, but the patient should always be consulted if personal information is to be discussed with others present to ensure that there is no objection. Failure to comply with HIPAA regulations can make a healthcare provider liable for legal action. **Privacy rule**: Protected information includes information in the medical record (electronic or paper), conversations between the doctor and other healthcare providers, billing information, and any other form of health information.

Issues of Confidentiality and Privacy Regarding Children and Adolescents

Children, especially adolescents, may have concerns about **confidentiality** in relation to their health or activities that they do not want divulged to their parents. Young people may be uncomfortable addressing concerns verbally and may be more forthcoming if given a questionnaire to fill out as a beginning point for discussion. The health educator is often faced with ethical concerns about dealing with confidentiality, but the best course is to deal with the issue directly by informing adolescents that what they say will be held in confidence within certain limitations:

- Mandatory reporting requirements must be upheld, including reports of child abuse, sexual abuse, and communicable diseases.
- Health endangerment, such as through the abuse of drugs or alcohol, eating disorders, or suicidal thoughts, must be reported to the parents, while assuring the child that the health educator will be there to support and help them to discuss these matters with parents.

Evaluation of Environment for Safety

Evaluation of the environment for safety may include ensuring that

- All alarms and fire-safety equipment are in place and functioning properly.
- Safety measures are posted in all laboratories, and adequate training of staff and students is conducted.
- Lighting is adequate.
- Access to the campus is controlled during school hours.
- Security cameras are in place and functioning properly.
- Staff members (and in large schools, students) wear identifying badges.
- The dress code (such as no wearing of gang colors) is enforced.
- Periodic checking for drugs is carried out (such as with dogs).
- Metal detectors are used.
- Eye protection and personal protective equipment (PPE) are available for high-risk areas (such as laboratories).
- Equipment is maintained and immediately repaired when necessary.
- The ventilation system is clean and functioning properly.
- Drinking water is assessed for contamination.
- Outdoor pollutants, such as pesticides, are controlled and limited.
- Toxic hazards, such as asbestos and chemicals, are identified and removed or stored safely.

Fire Prevention Procedures

Fire prevention procedures include the following:

- Ensure that exterior lighting is adequate and trees and shrubs are trimmed and intrusion alarms are in place and functioning.
- Store trash cans away from the building (in case of intentional fires).
- Ensure that sprinkler systems are properly inspected and functioning.
- Dispense adequate numbers of fire extinguishers throughout the campus.
- Ensure that all laboratory procedures are fire safe and monitored.
- Ensure that adequate smoke alarms are installed and maintained.
- Maintain the heating system and carry out routine service.
- Train kitchen staff in fire safety, maintain stoves and ovens, and install a fire suppression system in the stove hood.
- Conduct routine fire drills.
- Assess and maintain all electrical systems and equipment on a regular basis.
- Teach students fire safety awareness and how to respond to fires.
- Have annual (or more often) evaluations carried out by the fire department to identify risks.
- Develop a fire evacuation plan and widely disseminate it.

RACE and PASS in Relation to Fires

The acronym **RACE** is used to help staff members remember the steps to take in the event of fire:

- **R**emove students and others from danger.
- **A**ctivate alarm (call for help).
- **C**ontain the fire (close doors and windows if possible).
- **E**xtinguish the fire (using a fire extinguisher if the fire is small and you able to do so without risk).

Additionally, the acronym **PASS** is used to guide use of the fire extinguisher, The P.A.S.S. protocol covers these steps:

- **P** – Pull the pin of the fire extinguisher.
- **A** – Aim the nozzle at the fire.
- **S** – Squeeze the handle of the fire extinguisher.
- **S** – Spray from side to side, starting at the base of the fire.

For any fire, the fire department should be called by dialing 9-1-1 and staff members should not attempt to put out a fire that is large or dangerous. The primary concern must always be the safety of the students.

Primary Triage and Secondary Triage for Multiple-Casualty Incidents

Primary triage is a rapid method (30 to 60 seconds) of prioritizing patients based on the severity of their condition and is carried out at the scene of multiple-casualty incidents. All patients are triaged and tagged according to international color-coding priority (P) guidelines on the foot or wrist (not on clothing):

- P1—Red: Immediate care is needed for urgent systemic life-threatening conditions, such as airway/breathing problems, severe bleeding, severe burns (especially with breathing problems), decreased mental status, shock, and severe medical problems, Glasgow Coma Score ≤13.
- P2—Yellow: Delayed care and able to wait 45–60 minutes for treatment. Conditions include burns (without breathing problems), multiple bone/joint injuries, back and/or spinal cord injuries (unless in respiratory distress).
- P3—Green: Hold, able to wait hours for treatment of minor injuries.
- P4—Black: Deceased.

Patients coded black are left in place, but those with other color tags should be moved and segregated in separate sections of a holding area to await treatment and/or transport. The patients should be **retriaged (secondary triage)** as they are moved into the holding area to determine if the color tagging is still appropriate.

GCS

The **Glasgow Coma Scale (GCS)** measures the depth and duration of coma or impaired level of consciousness and is used for postoperative assessment. The GCS measures three parameters: Best eye response, best verbal response, and best motor response, with a total possible score that ranges from 3 to 15. The same scale is used with slight modifications for infants.

Eye opening	4: Spontaneous. 3: To verbal stimuli. 2: To pain (not of face). 1: No response.
Verbal	5: Oriented. (Infant: Smiles, exhibits appropriate interactions.) 4: Conversation confused, but can answer questions. (Infant: Crying but consolable.) 3: Uses inappropriate words. (Infant: Moaning, sometimes inconsolable.) 2: Speech incomprehensible. (Infant: Inconsolable, agitated.) 1: No response.
Motor	6: Moves on command. (Infant: Moves spontaneously or with purpose.) 5: Moves purposefully in response to pain. 4: Withdraws in response to pain. 3: Decorticate posturing (flexion) in response to pain. 2: Decerebrate posturing (extension) in response to pain. 1: No response.

Injuries/conditions are classified according to the total score: 3–8, coma; ≤ 8, severe head injury; 9–12, moderate head injury; 13–15, mild head injury.

First-Aid Procedures in Various Situations

Basic First Aid	
Anaphylaxis (allergic shock)	Immediately call 9-1-1. Administer epinephrine (EpiPen) per autoinjector if the person has one. Begin CPR if he or she is in respiratory arrest.
Animal bites	Minor (if no concern about rabies): Wash with soap and water and apply antibiotic cream/ointment and bandage. Major: Apply pressure to stop any bleeding with a dry, clean bandage and transport to the emergency department or call 9-1-1 if severe.
Black eye	Apply cold compresses, avoiding pressure on the eye. If blood is noted in the eye itself or vision is impaired, transport to the emergency department.
Chemical burns/eye splashes	Remove contaminated belongings and flush the burn area with copious tap water for at least 10 minutes. Transport to the emergency department or call 9-1-1 if burns are severe, the patient feels faint, or the burn is more than 3 inches in diameter. Flush eyes for at least 20 minutes, and then transport him or her to the emergency department.
Cut/Scrapes	Apply pressure with a clean bandage to stop any bleeding. Rinse with clear water and wash around the wound with soap and water. Apply antibiotic ointment and dressing. If the wound is deep and requires suturing, transport the person to the emergency department.
Heat cramps, exhaustion, stroke	Heat cramps and exhaustion: Remove the person to the shade, lay flat and elevate the legs, cool by spraying with cold water, have him or her drink cool water. Heat stroke: Call 9-1-1. Spray or immerse the person in cool water and fan, administer CPR if necessary.
Hypothermia	Call 9-1-1. Remove wet clothing, warm gradually with warm compresses to the trunk, and give warm drinks. Do not warm too quickly, and do not massage the limbs.

Basic First Aid	
Insect bites/stings	Remove stingers, wash the area with soap and water, and apply a cool compress. Apply cortisone cream to reduce itching. If there is a severe reaction or it is a bite with a known dangerous insect (such as a scorpion), call 9-1-1. Administer EpiPen if the person has one for allergy to the insect.
Bleeding	Minor: Apply pressure with a clean bandage to stop the bleeding, and apply a dry dressing. Severe: Call 9-1-1. Remove any large debris from the wound. Apply pressure with a clean bandage to stop the bleeding but not if debris is imbedded in wound, and don't apply pressure to an eye. In these cases, simply cover with a clean dressing. Lie the person flat and elevate his or her feet. Apply a tourniquet for bleeding that is life-threatening only if you are trained to do so.
Snakebites (venomous)	Call 9-1-1. Position the injury below the level of the heart, if possible. Cover the wound with a dry dressing. DO NOT apply ice, cut, or apply a tourniquet. Report a description of the snake to first responders.
Spider bite	Cleanse the bite with soap and water and apply antibiotic ointment and a cool compress. Transport the person to the emergency department if a poisonous spider, such as the black widow or brown recluse, is suspected.
Sprains/ Fractures/ Dislocations	Sprains: Use rest, ice, compress, elevate (RICE). Transport to the emergency department if he or she is unable to bear weight or use the joint. Fractures: Call 9-1-1 or transport the person to the emergency department. Apply pressure to stop any bleeding, cover wounds with a dry dressing, immobilize the injured limb, and apply an ice pack. Dislocation: Transport to the emergency department. Do not attempt to move the joint. Apply an ice compress to the joint.
Shock (any cause)	Call 9-1-1. Lay the person flat, elevate the legs and feet, and keep him or her still. Loosen the person's clothing. Begin CPR for cardiac or respiratory arrest.
Stroke	Call 9-1-1. Keep the head elevated.
Nosebleeds	Sit the person upright and pinch the nostrils for 5 to 10 minutes. Transport to the emergency department if bleeding follows an accident or if it persists for more than 20 minutes.

CPR Techniques

Hands-only **cardiopulmonary resuscitation (CPR)** is recommended for nonmedical rescuers for unconscious teens or adults who have no pulse or respirations. The rescuer should call 9-1-1 and place the victim supine on a hard surface. To find the correct hand position, run two fingers along the ribs to the center chest, place two fingers over the xiphoid process, and place the palm of the other hand on the sternum directly above the fingers. Then place the other hand on top of the first, fingers linked and elbows locked, to begin compressions, which should be done in a rocking movement, using the body to apply pressure. (Note, use two fingers for infants.) The rate of compressions is at least 100 per minute and at least two inches deep (1/3 chest depth for infants and small children). This rate corresponds roughly to the beat of the Bee Gees' song "Staying Alive" (dum, dum, dum, dum, stayin' alive, stayin' alive ...). With two trained rescuers, rescue breathing may be added at a compression-to-breathing ratio of 30:2.

Heimlich Maneuver

Adults and Children

The universal sign of choking is when a person clutches his or her throat and appears to be choking or gasping for breath. If the person can speak ("Can you speak?") or cough, the **Heimlich maneuver** is not usually necessary. The Heimlich maneuver can be done with the victim sitting, standing, or supine. The Heimlich procedure for children (≥1 year) and adults is performed as follows:

- Wrap your arms around the victim's waist from the back if sitting or standing. Make a fist and place the thumb side against the victim's abdomen slightly above the umbilicus. Grasp this hand with the other and thrust sharply upward to force air out of the lungs.
- Repeat as needed.
- If the victim loses consciousness, ease him or her into the supine position on the floor, and place your hands similarly to CPR but over the abdomen while sitting astride the victim's legs. Repeat upward compressions five times. If no ventilation occurs, attempt to sweep the mouth, and ventilate the lungs mouth to mouth. Repeat compressions and ventilations until recovery.

Infants (<1 Year)

Indications of choking in infants of younger than 1 year include lack of breathing, gasping, cyanosis, and inability to cry. Procedures for **Heimlich chest thrusts** include

- Position the infant in the prone (face-down) position along the forearm with the infant's head lower than the trunk, being sure to support the head so the airway is not blocked.
- Using the heel of your hand, deliver five forceful upward blows between the infant's shoulder blades.
- Sandwich the child between the two arms and turn the infant into the supine position and drape over the thigh with the head lower than the trunk and the head supported.
- Using two fingers (as for CPR compressions), give up to five thrusts (about 1.5 inches deep) to the lower third of the sternum.
- Only do a finger sweep and remove the foreign object if the object is visible. Repeat five back blows, five chest thrusts until the foreign body is ejected.
- If the infant loses consciousness, begin CPR. If a pulse is noted but spontaneous respirations are absent, continue with ventilation only.

Emergency Defibrillation with an AED

Emergency defibrillation is done for acute ventricular fibrillation or ventricular tachycardia with no audible or palpable pulse; it is ineffective for asystole or pulseless electrical activity. Defibrillation delivers an electrical discharge through paddles applied to both sides of the chest. Automated external defibrillators (AEDs) are frequently used by first responders, although manual defibrillators require less downtime from CPR. The procedure is as follows:

- Turn on the AED.
- Apply pads to the chest (the position may vary according to the manufacturer). For infants and small children: If pads may touch, apply one to the chest and one to the back.
- Plug in the connector if necessary.
- Do not touch the patient while the AED analyzes the heart rhythm.
- Follow directions for shocking, and warn others to stand clear.
- Continue CPR beginning with compressions for 2 minutes/five cycles between defibrillations.

If the patient is wet, wipe off the chest before applying the pads. Remove any transdermal patches on the chest, and shave excessive hair before applying the pads. If the patient has an implanted device, the pads should be placed at least 1 inch (2.5 cm) away.

Body Mechanics/Ergonomics

Things to Avoid

Proper body mechanics/**ergonomics** and prevention of repetitive strain injury include the following:

- Avoid bending at the waist to lift or reach for items. Stoop down with the knees bent.
- Avoid stretching overhead to reach for items on high shelves or out of reach (more than 20 inches). Use a step stool or a grabbing tool with an extension.
- Avoid pulling—push, roll, or slide instead.
- Avoid lifting—push, roll, or slide instead. Use lift devices rather than manually lifting heavy items and patients or get help.
- Avoid reaching, bending, or twisting to lift.
- Avoid prolonged periods of repetitive activity, such as keyboarding or stocking materials, and take note of numbness and tingling or discomfort (warning signs). Take frequent short breaks.

Guidelines

Ergonomics is the study of how to design work and products according to the principles of body mechanics to avoid injury, especially in the workplace:

- Lift with the leg muscles, not the back.
- Hold weight close to the body rather than at arm's length. Use the whole body to relieve strain on the arms and back.
- Flex at the hips and knees, not the waist.
- Maintain a straight back and avoid twisting.
- Assess weight and recognize limitations in lifting/carrying.
- Get help when necessary and communicate every step with your partner ("Lift on the count of three").
- Maintain a firm base of support with the feet apart (shoulder width) to stabilize your stance.
- Maintain the line of gravity (the imaginary line between your center of gravity and the ground) within the base of support.
- Stand close to the person or item to be lifted, bend the knees and hips, and use the muscles in the legs to support the weight rather than using the back or arms.

Issues of Environmental Protection

Hazardous Waste

Hazardous waste is waste that poses a threat to the health of individuals or to the environment. The Environmental Protection Agency classifies hazardous wastes according to the following characteristics:

- **Ignitable**: Liquids and nonliquids that can ignite and cause fires.
- **Corrosive**: Based on pH or the ability to corrode steel.
- **Reactive**: Wastes that are unstable, may react with water, or result in toxic gases. They may also explode.
- **Toxic**: Wastes that are harmful if ingested or absorbed.

Wastes may also be classified as listed wastes. These include wastes from manufacturing and industrial processes. Hazardous wastes are often produced in manufacturing, nuclear power plants (nuclear wastes), and healthcare facilities (needles, materials contaminated with body fluids). Nuclear wastes are classified as mixed waste because they contain a radioactive component as well as a hazardous component. Hazardous wastes can result in disease (such as from needle punctures), injury (from fire and explosions), and death (from toxic exposure, disease).

Waste Management

Waste management is the process by which waste products are collected, transported, and disposed of or recycled. Municipal waste management usually involves weekly collection with separate containers sometimes provided for garden waste, recyclables, and garbage, although garbage is mixed and then separated in some waste management plants. Waste management is regulated by the Environmental Protection Agency (EPA) through the *Resource Conservation and Recovery Act,* which regulates the handling and disposal of hazardous and nonhazardous waste. Because hazardous waste can result in disease, injury, or death, special handling is required. Hazardous waste cannot be disposed of with regular trash or in drains or the sewer system. In schools, chemistry labs often have hazardous wastes to dispose of, such as corrosive liquids, heavy metal solutions, and organic solvents. The art department and the school nurse may also have hazardous wastes, such as used paints, pigments, dyes, needles, and dressings contaminated with body fluids.

Disaster Preparedness

Each school should have protocols in place for responding to **environmental disasters** and should have adequate stores of food and water in case students and staff members have to shelter in place, as well as flashlights and batteries:

Earthquakes

Duck-cover-hold practices should be held periodically so students know what to do, and the health educator and teachers may need to shout directions to students who may be too frightened or confused to move.

Tornados

There may be little or no warning time, but students should be immediately directed to an enclosed hallway (on a lower floor if time permits) so they are protected from flying debris and broken glass. Students should not take shelter in large open areas, such as gymnasiums because of the danger of roof collapse.

Hurricanes

All staff should be assigned specific duties in securing a school, such as unplugging equipment, such as computers, and wrapping the exterior wall of the structure with plastic sheeting as a temporary barrier. School buses should be full of fuel and ready to evacuate students. Safe sites within the facility should be identified and secured. Generally, students are evacuated prior to the hurricane unless the school is to be used as a shelter. If a hurricane is imminent, water lines, utilities, and natural gas should be turned off and windows and exterior doors should be boarded. All chemicals in the laboratory must be inventoried and secured, and all outside equipment should be brought inside and secured.

Ice Storms

Usually, ice storms are accompanied by high winds and loss of electricity because of falling branches and trees. Students should be evacuated with the assistance of the police or fire department to ensure that the roads are safe. Precautions must be taken to prevent pipes from bursting if the heating system goes out.

Floods

Floods often accompany hurricanes but may occur with other storms as well. Flash floods can occur with little warning, and schools may become isolated by flood waters. Flood precautions, such as sandbagging, should be done in advance when possible, and the school should be evacuated if it is in danger, but if there is no time, then students should be directed to the safest area, such as an upper floor or bleachers in a gymnasium, avoiding contact with flood waters, which may be contaminated with hazardous chemicals. It is imperative that the road safety is verified before attempting to evacuate students to ensure they are not caught in flood waters. As with hurricanes, schools in danger of flooding should have adequate stores of food and water and flashlights and batteries.

When the threat is over, the health educator should immediately begin to assess damage and triage injured students, providing first aid as needed until first responders arrive and take over. If a partial or complete building collapse has occurred, the health educator should help direct other staff members to take students to a safe place and make lists of uninjured students and those accounted for to help determine which students are missing.

School Shooting or Terrorist Attack

If a **school shooting or terrorist attack** occurs, the health educator should first assess the situation for personal safety before rendering assistance. If an active shooting is taking place, the health educator should help students barricade or hide themselves if possible, shout for those being fired upon to hit the ground and/or seek shelter, and call 9-1-1. When the shooting ceases and it's safe to approach those who are injured, the health educator should immediately begin to triage students, identifying those most in need of assistance and rendering first aid. The health educator may need to provide direction to other school personnel, such as teachers, to help with the following:

- Apply pressure to bleeding wounds.
- Get supplies.
- Take unharmed students to a separate area.
- Stay with and comfort frightened students.
- Make lists of injured students.

First responders will address the needs of the injured, but uninjured students may be severely traumatized and should not be left unattended until their families can come to retrieve them.

Cycle/Chain of the Infectious Process

The **cycle of the infectious process** contains six links, and the infectious process can be interrupted at any of these links:

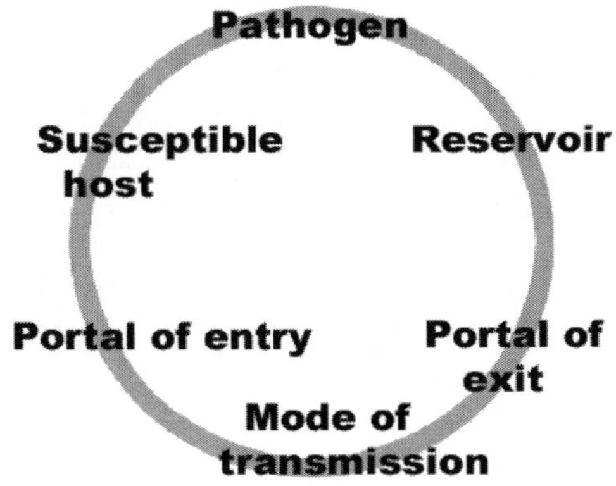

- **Pathogen**: Disease-causing organism (generally bacteria or virus). Pasteurization and disinfection are both methods to break this chain.
- **Reservoir**: May be a human, animal, or environmental component required by the pathogen to survive. This link may be broken by quarantine or medical treatment.
- **Portal of exit**: Body fluids; respiratory, gastrointestinal, urogenital tracts; wounds. This link may be broken by face masks, dressings, and isolation procedures.
- **Mode of transmission**: Direct or indirect contact; contaminated food, water, or dust particles; insect bites. This link may be broken by air cleaning systems, boiling water, using insect spray, and wearing face masks.
- **Portal of entry**: Respiratory, gastrointestinal, urogenital tracts and wounds. Link may be broken by wearing face mask, wearing protective clothing and gloves, and washing hands.
- **Susceptible host**: Human or animal, especially those who are young, old, or immunocompromised. The link may be broken by improving nutrition and immune status and vaccinations.

Nosocomial Infections

A **nosocomial infection** is defined by the CDC's National Nosocomial Infections Surveillance system as a hospital-acquired infection, either localized or systemic, caused by a pathogen or toxin that was not present (or incubating) in the patient at the time he or she entered the hospital. In some cases, infection may be obvious within the first 24–48 hours, but other infections may not be obvious until after discharge from the hospital because incubation times and resistance vary. An infection that occurs after discharge but is hospital acquired is nosocomial. Identifying a nosocomial infection should result from analysis of laboratory findings as well as clinical symptoms. A diagnosis of infection by an attending physical or surgeon is also considered acceptable identification. Placentally transferred infections are not considered nosocomial, but perinatal infections are, even if they are acquired from the mother during delivery. Colonization that is not causing an inflammatory response or evidence of infection is not considered nosocomial for reporting purposes.

CDC Guidelines

Standard Precautions

The **2007 CDC isolation guidelines** include standard precautions that apply to all patients and transmission-based precautions for those with known or suspected infections. **Standard precautions** should be used for all patients because all body fluids (e.g., sweat, urine, feces, blood, and sputum) and nonintact skin and mucous membranes may be infected:

Hand Hygiene	Wash hands before and after each patient contact.
Protective Equipment	Use PPE, such as gloves, gowns, masks, eye protection, and/or face shields, depending on the patient's condition and degree of exposure.

Respiratory Hygiene/ Cough Etiquette	Educate staff, patients, family, and visitors. Post instructions (language appropriate). Use source control measures, such as covering a cough, disposing of tissues, using a surgical mask on a coughing person or on staff to prevent inhalation of droplets, and properly disposing of dressings and used equipment. Wash hands after contacting respiratory secretions. Maintain a distance of >3 feet from a coughing person when possible.
Safe Injection Practice	Use a sterile single-use needle and syringe one time only and discard them safely.

Transmission-Based Precautions

The **2007 CDC isolation guidelines** include standard precautions that apply to all patients and **transmission-based precautions** for those with known or suspected infections as well as those with excessive wound drainage, other discharge, or fecal incontinence. Transmission-based precautions include the following:

Contact	Use PPE, including gown and gloves, for all contact with the patient or the patient's immediate environment. Maintain the patient in a private room or >3 feet away from other patients.
Droplet	(Appropriate for influenza, streptococcus infection, pertussis, rhinovirus, and adenovirus and pathogens that remain viable and infectious for only short distances.) Use a mask while caring for the patient. Maintain the patient in a private room or >3 feet away from other patients with a curtain separating them. Use a patient mask if transporting a patient from one area to another.
Airborne	(Appropriate for measles, chickenpox, TB, and severe acute respiratory syndrome because pathogens remain viable and infectious for long distances.) Place the patient in an airborne infection isolation room. Use ≥N95 respirators (or masks) while caring for the patient.

Medical Regulatory Acts/Agencies

Medical Legislation	
Act/Agency	**Purpose**
Pure Food and Drug Act	Consumer protection act intended to prevent the manufacture, sale, and transportation of adulterated foods, drugs, and alcoholic beverages.
Federal Food, Drug, and Cosmetic Act	Provides authority to the FDA to oversee food, drug, and cosmetic safety.
Harrison Narcotic Act	Provides authority for regulation and taxation of production, importation, and distribution of coca/opium products, such as narcotics.
Controlled Substances Act	Establishes US drug policy and gives five schedules under which drugs are classified, implemented by the DEA and FDA.
Food and Drug Administration (FDA)	Consumer protection agency that protects public health through the control and supervision of drugs, vaccines, blood transfusions, medical devices, cosmetics, foods, tobacco, and dietary supplements.
Drug Enforcement Agency (DEA)	Law enforcement agency, part of the Department of Justice, that enforces the Controlled Substances Act and combats drug smuggling/use.

OSHA

The **Occupational Safety and Health Association** (OSHA) is a federal agency that ensures worker safety and protection. Agents carry out inspections and investigate accidents and reports of noncompliance. OSHA has established different regulations for all types of industries, including health. Healthcare providers must comply with OSHA regulations. Regulatory areas include the following:

- Bloodborne pathogens: Provides guidelines, along with the CDC, to prevent transmission of bloodborne pathogens.
- Chemical/Biologicals: Includes all hazardous chemicals/biologicals.
- Ergonomics: Sets requirements for work surfaces, chairs, and assistive devices.
- Surgical safety: Includes design and airflow, safeguards.
- Construction: Includes heating and cooling, ADA compliance, safety bars, and industry standards.
- Infection control: Includes all aspects of infection control with a special emphasis on preventing the spread of MRSA.
- Medical equipment: Includes all electrical, mechanical, or digital equipment.
- Personal protection: Includes requirements for face and eye protection and respiratory masks.

FDA

The **Food and Drug Administration** (FDA), an agency of the US Department of Health and Human Services, is funded through congressional allocation and fees paid by pharmaceutical companies. The FDA develops regulations in support of the Federal Food, Drug, and Cosmetic Act (FD&C Act) and is responsible for ensuring public health through regulation of consumer goods:

- Food products to ensure safety.
- Prescription drugs, over-the-counter drugs, and veterinary products. This includes regulating clinical trials and all phases of manufacturing, labeling, and marketing.
- Dietary supplements.
- Biological products.
- Tobacco products, including regulations regarding warnings on labels.
- Protection of human subjects in research.
- Cosmetics.
- Vaccines.
- Medical devices such as blood pumps and ventilators.
- Blood transfusions.
- Devices that emit electromagnetic radiation.
- Animal food products.

CDC

The **Centers for Disease Control and Prevention** (CDC) is an agency of HHS and is charged with protecting the public health through disease prevention. Activities include data collection (some diseases must be reported to the CDC), research, preparedness activities, outbreak monitoring, and interventions. The CDC focuses on infectious diseases, antibiotic resistance, vaccines, noninfectious conditions that affect general health (e.g., obesity, diabetes mellitus), travelers' health, foodborne diseases, worldwide health issues, safety issues, injury prevention, occupational and environmental health, and health promotion. When an outbreak occurs, the CDC carries out investigations in the United States and in other countries to identify the pathogen and the source of the infection as well as necessary interventions in order to prevent further spread. The CDC issues warnings to travelers and provides immunization recommendations for travelers. The CDC maintains websites with extensive credible health information for healthcare providers and consumers and provides educational materials such as posters and pamphlets.

School Laboratory Safety Guidelines

The National Institute for Occupational Safety and Health publishes guidelines for **school laboratory safety**. Guidelines include the following:

- Safety and first aid equipment should be routinely inspected and readily available (including safety showers, eyewash station, first-aid kits, and fire safety equipment).
- The administration should be notified of any safety hazards in the laboratory, and all defective equipment should be removed.
- Staff training records should be maintained.
- Students should receive verbal and printed safety procedures and should be trained in the safe use of laboratory equipment.
- Staff should be trained on how to turn off the water, gas, and electricity in the laboratory.
- All chemicals should be inventoried and inspected, clearly labeled, and stored and used according to the manufacturers' directions.
- Chemicals should be used in accordance with their Safety Data Sheets and disposed of in accordance with hazardous materials regulations.
- Appropriate PPE must be worn during laboratory procedures.
- Students should always be supervised in the laboratory.
- Personal items should be stored away from work areas, and aisles should be kept clear.
- All spills should be cleaned immediately, using appropriate safety precautions.

SDS

Safety Data Sheets (SDS), formerly known as Material Safety Data Sheets (MSDS), explain how to handle caustic substances in the event of an accident or injury and provide pertinent information on the composition and toxic effects of the chemicals in the lab. SDS outline the proper storage of chemicals, procedures for cleanup, and dumping of caustic substances as well as procedures in the event of a chemical spill or injury and proper locations in the facility for cleanup. The SDS should also contain information indicating which substances may cause allergic effects or asthma from contact or inhalation. Emergency rescue services should obtain SDS for common chemicals and products. Manufacturers and suppliers should have SDS on file and can be contacted for copies. OSHA/EPA Occupational Chemical Database provides links for SDS for some products. SDS are available from various other sources, including the Toxicology Data Network, Pathogen Safety Data Sheets (biological hazards), and poison control centers.

School Workplace Safety Guidelines

The National Institute for Occupational Safety and Health publishes dozens of guidelines for all aspects of **workplace school safety**, such air pollution control, fire protection for cooking areas, and electrical safety work practices. Additionally, individual states often provide safety guidelines, such as the Texas School and Firearm Safety Action Plan (May 2018), developed in response to school shootings. The Texas School Safety Center, under the Texas Education Agency, provides school safety information for schools throughout the state as well as research, training, and technical support. Toolkits provided the Texas School Safety Center (https://txssc.txstate.edu/tools/) include High Quality Emergency Operations, Threat Assessment and Management, Safety and Security Agreements, Youth Preparedness Events, K–12 Standard

Response Protocol, Before You Text: Sexting and Bullying Protection, Tobacco Law, School Safety Spotlight Program, and Severe Weather. Each area of the school and each discipline should follow the appropriate safety guidelines to ensure a safe workplace.

Professional Responsibilities

Communication Strategies

Communication strategies may involve verbal, nonverbal, and visual communication, depending on the situation. Communication strategies include the following:

- **Intrapersonal**: Dialog with the self is used in decision making and aids in comprehension of input, planning for output, and personal assessment.
- **Interpersonal**: Face-to-face communication with others may be direct or electronic (such as Skype). Face-to-face communication facilitates all forms of communication, so many different types of communication may occur simultaneously, increasing the chance of the message being correctly received and persuading others.
- **Small group**: Small groups (three to six individuals) allow many different relationships to develop and facilitate communication; however, if the group is too large, cliques may form. Members may be influenced positively or negatively by others, depending on the degree of cohesiveness.
- **Organizational**: May include intrapersonal, interpersonal, small group, and public communication, depending on the purpose of communication. Communication is often based on the hierarchical structure.
- **Public**: Information shared from the individual to a large group to inform, persuade, or entertain.

Communication Characteristics

Characteristics of communication include the following:

- **Process**: Communication is a complex dynamic process that is bidirectional and involves both verbal and nonverbal interactions.
- **Symbolic**: Communication always uses symbols of some type to transmit thoughts and ideas. Almost anything can become a symbol to transmit information: images, words, appearance, color, and tone of voice. The same symbol may transmit something very different to different receivers, who translate the symbol received into meaning.
- **Receiver-based**: Communication occurs with the receiver when meaning is attached to symbol. All behavior communicates whether intended or not.
- **Irreversible**: Once communication occurs, it cannot be withdrawn or reversed. Correction of unintended communication may communicate a different message, but the original remains.
- **Unrepeatable**: An original communication can never be repeated in the exact same way because the communication process is dependent on the receiver.

Communication Recipient Characteristics

Communication is dependent on the **recipient** of the intended or unintended message because the transfer of information is affected by the recipient's motivation to decode the message and his or her ability to comprehend the message. If a recipient lacks motivation, then communication as intended may be effectively blocked or a completely different message may be received. For example, if the recipient does not want to hear a message and pays no attention to the actual content, the message received may be that the communicator is annoying or overbearing. Therefore, for effective communication to occur, the recipient must be motivated to receive the message. The ability of the recipient to comprehend a message depends on many complex factors, such as cognitive ability, knowledge base, emotional status, sensory impairment, and health status. For example, if a person is hard of hearing, a spoken message may be incomprehensible.

Communication via Social Media

Social media include such sites as Facebook, LinkedIn, Twitter, and Snapchat. Social media sites are increasingly used for marketing, especially to younger generations that grew up with computers and the Internet. Content developed for social media should be highly focused and of good quality if it is to attract an audience. Taking the time to identify and target influential individuals is an essential strategy in marketing because they can share content and expand outreach at no additional cost over social media. Personal communication via social media is more problematic because of the possibility of transmitting confidential or damaging information. Some organizations now prohibit their employees from making any mention of the organization in any social media, so any comments about employment or pictures must be avoided whether positive or negative. One should never communicate negatively about an employer or anyone else on any social media site with an expectation of privacy and should avoid all comments that may be construed as racist, misogynistic, or bigoted.

Cultural and Spiritual Competence Regarding Communication

There are many issues related to **cultural and spiritual competence** in communicating with others:

- **Eye contact**: Many cultures use eye contact differently than is common in the United States. They may avoid direct eye contact, considering it to be rude, or may look away to signal disapproval, or may look down to signal respect. Careful observation of the way family members use eye contact can help to determine what will be most comfortable for the patient/family.
- **Distance**: Some cultures stand close to others (<4 feet) when speaking (Middle Easterners, Hispanics), and others stand at a farther distance (>4 feet) (Northern Europeans, many Americans). There is considerable difference relating to concepts of personal space among cultures. Allowing the family to approach or observing whether they tend to move closer, lean forward, or move back can help to determine a comfortable distance for communication.
- **Time**: Americans tend to be time oriented and expect people to be on time, but time is more flexible in many cultures, so scheduling may require flexibility.

Barriers to Effective Communication

Barriers to effective communication include the following:

- **Psychological factors**: The communicator's or recipient's emotional status, such as having increased anxiety, can negatively impact communication. Biases, prejudices, and belief systems may also interfere with a person's ability to attend to the ideas of another person.
- **Physical factors**: Communication may be impaired if there is excessive noise or distracting activities are taking place or if the person is hearing or vision impaired. Some environments are not conducive to communication, especially if too great a distance separates the communicators.
- **Gender factors**: Communication styles often vary between males and females, and this can lead to misunderstandings. However, communication styles may also vary among those of the same gender depending on many social and psychological factors.

- **Semantic factors**: Communicators may have a different understanding of the same words. For example, a speaker of English as a second language may have a more literal interpretation of words than a native speaker, and this can lead to misunderstandings.

Selection of Appropriate Communication Methods

Selecting appropriate communication methods requires many steps:

1. Consider the purpose of the communication.
2. Identify the person or persons who will be the recipients and obtain or consider information about them, what influences them, and how best to reach them.
3. Consider the message to be conveyed and the best way to communicate so that the message is received as intended.
4. Determine whether the communication is intended as one-way or requires feedback. Choose an interactive channel if feedback is desired.
5. Determine the cost or effort involved in communicating through the chosen channel.
6. Develop the correct format for the communication (letter, fax, email), using or developing a template as appropriate.
7. Complete the message and carry out the communication using the selected channel.
8. Monitor any feedback if appropriate.

Verbal/Spoken Communication

Verbal (spoken) communication can vary from very formal (such as a conference presentation) to very informal (such as a chat with a friend), but every aspect of the communication process has meaning—the words, the posture, the tone of voice, the expression on the face, silence times, and the general appearance. The communication of the same words will be very different if heard over the phone, read in an email, or heard face to face. In any professional communication, formal or informal, the individual should come prepared and should have some idea of what to say, although memorizing word for word is not advisable because communication should appear spontaneous even when it is not. The average person speaks about 200 words per minute, and each sentence is a new creation; therefore, without proper planning, the message can easily become muddled. For a formal presentation, brief outline notes or presentation software may be helpful to keep the speaker focused on the topic.

Steps of Data Analysis

Steps to data analysis include the following:

1. **Organize**: Before beginning analysis, the data should be organized in some meaningful way, such as by entering them into a database or spreadsheet, organized chronologically. Organization may vary depending on the type of data.
2. **Convert text to numerical data**: Numerical data is easier to quantify. For example, "Yes" could be converted to 00 and "No" to 01.
3. **Group**: Separate data into meaningful categories, such as by grade (if related to students), by topic, or by gender.
4. **Conduct an error review**: Check the data carefully to ensure that there are no errors in the original data or in the organized or grouped data before proceeding.
5. **Choose a statistical method of analysis**: May include various statistical tests, such as the T-test, analysis of variance, and linear regression.
6. **Begin analysis**: Determine research questions and consult a statistician, if necessary, to ensure that the appropriate analysis is carried out.

7. **Carry out statistical measures**: Review the results for accuracy and patterns.
8. **Summarize and present results**: May include raw data, summary, and charts and graphs to demonstrate results.

Issues of Concern

Issues of concern when analyzing data, records, and technical reports include the following:

- **Type of statistical analysis**: If based on averages, it's important to assess the outliers, because they may skew the mean to one side and give an inaccurate portrayal. A similar problem may occur with standard deviation. Percentages are generally the weakest form of statistics, so the raw data must be analyzed.
- **Sample size**: If data are based on research studies, then the type of sampling and the sample size are critical to understanding the results.
- **Placebo effect**: Bias in the form of expectations may result in finding a result in support of the bias.
- **Hawthorne effect**: Those involved in a study may skew the results because they realize they are in a study and change behavior to meet expectations.

Importance of Matching Communication Needs with Communication Vehicles

The communication vehicle should best meet the communication needs:

- **Mail**: Use to add a personal touch to messages and to deliver documents securely. Mailings can reach large populations, although the cost may be relatively high.
- **Email**: Allows for fast communication and mass mailings at little cost, but emails are often screened and may be ignored if the receiver doesn't know or recognize the sender. Documents can be easily transmitted through email as text or PDF files.
- **Telephones (land line)**: Use when interaction and discussion are needed or for personal appeals. The system should include voice mail. This is a relatively inexpensive form of communication, but the ubiquitous use of voice mail often means delays in actual communication.
- **Smartphones**: Use when rapid communication by phone, email, or text messaging is needed as well as Internet access. This is especially useful when the person is mobile.
- **Video/Web conferencing**: This is valuable when participants cannot otherwise meet face to face and can save money associated with travel expenses. This vehicle allows participants to communicate verbally and nonverbally.
- **Internet/Web pages**: Internet communication can be synchronous or asynchronous, and it allows for the presentation of information (such as on a web page) as well as verbal communication (such as with messaging).
- **Social media**: These provide the opportunity to share professional or organizational information (such as with LinkedIn and Facebook). Twitter may be used to communicate short messages, and the messages should contain hashtags so that interest can be assessed.
- **Fax**: This allows for the transfer of documents or images quickly and may be used, for example, to send an agenda prior to a meeting or to send documents that must be reviewed. Almost any type of document can be scanned and faxed.

Active Listening

Active listening requires more than passively listening to another individual. Active listening includes observing the other individual carefully for nonverbal behaviors, such as posture, eye contact, and facial expression, as well as understanding and reflecting on what the person is saying. The listener should observe carefully for inconsistencies in what the individual is saying or comments that require clarification. Feedback is critical to active listening because it shows the speaker that one is paying attention and showing interest and respect. Feedback may be as simple as nodding the head in agreement, but it should also include asking questions or making comments to show full engagement. Listening with empathy is especially important because it helps to build a connection with the speaker. The listener should communicate empathy with words: "You feel (emotion) because (experience)" because the speaker may not be sensitive to what the listener is comprehending.

Assertiveness in Communication

Assertive communication occurs when the individual expresses opinions directly and actions correlate with words. Assertive communicators are respectful of others and not bullying but firm and honest about opinions. They frequently use "I" statements to make their point: "I would like ..." Communication usually includes cooperative statements, such as "What do you think?" and distinguishes between fact and opinion. Assertive communicators often engender trust in others because they are consistent, honest, and open in communicating with others. The assertive communicator feels free to express disagreement and anger but does so in a manner that is nonthreatening and respectful of others' feelings. Assertive communication requires a strong sense of self-worth and the belief that personal opinions have value. Assertive communicators tend to have good listening skills because they value the opinions of others and feel comfortable collaborating.

Teaming Skills

Leading Intra- and Interdisciplinary Teams

There are many skills that are needed to lead and facilitate coordination of **intra- and interdisciplinary teams**:

- Communicating openly is essential, and all members should be encouraged to participate as valued members of a cooperative team.
- Avoiding interrupting or interpreting the point that another is trying to make allows free flow of ideas.
- Avoiding jumping to conclusions, which can effectively shut off communication.
- Active listening requires paying attention and asking questions for clarification rather than to challenge others' ideas.
- Respecting others' opinions and ideas, even when opposed to one's own, is absolutely essential.
- Reacting and responding to facts rather than feelings allows one to avoid angry confrontations or defuse anger.
- Clarifying information or opinions stated can help avoid misunderstandings.

Keeping unsolicited advice out of the conversation shows respect for others and allows them to solicit advice without feeling pressured.

Leadership Styles

Leadership styles often influence the perception of leadership values and commitment to collaboration. There are many different leadership styles:

Charismatic	Depends upon personal charisma to influence people, and may be very persuasive, but this type of leader may engage "followers" and relate to one group rather than the organization at large, limiting his or her effectiveness.

Bureaucratic	Follows organization rules exactly and expects everyone else to do so. This is most effective in handling cash flow or managing work in dangerous work environments. This type of leadership may engender respect but may not be conducive to change.
Autocratic	Makes decisions independently and strictly enforces rules, but team members often feel left out of the process and may not be supportive. This type of leadership is most effective in crisis situations, but these leaders may have difficulty gaining the commitment of the staff.
Consultative	Presents a decision and welcomes input and questions, although decisions rarely change. This type of leadership is most effective when gaining the support of the staff is critical to the success of proposed changes.
Participatory	Presents a potential decision and then makes a final decision based on input from staff or teams. This type of leadership is time-consuming and may result in compromises that are not wholly satisfactory to management or staff, but this process is motivating to staff who feel that their expertise is valued.
Democratic	Presents a problem and asks staff or teams to arrive at a solution, although the leader usually makes the final decision. This type of leadership may delay decision making, but staff and teams are often more committed to the solutions because of their input.
Laissez-faire (free rein)	Exerts little direct control but allows employees/teams to make decisions with little interference. This may be effective leadership if teams are highly skilled and motivated; however, in many cases, this type of leadership is the product of poor management skills and little is accomplished because of this lack of leadership.

Delegation of Tasks in Teams

One major responsibility of leadership and management in teams is using **delegation** effectively. The purpose of having a team is so that the work is shared: Leaders can cripple themselves by taking on too much of the workload. Additionally, failure to delegate shows an inherent distrust in team members. Delegation includes the following:

- Assessing the skills and available time of the team members, determining if a task is suitable for an individual.
- Assigning tasks, with clear instructions that include an explanation of the objectives and expectations, including a timeline.
- Ensuring that the tasks are completed properly and on time by monitoring progress but not micromanaging.
- Reviewing the final results and recording the outcomes.

Because the leader is ultimately responsible for the delegated work, mentoring, monitoring, and providing feedback and intervention as necessary during this process are necessary components of leadership. Although delegated tasks may not always be completed successfully, they represent an opportunity for learning.

Facilitation

Leading and facilitating teams require using good facilitation. Considerations include the following:

- **Scheduling**: The time and the place must be convenient and conducive to working together, so the leader must review the work schedules of those involved, finding the most convenient time. Venues or meeting rooms should allow for sitting in a circle or around a table to facilitate the equal exchange of ideas. Any necessary technology, such as computers or overhead projectors, or other equipment, such as white boards, should be readily available.
- **Preparation**: The leader should prepare a detailed agenda that includes a list of items for discussion.
- **Conduction**: Each item on the agenda should be discussed, soliciting input from all group members. Tasks should be assigned to individual members based on their interest and their part in the process in preparation for the next meeting. The leader should summarize all input and begin a tentative future agenda.
- **Observation**: The leader should observe the interactions, including verbal and nonverbal communication, and respond.

Team Structure

The appropriate **team structure** is very important in performance because creating a team does not in itself assure teamwork. The team must be comprised of individuals whose skills complement each other and who have a shared purpose because outcomes will depend on the collaborative efforts of the group rather than individuals within the group. Accordingly, the collective team is accountable for outcomes rather than individuals. When creating teams, the team structure, and other important elements must be considered:

- **Size**: Teams of <10 members are most effective.
- **Skills**: Team members should have complementary skills that encompass technical, problem solving, decision making, and interpersonal communication.
- **Performance goals**: Teams should be allowed a degree of autonomy in producing action plans for performance improvement, based on strategic goals and objectives.
- **Unified approach**: The teams should be created according to the model of performance improvement, but members should have some flexibility in working together.
- **Accountability**: The team members are collectively accountable rather than individually.

Group Process Phases

Group Process Phases	
1	**Orientation**: The task is identified and members learn the mission, depending primarily on the leader in the beginning but they are beginning to explore their own roles in the group and accept that change can occur.
2	**Organization**: Members make group decisions about rules, limits, criteria, and the division of labor. Some resistance or fear of change may occur as members doubt the possibility of change, but members gain confidence as the work of the group becomes better organized.
3	**Flow of information**: Members become more able to express feelings and opinions and accept their roles in the group as interpersonal conflict lessens and group cohesion increases.
4	**Problem solving**: Members have a clear idea of the task and are able to work collaboratively and interdependently. They feel satisfaction with the group and have confidence regarding reaching goals. However, some members or groups may reach an impasse and decide that goals cannot be met and actively resist change.

Networking

Networking, creating a network of contacts throughout the education and healthcare community, not only helps a health educator to find employment but it also provides valuable professional resources in achieving career goals. Networking should begin with professors and instructors while the person is still a student through demonstration of competence. The health educator can cooperate with others involved in clinical tasks or research, gaining experience and credibility. Those involved in the sales of supplies, books, and equipment are resources who can provide the health educator with current trends and changes. One of the most effective ways to network is to become involved in national organizations, such as the American Association for Health Education, and to participate in conferences through attendance and conference presentations. The health educator should make an effort to maintain periodic contact with others in an informal network by telephone, mail, or email.

Problem-Solving Steps

Problem solving to anticipate or prevent recurrences of dissatisfaction involves taking steps to resolve the immediate problem, but this is only the first step if recurrence is to be avoided:

1. **Define the issue**: Talk with those involved to determine if the problem is related to a failure of communication or to other issues, such as culture or religion.
2. **Collect data**: This may mean interviewing additional people or reviewing documentation, gaining a variety of perspectives.
3. **Identify important concepts**: Determine if there are issues related to values or beliefs.
4. **Consider the reasons for actions**: Distinguish between motivation and intention on the part of all parties to determine the reason for the problem.
5. **Make a decision**: A decision on how to prevent a recurrence of a problem should be based on advocacy and moral agency, reaching the best solution possible for the people involved.

Conflict Resolutions

Conflict is an almost inevitable product of teamwork, and the educator must assume responsibility for **conflict resolution.** Although conflicts can be disruptive, they can produce positive outcomes by forcing team members to listen to different perspectives and opening dialogue. The team should make plans for dealing with conflict resolution. The best time for conflict resolution is when differences emerge but before open conflict and hardening of positions occur. The leader must pay close attention to the people and problems involved, listen carefully, and reassure those involved that their points of view are understood. Steps to conflict resolution include the following:

1. Allow both sides to present their side of conflict without bias, maintaining a focus on opinions rather than on individuals.
2. Encourage cooperation through negotiation and compromise.
3. Maintain the focus, providing guidance to keep the discussions on track and avoid arguments.
4. Evaluate the need for renegotiation through a formal resolution process or third party.
5. Use humor and empathy to defuse escalating tensions.
6. Summarize the issues, outlining key arguments.
7. Avoid forcing a resolution, if possible.

APPROACHES

Approaches to Conflict Resolution	
Accommodating	One party ceding to the other, usually when the other has more power.
Avoiding	Taking steps to avoid dealing with the conflict.
Collaborating	Trying to find a solution that pleases both parties.
Competing	One party is trying to win at all costs.
Compromising	Each party is ceding something in return for harmony.
Confronting	Using "I" messages and assertive problem solving.
Forcing	One party issuing orders to force a solution.
Negotiating	Similar to collaborating with back-and-forth bargaining.
Reassuring	Attempting to make everyone happy.
Problem solving	Trying to find a solution that works for everyone using a step-by-step approach.
Withdrawing	One party withdrawing from the conflict, leaving the conflict unresolved.

RESOURCES FOR KEEPING INFORMED ABOUT CURRENT KNOWLEDGE IN HEALTH SCIENCE

Resources for keeping informed about current knowledge in health science includes the following:

- **Internet**: The government has many websites devoted to current knowledge, such as the CDC site. A valuable online resource is the E-Updates and News in Adolescent Health provided by the *Office of Adolescent Health* (HHS). Major news sites, such as CNN, have daily health news. *Medical News Today* provides links to medical news articles.
- **Professional journals**: Journals such as the *Journal of School Health* and the *American Journal of Health Education* provide health information of particular interest to health educators.
- **Public health/Local health agencies**: These agencies provide updates to the community about issues of current concern, such as outbreaks or emerging infections.

Professional organizations: Organizations such as the American School Health Association and the American Association for Health Education carry out research and provide information and support to members as well as sponsoring state and national conferences, various workshops, and informative websites.

Various Health-Related Careers and Educational Requirements

Physician	Requires bachelor's degree, 4 years of medical school, internship, and residency and licensure.
Nurses (registered nurses [RNs], licensed vocational nurses [LVNs], and advanced practice nurses [APNs])	RNs are required to attend 2- to 5-year training programs (associate of science in nursing [ASN], bachelor of science in nursing [BSN]) and licensure as well as additional training for APNs. LVNs require 18 months to 2 years of training and licensure and work under RN supervision.
Nutritionists	Requires a BSN or master's degree.
Certified nurse assistant (aide)	Requires 6 to 8 weeks of training and works under supervision of RNs and LVNs. Must be 18 in Texas.
Physician assistant	Requires a 2-year master's degree program. PAs carry out many of the tasks of physicians.
Technicians	Technicians include X-ray technicians, laboratory technicians, ultrasound technicians, dental hygienists, pharmacy technicians, emergency medical technicians, echocardiogram technicians, and phlebotomists. Training varies but is often about 2 years, whereas those that require one skill, such as phlebotomists, may be trained in a matter of weeks. Some require licensure.
Medical assistant	Programs vary from 1 to 2 years and include certificate and/or an ASN degree.

Community Resources for Students

Community resources to prepare students for transition from secondary to postsecondary education and provide work-based learning opportunities include the following:

- **Youth employment**: Helps students gain confidence, learn work skills, develop leadership, and make decisions about postsecondary work or education.
- **Shadowing**: Exposure to real-life work experience in fields of interest can help students make informed career choices.
- **Volunteer work**: Improves communication and socialization skills, promotes confidence, and provides opportunities for skill building.
- **School-to-work**: Programs and resources available for school-to-work transitions vary according to the community but may include those covered under the School-to-Work Act (1994), such as vocational instruction at the high school or postsecondary level, workplace mentoring and work experience programs, and apprenticeships. In addition, special programs may include training programs, sheltered workshops, and individual placement and support models.
- **Texas Internship Challenge**: A Texas state program that matches employers with interns.

Professional Characteristics of Healthcare Workers

Professional characteristics of healthcare workers include the following:

- Communication and interpersonal skills: Able to listen and speak effectively and to work well with others.
- Empathetic: Has compassion and empathy for others.
- Emotionally stable: Does not anger easily or lose control of emotions.
- Detail oriented: Recognizes the importance of all information.
- Problem-solving skills: Able to evaluate a problem effectively and reach a solution.

- Neat, clean appearance: Practices good hygiene and ensures that clothing/uniforms are appropriate for the situation.
- Respectful: Treats all others with respect and refrains from judgmental opinions based on differences.
- Reliable: Keeps their word and can be relied upon to carry out assigned duties and responsibilities.
- Competent: Keeps current in the healthcare field through continuing education courses, further degrees, observation, and self-study.
- Organized: Can prioritize based on needs and plan the workload effectively.
- Able to multitask: Is comfortable dealing with many different issues at the same time.
- Ethical: Understands ethical dilemmas and makes decisions based on ethical standards.
- Adaptable: Can adapt easily to changes.

Sources of Employer and Career Opportunity Information

Sources of **employer and career opportunity** information include the following:

- **Newspaper advertisements/Craigslist**: Job postings are regularly updated and may provide some information about opportunities.
- **Professional journals**: Often provide information about professional careers and job postings.
- **Websites**: Professional organizations and companies often post information about careers and job opportunities as well as requirements in terms of education and work experience.
- **Career guides**: Provide information such as work responsibilities, educational requirements, job market, and potential earnings.
- **Texas Workforce Commission**: Provides assistance with posting of jobs, job searching, placement, recruitment, and career development, matching employees and employers. Links to Texas Interactive Workforce Data that provides labor market information (labor analysis, market statistics, career descriptions, military transition to work) and tools such as Texas Career Check, Texas Work Prep, Texas CREWS and Texas OnCourse.
- **Colleges and universities**: Offer information about different careers and the courses of study required. Provide career interest assessment to help guide students to a career that fits their preferences.

Steps to Seeking Employment

Steps to seeking employment include the following:

- **Research the job market**: Read job postings (print and online), register with the Texas Workforce Commission, and ask friends and associates about possible job openings.
- **Write/Update a résumé**: Include education, work experience, and skills (keyboarding, software, tool handling) appropriate for the type of employment.
- **Edit social media profile**: Assume an employer will check, and remove any information or pictures that may be deemed inappropriate.
- **Narrow job search/Begin application process**: Apply directly to companies or through the Texas Workforce Commission.
- **Research companies** when applying to ensure your ability to answer questions knowledgeably.
- **Practice job interviews**: Look at lists of different types of interview questions and practice answering to avoid being intimidated during the interview process.

- **Attend the interview**: Dress neatly, remain respectful, answer questions honestly, and be prepared to ask questions about the company. Thank the interviewers.
- **Receive job offers and accept a position**: Do not assume that the first job offer is the best choice, but consider all of the options.
- **Work**: Be punctual, respectful, cooperative, and carry out all assigned duties.

Guiding Students to Prepare Professional Portfolios

A **portfolio** is usually created in paper format but is then scanned into an electronic format so that it demonstrates technical skills and can be easily transmitted to employers or other interested parties and can include videos as well as text and photos. Students should not include information about religion, hobbies, or sports activities unless they are associated with a career or demonstrate leadership skills (e.g., you were captain of the basketball team). Components of a portfolio generally include the following:

- Statement regarding job or career interests and goals.
- Current résumé/curriculum vitae. Birthdate, race, and gender should be omitted.
- Narrative descriptions of special skills or work experience, such as the ability to use software, tools, or speak a second language.
- Academic achievements: May include a list of coursework, degrees, and internships. In some cases, it may include transcripts.
- Work experience: List employer, address, telephone number, dates of employment, and name of supervisor. If no work experience, you may substitute a list of volunteer activities.
- Performance reviews, certificates, awards, and letters of recognition.

Preparing Students for Productive Work Habits

Productive work habits include the following:

- **Punctuality**: Always plan to arrive at the worksite a few minutes before work begins to avoid a last-minute rush or the need to speed on the way to work.
- **Regular attendance**: Avoid taking sick time for recreational activities. Ask for time off well in advance, and try to take no extra time off for at least the first 6 months of employment.
- **Demonstrate initiative**: Do things that need to be done and are within the job description without always waiting for direction. Look for opportunities to work more efficiently.
- **Remain organized**: Be neat and efficient at work, ensuring that tasks are completed in a timely manner.
- **Appearance**: Dress appropriately for the work environment and maintain adequate hygiene.
- **Time management**: Plan out and complete assignments/duties efficiently within the allotted time.
- **Comportment**: Be polite and respectful of others. Avoid complaining. When working with customers, do not carry on personal conversations with coworkers.

TIME MANAGEMENT

TIME Grid

Time management is an important skill and can often be best managed with a time grid because it helps the person to visualize each day and provides a realistic picture of activities. Steps include the following:

1. Develop a time grid that shows all 7 days and time grids in half-hour increments, such as from 5 a.m. to 1 a.m.).
2. Place all required attendance within the appropriate grids, such as class hours and/or work hours.
3. Include travel time to and from school/work on the grid.
4. Add time needed for bathing, showering, dressing/undressing in the morning and evening.
5. Add meal times.
6. Add sleep time of at least 8 hours.
7. Add study time. (Generally, 2 hours of study time are necessary for every class hour.)
8. Add recreation time: Gym, running, reading, watching TV.
9. Review the grid to determine if everything fits into the grid and if there is any free time available. Modify times as necessary.

STEPS

Time management is an important function of leaders for managing their own time, modeling time management, and using the time of others effectively. Steps for effective time management include the following:

1. **Plan**: Create goals and establish schedules for yearly, monthly, and daily activities. Plan for each day in advance.
2. **Create a list**: A daily list should be created/updated, including routine tasks, so that all can be completed.
3. **Prioritize**: Determine the order in which tasks needs to be accomplished, beginning with high-priority items.
4. **Minimize paper handling**: Try to handle a paper/task once only instead of shuffling it about and dealing with it repeatedly.
5. **Use time effectively**: Avoid wasting time. Start meetings on schedule and monitor time. Work efficiently, paying attention to necessary details
6. **Delegate**: Determine which tasks can be delegated to others.
7. **Use computer technology**: Avoid paper when possible. Keep calendars and lists on the computer for easy updating. Use email and the Internet.
8. **Avoid procrastination**: Just do it.

STEPS TO GUIDING STUDENTS TOWARD REALISTIC CAREER GOALS

Steps to guiding students toward realistic **career goals** include the following:

- **Assessment of interests**: Many standardized career interest tools are available to help students gauge their interests and aptitudes.
- **Presentation of career options**: Based on the interest assessment, the student should be provided lists of potential careers and encouraged to research online, such as in the Occupational Outlook Handbook. The student must consider the preparation needed for a career. For example, a student who dislikes academic work and does not plan to go to college may be more interested in a trade and an apprenticeship in which most of the learning is done on the job.

- **Job shadowing**: The student should contact professionals or workers in fields of interest in order to shadow them in their work in order to obtain a more realistic idea of what the job entails.
- **Volunteer work**: Working as a volunteer in an area of interest may give the student a change for some hands-on activities and allows the student to make observations over time.
- **Internships**: Allows the student to have hands-on experience and to conduct a more in-depth study of a certain career and may help to develop relationships with others in the field.

New and Emerging Careers in Health Care

The **fastest growing jobs in health care** include those that attend to the needs of older adults because of the aging of the population:

- Certified nurse aides and personal care aides.
- Home health nurses and aides.
- Diagnostic medical sonographers.
- Occupational and physical therapist assistants.
- Estheticians, especially with an understanding of plastic surgery and medical beauty treatments.

Emerging jobs in health care include the following:

- 3D printing specialists to design and print body parts for transplant.
- Developers of virtual assistants and content for voice assistants (such as Alexa and Siri) regarding health issues.
- Documentation scribes with training in medical terminology to document for physicians.
- Managers of virtual hospitals connecting with patients through telehealth.
- Robotic controllers and managers.
- Genetic and epigenetic counselors.
- Healthcare financial advisors.
- Data security experts.
- Informatics, managing data.

TEKS for Health Science Technology Education

The Texas State Board of Education updated the **Texas Essential Knowledge and Skills (TEKS)** for career and technical education in 2015 and 2018. TEKS contains 16 career clusters with Health Science in Subchapter H.

Recommended Courses for Health Science Skills

Health Science skills include these recommended courses:

- Principles of Health Science (1 credit): Grades 9–10.
- Medical Terminology (1 credit): Grades 9–12.
- Anatomy and Physiology (1 credit): Grades 10–12. Prerequisites: Biology and Chemistry.
- Medical Microbiology (1 credit): Grades 10–12. Prerequisites: Biology and Chemistry.
- World Health Research (1 credit): Grades 11–12. Prerequisites: Biology and Chemistry.
- Pathophysiology (1 credit): Grades 11–12. Prerequisites: Biology and Chemistry.
- Health Informatics (1 credit): Grades 11–12. Prerequisites: Business Information Management I and Medical Terminology.

- Mathematics for Medical Professionals (1 credit): Grades 11–12. Prerequisites: Geometry and Algebra II.
- Pharmacology (1 credit): Grades 11–12. Prerequisites: Biology and Chemistry.
- Health Science Theory (1 credit): Grades 10–12. Prerequisites: Biology. Recommended corequisite: Health Science Clinical.
- Health Science Clinical (1 credit): Grades 10–12. Prerequisites: Biology. Recommended corequisite: Health Science Theory.
- Practicum in Health Science (2 credits): Grades 11–12. Requires prerequisites of Health Science Theory and Biology.
- Extended Practicum in Health Science (1 credit): Grades 11–12. Prerequisites: Health Science Theory and Biology. Corequisite: Practicum in Health Science.

Integrating Technology and Other Educational Media into the Health Education Process

Technology and other educational media can be integrated into the health education process in a variety of ways:

- **High-fidelity simulations**: These can include various equipment, such as mannequins, AEDs, blood pressure cuffs, and thermometers. These allow students to manipulate equipment and practice in a way that builds skills.
- **Computer-assisted instruction**: Interactive instructional modules are available on many health topics and help to engage the student.
- **Smartphone apps**: Multiple apps allow students to monitor activity and diet on an individual basis or as part of a group. Other apps support smoking cessation through financial calculators (showing savings), timers, self-hypnosis, virtual smoking, and count-down calendars.
- **Fitness trackers/Pedometers**: These devices, which may be worn like a watch or attached to clothing, encourage activity, for example, by keeping track of feet walked per day. Some fitness trackers also monitor heart rate, and some sync information with other mobile devices, such as a smartphone.

High- and Low-Fidelity Simulations

High-fidelity simulations are those that use real and/or realistic equipment and materials as part of learning. This can include ECG machines, mannequins, or specialized equipment used in the work environment, so that the learners can actually practice the tasks or procedures that they will carry out as part of their job functions. High-fidelity simulations are often the most helpful for the learner but are also the costliest because equipment may need to be dedicated for learner use. Additionally, training that involves practice and assessment of performance is often more time-consuming. **Low-fidelity simulations** rely on verbal, print, video, or audio descriptions and often involve discussion of potential actions rather than actual practice. Thus, learners may be presented with a case study or scenario with specific problems and be asked to describe the process for dealing with the problems. Low-fidelity simulations are less expensive and can usually be completed more quickly, but evaluation may not adequately measure clinical expertise.

Selecting Appropriate Teaching Tools

Print materials	Print materials may be provided before, during, or after class, and they can include books, journals, copies of articles, handouts, reference cards, and posters.

Electronics/ Audiovisual	Computer-assisted learning modules tablet (iPad, Nook, Kindle Fire) applications, and podcasts are especially valuable for independent study. Videos and audio recordings may be used independently or to supplement a class presentation. For example, videos may be used for demonstrations if equipment is not available or to show how to use equipment.
Display	Various types of displays can be used, including whiteboards, electronic whiteboards, flipcharts, and slide show presentations.
Internet resources	Databases (Cochrane, Medscape Reference, PubMed), NIH/CDC sites, Medline can provide excellent reference materials. Government sites often offer brochures and pamphlets or guidelines for free download or purchase at low cost.
Equipment	Various types of medical equipment, mannequins, simulations.
Guest speakers	Physicians, advance practice nurses, social workers, infection control nurses, administrators, risk managers, and human resources personnel all may serve as guest speakers.

Advantages of Students' Participation in Professional Development Opportunities

Professional development may include formal educational opportunities, such as conferences and online courses, and seminars, but it can also include such diverse activities as job shadowing, informal discussions, independent study, volunteering, and interning. Professional development opportunities should help students hone their skills and gain knowledge. The advantages of students' participation in professional development opportunities include the following:

- Increased retention and improved performance in the healthcare program.
- Increased knowledge and confidence in their ability to work in the field.
- Valuable networking and contacts throughout the healthcare community.
- Acquisition of new skills sets and more efficient ways to carry out activities.
- Maintenance of skills, which helps the student stay up to date.
- Increased benefits to the entire program because the student can share information.
- Increased satisfaction and pride in achievements.
- Establishment of habits of continual learning in the field of choice.
- Provision of opportunities for extra credit.

Ethical Frameworks

An **ethical framework** may facilitate decision making in complex healthcare situations:

Identification of issues	Objectively describe the ethical issue, acknowledging emotional biases.
Values clarification	Determine if decision making is impacted by personal values or the values of others and whether there is conflict in these values.
Influences and barriers	Consider the medical condition, risk factors, socioeconomic status, religion, support systems and barriers, such as conflicts, differing professional assessments, regulations, and control issues.
Principles	Use and apply ethical principles (autonomy, beneficence, nonmaleficence, justice, privacy, confidentiality, veracity, and fidelity).
Alternative solutions	Explore alternate solutions, considering the pros and cons, ethical issues, and outcomes.

Conflict resolution	Use collaboration, compromise, and/or accommodation rather than coercion or avoidance in reaching a solution.
Implementation	Select and carry out a solution that is defensible as an ethical decision.
Assessment	Assess the process of reaching an ethical solution and the outcomes.

Ethical Decision-Making Models

Do no harm	This model is based on nonmaleficence, the requirement that the treatment provided does no harm; however, by their nature, some treatments can and often do harm patients, so the underlying intent and goal of treatment must be considered when making decisions. For example, CPR may be carried out to save a patient's life and done with correct technique but still may result in rib fractures.
In good faith	The motive for a decision should be honest and fair, and decisions should be made with sincere intention to do good even though the outcome may be negative. For example, emergency medical services personnel may provide a treatment for a patient in good faith although the treatment proves to be ineffective.
Patient's best interest	Making a decision in the patient's best interest includes considering the patient's or parents' (in the case of children) wishes, the best clinical judgment, the best choice of various options, the chances for improvement/decline, and religious/cultural preferences.

Promotion of Autonomy

Autonomy is the ethical principle that the individual has the right to make decisions about his or her own care. In the case of children or patients with dementia who cannot make autonomous decisions, parents or family members may serve as the legal decision maker. The right of patients to make decisions about end-of-life care through advance directives, to refuse care, and to make informed consent was formalized in the Patient Self-Determination Act (1991). However, with hospice and palliative care, the healthcare provider must encourage active participation by patients and families and must respect cultural differences that may impact decision making. In some cultures, decisions are often made by the family or the head of the family rather than the individual. Additionally, there are limitations to autonomy. In most states, even if patients want physician-assisted suicide, the practice is illegal.

Promotion of Beneficence

Beneficence is an ethical principle that involves performing actions that are for the purpose of benefiting another person. In the care of a patient, any procedure or treatment should be done with the ultimate goal of benefiting the patient and any actions that are not beneficial should be reconsidered. Although some care may focus on comfort needs rather than on the extension of life, all of the patient's needs must be considered. Beneficence applies not only to obligatory acts (such as medical treatments) but also to nonobligatory acts (such as taking time to sit and talk with a patient). Patients' physical needs and emotional needs should have equal importance in the provision of care. The healthcare provider has a responsibility to promote beneficence in all aspects of the care plan and to actively work to prevent harm.

Promotion of Veracity

Veracity refers to the obligation that the healthcare provider has to tell patients and families the truth and to avoid lying or making misleading statements. The healthcare provider should not purposefully withhold information that the patient is entitled to, such as when a medication or treatment error has occurred, although the reality is that patients are often not informed about such occurrences. In Western culture, the idea that people are entitled to truthful information about their condition is paramount and is supported by law, but not all cultures view veracity in the same manner. In some cultures, bad news, such as a diagnosis of cancer, is routinely withheld from patients and telling them is considered cruel. Healthcare providers should consider the cultural implications of veracity and discuss the issue with the patient and family members when appropriate, keeping in mind that the truth may be negative but it should never be unkind.

Promotion of Nonmaleficence

Nonmaleficence is an ethical principle that means healthcare workers should provide care in a manner that does not cause direct intentional harm to the patient:

- The actual act must be good or morally neutral.
- The intent must be only for a good effect.
- A bad effect cannot serve as the means to get to a good effect.
- A good effect must have more benefit than a bad effect has harm.

With provision of care to patients, the healthcare provider must continually reevaluate patient care and treatments that may be beneficial initially but later negatively impact the patient's comfort needs. Nonmaleficence is a consideration when patients are receiving chemotherapy or radiotherapy that results in severe adverse effects. These effects must be balanced against the potential for long-term improvement in condition or prolonged survival, considering the patient's wishes.

Promotion of Justice

Justice is the ethical principle that relates to the distribution of the limited resources of healthcare benefits to the members of society. This issue may arise when there are more patients than can be accommodated. Decisions should be made according to what is best or most just for the patients and not colored by personal bias. The healthcare provider should apply the principle of justice in ensuring that all patients have equal consideration of their needs and that resources are distributed fairly; however, the realities of healthcare access (insured versus uninsured) present a challenge to upholding justice because some people can afford necessary care and others cannot. The healthcare provider has a responsibility to try to compensate by helping people in finding additional sources of financial assistance and supplies that they cannot otherwise afford. Some hospice and palliative care programs have fund-raising programs so they can serve patients who lack adequate insurance and/or income.

Bioethics

Bioethics is a branch of ethics that involves making sure that the medical treatment given is the most morally correct choice given the different options that might be available and the differences inherent in the varied levels of treatment. In the clinical unit, if the patients, families, and the staff are in agreement when it comes to values and decision making, then no ethical dilemma exists; however, when there is a difference in value beliefs between the patients/families and the staff, there is a bioethical dilemma that must be resolved. Sometimes, discussion and explanation can resolve differences, but at times the institution's ethics committee must be brought in to resolve the conflict. The primary goal of bioethics is to determine the most morally correct action using the set of circumstances given.

Environmental Ethics

Environmental ethics focus on the belief that human beings have an ethical obligation to the environment and that ethical considerations should be applied to the environment as well as to living things. This includes such things as consideration of the carbon footprint of not only individuals and groups but organizations and governments. Environmental ethics focuses on protection of the environment and prevention of damage and recognizes that all things, living and nonliving, are related and affect each other, negatively or positively. Environmental ethics extends moral standings to animals as well. When applying environmental ethics to healthcare organizations, considerations include the following:

- Reducing waste and recycling materials.
- Reducing heating/cooling use through better construction practices.
- Providing appropriate waste management.
- Using environmentally friendly materials in construction.
- Identifying alternative products to those that contain toxins or harmful substances.
- Preventing downstream pollution from medical waste.

CONFIDENTIALITY

Confidentiality is the obligation that is present in a professional-patient relationship. Healthcare providers are under an obligation to protect the information they possess concerning the patient and family. Care should be taken to safeguard that information and provide the privacy that the patient deserves. This is accomplished through the use of required passwords when family members call for information about the patient and through the limitation of who is allowed to visit. The healthcare provider should not assume that family members can be apprised of an older adult's health information without that person's consent. There may be times when confidentiality must be broken to save the life of a patient or others, but those circumstances are rare. The healthcare provider must make all efforts to safeguard patient records and identification. Computerized record keeping should be done in such a way that the screen is not visible to others, and paper records must be secured.

SCOPE OF PRACTICE

Each state has a nurse practice act (such as the Texas Nursing Practice Act) that delineates the **scope of practice** for all levels of nursing from certified nurse's aides to advance practice nurses, such as nurse practitioners. Scope of practice refers to those duties and responsibilities that the person is expected to perform as part of employment. Additionally, practice acts are usually in place for other healthcare providers who are licensed such as the Texas Physical Therapy Practice Act that established the scope of practice for physical therapists. Healthcare providers who are certified may have additional guidance regarding the care that they are trained to provide, but the power to control practice always rests ultimately with the state. It is the responsibility of the healthcare provider to be familiar with the appropriate state practice act and to ensure that the care provided is within the limits outlined because failure to do so may result in malpractice.

CLIENT'S RIGHT TO REFUSE

The **right to refuse** services rests with adults, so ordinarily an adult (or an emancipated minor who has been granted the rights of adulthood) can refuse any medication, treatment, counseling, or placement, although this is not always true. Court orders override these rights, and if the court has declared that a person is incompetent, this person's guardian makes the decisions. Additionally, if the court has ordered specific treatment, therapy, or placement, then the client must comply even against his or her wishes. Children, including adolescents, have no rights to refusal, but they should be consulted as much as possible, and their wishes should be respected and incorporated into the plan of care. For example, if an adolescent does not want to have a particular treatment, then options should be explored because forcing an adolescent to do something often results in poor outcomes.

Client's Rights and Responsibilities

People are empowered to act as their own advocates when they have a clear understanding of their **rights and responsibilities.** These should be given (in print form) and/or presented (audio/video) to parents/guardians on admission to the health care facility or as soon as possible:

- **Rights** should include competent, nondiscriminatory medical care that respects privacy and allows participation in decisions about care and the right to refuse care. They should have clear, understandable explanations of treatments, options, and conditions, including outcomes. They should be apprised of transfers, changes in the care plan, and advance directives. They should have access to medical record information about charges.
- **Responsibilities** should include providing honest and thorough information about health issues and medical history. Parents/guardians should ask for clarification if they don't understand the information that is provided to them, and they should follow the plan of care that is outlined or explain why that is not possible.

Issues Related to Malpractice and Negligence

Necessary Elements of Negligence

The four necessary elements of **negligence** (failure to follow standards of care) are as follows:

- **Duty of care**: The defendant (the healthcare provider) had a duty to provide adequate care and/or protect the plaintiff's (the patient's) safety.
- **Breach of duty**: The defendant failed to carry out the duty to care, resulting in danger, injury, or harm to the plaintiff.
- **Damages**: The plaintiff experienced illness or injury as a result of the breach of duty.
- **Causation**: The plaintiff's illness or injury is directly caused by the defendant's negligent breach of duty.

Abandonment occurs if the healthcare provider withdraws from providing care contrary to patient's desire or knowledge and fails to arrange for appropriate care by others, resulting in harm to the patient. **Assault** occurs if a healthcare provider threatens a patient in some way such that the patient becomes fearful of harm, whereas **battery** occurs when the healthcare provider intentionally injures a patient, such as by hitting or shoving the person. Assault and battery often occur together.

Types of Negligence

Negligence indicates that *proper care* has not been provided, based on established standards. Reasonable care uses a rationale for decision-making in relation to providing care. State regulations regarding negligence may vary, but all have some statutes of limitation, governmental immunity, and Good Samaritan laws that may provide a defense. Types of negligence include the following:

- **Negligent conduct**: An individual failed to provide reasonable care or to protect/assist another, based on standards and expertise.
- **Gross negligence**: An individual willfully provided inadequate care while disregarding the safety and security of another.
- **Contributory negligence**: The injured party contributed to his/her own harm.
- **Comparative negligence**: Individuals involved are assessed for the percentage of negligence attributed to each.

If the charge of negligence is supported, the patient may collect physical (lost earnings due to injury), psychological (pain and suffering), and punitive damages. A finding of negligence can lead to a malpractice suit.

Threats of Malpractice

If a patient **threatens a malpractice lawsuit**, it's important to avoid arguing or making excuses. In order to prove malpractice, the patient must be able to show that he or she suffered an injury of some type as the result of health care. The healthcare provider should listen patiently and should carefully document any specific complaints that the patient makes, using quotations and including the date and time and any witnesses. If the patient is angry, sometimes simply being allowed to vent may solve the problem, but if the patient is in a public area, the healthcare provider should suggest a more private area and should advise the patient to discuss the matter with the physician. Because malpractice is a legal issue that is generally handled by attorneys, the organization may have an established protocol for dealing with complaints, and that protocol should be followed exactly.

Advance Directives, DNR Orders, and Durable Power of Attorney

In accordance to federal and state laws, individuals have the right to self-determination in health care, including decisions about end-of-life care through **advance directives** such as living wills and the right to assign a surrogate person to make decisions through a **durable power of attorney**. Patients should routinely be questioned about an advance directive because they may present to a healthcare organization without the document. Patients who have indicated that they desire a **do-not-resuscitate** (DNR) order should not receive resuscitative treatments for terminal illness or conditions in which meaningful recovery cannot occur. Patients and families of those with terminal illnesses should be questioned as to whether the patients are hospice patients. For those with DNR orders or those withdrawing life support, staff should provide the person palliative rather than curative measures, such as pain control and/or oxygen and provide emotional support to the patient and family. Religious traditions and beliefs about death should be treated with respect.

Issues Related to Death and Dying

Treatment	Benefits	Risks
Opioid analgesia	Relieves pain, relieves dyspnea	Excessive sedation, respiratory depression, constipation, confusion, myoclonus, itching.
Antibiotics	Reduce infection	Prolonged life and suffering, nausea, diarrhea, increased risk of *Clostridioides difficile* infection.
Oxygen	Reduces dyspnea	Increases dryness of the mucous membranes, interference with the ability to communicate, depressed respiratory drive.
Tube feedings/ Percutaneous endoscopic gastrostomy tube	Improve nutrition, hydration	Infection, local irritation, prolonged suffering, tube leakage, aspiration pneumonia, abdominal discomfort, gastric perforation.
Mechanical ventilation	Relieves dyspnea, prolongs life	Prolonged suffering, inability to communicate.
Antimuscarinic agents (glycopyrrolate, atropine)	Reduces death rattle	Xerostomia, increased sedation, increased delirium.

Glucocorticoids	Reduces intracranial pressure, increases appetite, controls pain, reduces fatigue	Insomnia, GI upset, delirium, depression, increased risk of infection and hyperglycemia, Cushingoid syndrome, anxiety, increased risk of thromboembolism, myopathy, interference with other medications.

ADVANTAGES AND DISADVANTAGES OF TREATMENT OPTIONS

There are many ethical concerns that healthcare providers and families must face when determining the treatments that are necessary and appropriate for a **dying patient.** It is the healthcare provider's responsibility to provide support and information to help parents/families make informed decisions:

Treatment	Advantages	Disadvantages
Analgesia	Provide comfort. Ease the dying process.	Increase sedation and decrease cognition and interaction with family. Side effects. May hasten death.
Active treatments (such as antibiotics, chemotherapy)	Prolong life. Relieve symptoms. Reassure family.	Prolong the dying process. Side effects may be severe (as with chemotherapy).
Supplemental nutrition	Relieve the family's anxiety that the patient is hungry. Prolong life.	May cause nausea, vomiting. May increase tumor growth with cancer. May increase discomfort.
Intravenous fluids for hydration	Relieve the family's anxiety that the patient is thirsty. Keep the mouth moist.	May result in congestive heart failure and pulmonary edema with increased dyspnea. Increased urinary output and incontinence may cause skin breakdown. Prolong the dying process.
Resuscitation efforts	Allow the family to deny that death is imminent.	Cause unnecessary suffering and prolong the dying process.

DISTRESS, HOPELESSNESS, AND DEATH ANXIETY

Patients receiving palliative and hospice care often experience **distress, hopelessness, and death anxiety.** Patients may focus on their fear of dying, resulting in feelings of distress and hopelessness. Some patients with chronic disease may express death anxiety even though their death is not imminent, and this fear may negatively impact their ability to enjoy life. Others experience death anxiety as they near death, especially those who feel that they have things that must be attended to before death or those who fear the process of dying, especially pain and difficulty breathing. Patients with death anxiety should be encouraged to express feelings and talk about their fears and carry out a review of life. Reassuring patients that they can receive adequate medication to relieve pain and dyspnea may help to alleviate some fears. Some patients may benefit from CBT or relaxation exercises.

TExES Practice Test

1. Which of the following is not an historical event in the development of modern health care?

a. The first reproductive cloning of a human being was done in 1997.
b. The first baby conceived by in vitro fertilization was born in 1978.
c. The first successful heart transplantation was done in 1967.
d. The human genome project was completed in 2000.

2. Which of the following agencies is not under the auspices of the Department of Health and Human Services?

a. The Centers for Disease Control and Prevention (CDC)
b. The National Institutes of Health (NIH)
c. The World Health Organization (WHO)
d. The Food and Drug Administration (FDA)

3. Which of the following represents a way in which cultural influence can impact health care delivery?

a. A hospital provides a chapel as a place for patients and family members to express their spirituality
b. An American patient and health care provider keep a physical distance of three feet between them
c. A second-generation immigrant undergoes acculturation to the dominant culture
d. A culture practices religious fasting, which can affect medication schedules and interfere with drug absorption

4. Which of the following is not a health care-related technological advance currently in demand?

a. In-vitro fertilization
b. Eugenics
c. Gene therapy
d. Gene sequencing

5. A health insurance plan where health care is given by a network of providers with increased fees for use of out-of-network providers is called a(n)

a. Preferred Provider Network (PPO).
b. Medicare.
c. Health Maintenance Organization (HMO).
d. Fee-for-service plan.

6. Which of the following is a reasonable claim regarding a nutritional supplement?

a. The supplement makes weight loss easy
b. The supplement remedies vitamin deficiency
c. Most Americans are poorly nourished
d. Recommended Daily Allowances (RDAs) are set too low

7. The human body wants glucose levels to be maintained within a very narrow range. The hormones insulin and glucagon control glucose levels. The schematic below shows the pattern of insulin and glucagon release in the body. Based on this schematic, going on a diet with severely restricted caloric intake will cause which of the following hormone balances in the body?

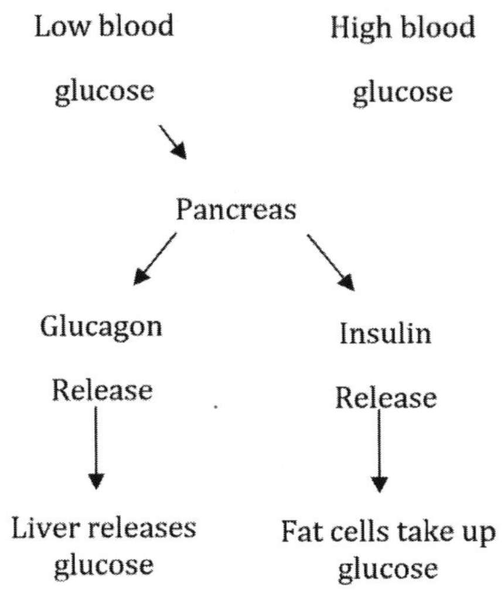

a. Glucagon > Insulin
b. Insulin > Glucagon
c. Glucagon = Insulin
d. Glucagon = Glucose

8. The most common blood types are O positive and A positive. The rarest blood type is AB negative. Which of the following donors would be most valuable to a blood bank?

a. O positive
b. O negative
c. AB positive
d. A negative

9. The digestive juices of the stomach are the most acidic body fluid. Antacids are medications taken to reduce heartburn and other digestive problems. If an antacid containing calcium carbonate ($CaCO_3$) is taken, the concentration of which of the following ions in the stomach will be reduced?

a. Ca^{2+}
b. OH^-
c. H^+
d. Cl^-

10. A researcher wants to test the osmotic pressure of different concentrations of a sucrose solution by placing water on side A of a semi-permeable membrane and various sucrose solutions on side B. On side B she places pure water, 0.1 M sucrose, 0.2 M sucrose, and 0.5 M sucrose. What is the purpose of the pure water on side B in this experiment?

a. It regulates the osmotic pressure on side A
b. It tests the integrity of the membrane
c. It makes the membrane permeable to small molecules
d. It is the control in the experiment

11. If a doctor prescribes drops for an eye infection and writes "q.d. OU" on the prescription, the patient should

a. Use the drops every day in both eyes.
b. Use the drops every day in the right eye.
c. Use the drops every day in the left eye.
d. Use the drops as needed in both eyes.

12. If a patient has post-op hypoglycemia and gastric distension, she

a. Has low blood sugar and a stomachache after leaving the hospital.
b. Has low blood sugar and a bloated stomach following surgery.
c. Has high blood sugar and a bloated stomach following surgery.
d. Has normal blood sugar and a stomachache following surgery.

13. If an otherwise healthy three-year-old complained of pain in his left ear and had a temperature of 39° Celsius, how would a doctor correctly notate this?

a. WDWN 3 y.o. c/o pain in L ear temp 39
b. WDWN 3 y.o. c/o pain in AS T 39 C
c. 3 y.o. has pain in left ear T 39 C
d. Healthy 3-year-old boy has pain in left ear and fever

14. If after a bee sting you notice a student's hand becoming red and swollen, you could report that he had

a. Dermatitis.
b. Dememia.
c. Dermogenesis.
d. Dermopexy.

15. The study of blood is called

a. Nephrology.
b. Pathology.
c. Hematology.
d. Osteology.

16. An ectopic pregnancy is

a. A case where the placenta has prematurely detached from the uterine wall.
b. Extra-uterine implantation of an embryo.
c. A pregnancy that terminates within the first three months of gestation.
d. A case where the mother has pregnancy-induced hypertension.

17. The part of the digestive tract responsible for water and mineral reabsorption is the

a. Esophagus.
b. Stomach.
c. Small intestine.
d. Large intestine.

18. A group of cells that derive from a common source and perform similar biological functions is called a(n)

a. Carcinoma.
b. Organ.
c. Tissue.
d. Organ system.

19. Acromegaly is a disease characterized by enlarged features, especially the face and hands, caused by hypersecretion of pituitary hormone after normal growth has stopped. It is a disease of the

a. Integumentary system.
b. Blood and lymph systems.
c. Nervous system.
d. Endocrine system.

20. At the neuromuscular junction, vesicles containing neurotransmitters are released from the _________, after which neurotransmitter receptors bind their ligands and allow ions to flow in the muscle cell, resulting in a muscle contraction.

a. Synaptic terminals
b. Dendrites
c. Axons
d. Glia

21. The diagrams below are examples of breathing patterns.

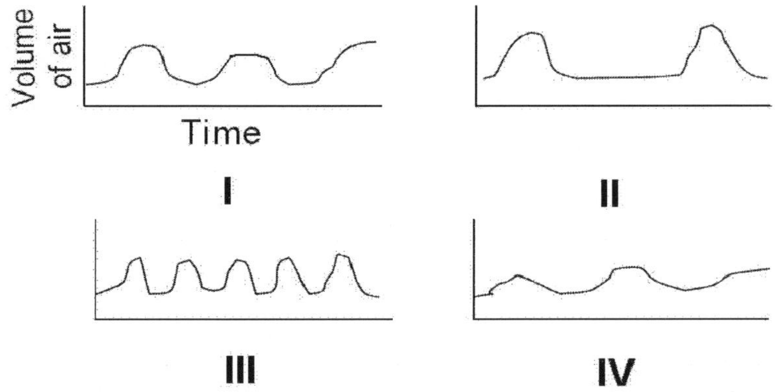

Example I represents eupnea and the others are abnormal. Which is an example of bradypnea?

a. I
b. II
c. III
d. IV

22. Bones provide shape and support to the body, protect internal organs, and assist in movement. These functions require bones to be strong and hard. However, bones must also have some flexibility to absorb torque and tension. The component of bones that provides for this flexibility is

a. Marrow.
b. Calcium phosphate.
c. Collagen.
d. Nerve cells.

23. Which of the following is true of both skeletal muscle and visceral muscle?

a. Both are under voluntary control
b. They make up approximately equal proportions of a person's body weight
c. They have two components in opposition to each other: the prime mover, which causes movement, and the antagonist muscle, which releases during movement
d. They contract when stimulated by neural impulses

24. Muscle fibers must burn energy to function. Which molecule directly transfers its chemical energy to actin and myosin in a muscle fiber?

a. Glycogen
b. Glucose
c. ATP
d. Lactic acid

25. The kidney is part of which of the following organ systems?

a. The integumentary system
b. The blood and lymph system
c. The endocrine system
d. The urinary system

26. For which of the following body fluids would the presence of microorganisms constitute an infection?

a. Saliva
b. Upper respiratory mucus
c. Urine
d. Feces

27. Campers in a remote area plan to drink water from a stream and are worried about the presence of pathogenic microorganisms in the water. Which of the following would not be an effective way of removing the most common sources of infection for humans: bacteria, fungi, protozoans, and viruses?

a. Boiling water prior to drinking it
b. Filtering the water through a sub-micron filter
c. Treating water with an antimicrobial chemical agent
d. Allowing the water to settle so that particles sediment to the bottom of a container

28. Which of the following parts of the body would create the most ideal environment for microbial reproduction and growth?

a. The mouth
b. The skin
c. The eyes
d. The scalp

29. Preparation of a bacterial culture requires preparing sterile agar growth media, flaming an inoculating loop, taking a specimen sample using the inoculating loop, and then streaking the agar plate to promote even growth of the microorganism. The inoculating loop is then flamed to kill microorganisms before it is touched to any other surface. This technique is known as

a. Culture technique.
b. Sterile technique.
c. Clinical technique.
d. Transmission-based technique.

30. Which of the following is not a way in which microscopes are used in a clinical laboratory?

a. Counting cells, such as the number of red blood cells per unit volume of blood
b. Distinguishing one type of microorganism from another, for example to distinguish a yeast infection from another kind of infection
c. Distinguishing different types of viral infections
d. Identifying solid particles in the urine

31. When a patient is admitted to the emergency room, a nurse will immediately measure body temperature, pulse rate, blood pressure, and respiratory rate. These measures, called vital signs, are important because

a. They are key factors in determining whether the patient requires medication.
b. Changes in homeostasis are associated with disease processes.
c. Changes in vital signs are associated with congenital disorders.
d. Changes in homeostasis may require that the patient be quarantined.

32. The most important and most effective protection against the transmission of infectious diseases is:

a. Hand washing,
b. Sterilization of work surfaces and door handles.
c. Vaccinations.
d. Wearing protective equipment such as gloves and facemasks.

33. If the skin is wounded, the body's defense against infection is to increase blood flow to the wound so that it becomes red and inflamed. Which of the following cell types would be active in fighting pathogens in the wound?

a. Epithelial cells
b. Red blood cells
c. Macrophages
d. Squamous cells

34. Spina bifida is a condition in which a child is born with an incompletely formed spinal cord. The vertebrae overlying the spinal cord may be open, with the incompletely formed spinal cord sticking out through the opening in the bones. Spina bifida is a ________ disorder.

a. Chronic
b. Acute
c. Congenital
d. Contagious

35. A vaccine against the varicella, or chickenpox virus, became available in 1995. Prior to that time, nearly all individuals in the United States had suffered from chickenpox by adulthood. If a child does not receive a varicella vaccination, he or she will be at risk of

a. Not getting chickenpox until adulthood.
b. Acquiring chickenpox from another child who recently received the vaccine.
c. Having multiple cases of chickenpox.
d. Infecting other children who are too young to receive the vaccine.

36. A child who had a runny nose but seemed otherwise healthy at school on Monday stayed home on Tuesday with the flu. On Thursday several other children in his class stayed home from school with flu systems. The child who stayed home on Tuesday was in the ________ phase of infection.

a. Remission
b. Symptomatic
c. Prodromal
d. Incubation

37. Bubonic plague is a disease caused by the bacteria Yersinia pestis. Rodents harbor the bacteria and may pass it to humans. Humans in turn pass the infection to other humans. In this disease process, the rodent is the

a. Reservoir.
b. Host.
c. Incubator.
d. Sleeper.

38. An elderly man's internist has noticed over the past year that he has had difficulty walking, poor balance, and tremors. He is most likely suffering from

a. Cardiovascular disease.
b. A neurological disorder such as Parkinson's disease.
c. An autoimmune disorder such as arthritis.
d. A cerebrovascular disorder such as stroke.

39. A stroke victim is unable to walk and spends all of her time in bed or in a chair. A significant risk of this kind of immobility is

a. Pressure ulcers.
b. Osteoporosis.
c. Malnutrition.
d. Injuries from falling.

40. Aging individuals often experience a loss of acuity in their senses, including vision, hearing, and taste. Sensory loss could put an aging individual at risk of which of the following health problems?

a. Sleep problems
b. Dementia
c. Parkinson's disease
d. Malnutrition

41. An elderly woman has an advance health care directive stating that she does not wish to be resuscitated in the event of a heart attack. While her daughter is visiting, the woman goes into cardiac arrest. Which of the following actions taken by the hospital staff would be the most ethical response to this situation?

a. No resuscitation, even if requested by the daughter
b. Resuscitation if requested by the daughter
c. Resuscitation if the daughter signs a statement acknowledging that it was done with her permission
d. Resuscitation if the elderly woman looks like she is in pain or distressed

42. When a man with high cholesterol examines the nutrition label on food to check its cholesterol content, he should also note

a. The serving size.
b. The vitamin A content.
c. The total carbohydrate content.
d. The protein content.

43. The gallbladder secretes bile salts that assist in fat digestion. Which of the following therapeutic diets should a patient who has had his gallbladder removed be on?

a. High calorie – more than 2000 calories per day
b. Restricted residue – low in bulk and low fiber
c. Low fat – high carbohydrate, low protein
d. High protein – low carbohydrate, high protein

44. Which of the following diets would be the most healthful and effective ways for an overweight person to lose weight?

a. Full liquid – strained, semi-liquid, and clear liquid foods
b. Low fat
c. A balanced diet that contains 500 calories less per day than a person expends
d. A varied diet that contains 1000 calories less per day than a person expends

45. In working with a patient with hyperglycemia, what should a health care worker first ask the patient before making dietary recommendations?

a. What are the patient's dietary preferences?
b. How much exercise does the patient get per day?
c. Does the patient know how to read a nutrition label?
d. Which dietary supplements does the patient take?

46. At a birthday party, a child has an itchy throat, a cough, a runny nose, and red, itchy eyes shortly after eating a chocolate chip cookie with walnuts. He has eaten walnuts once before with no noticeable effects. He eats bread on a regular basis. What is the most likely cause of the child's symptoms?

a. A food allergy to walnuts
b. Rapid onset of a cold
c. Rapid onset of seasonal allergies
d. A food allergy to wheat

47. Asthma is a chronic condition where the bronchi become inflamed and constricted due to a hypersensitive immune reaction to environmental irritants. Airways can be opened with fast-acting drugs called bronchodilators. What would be the most effective route of administration for bronchodilators?

a. Intranasal
b. Inhalational
c. Enteral
d. Topical

48. Generic drugs are cheaper than name-brand drugs because

a. They contain a lower concentration of active ingredients than name-brand drugs.
b. They do not have to go through FDA approval, saving the costs of regulatory compliance.
c. They do not have the overhead cost of drug development associated with them - generics are produced after a patent has expired.
d. They are made with less effective drug derivatives than name-brand drugs.

49. If a drug has a contraindication for use in infants, it means that

a. Risks of negative side effects are increased when the drug is used in infants.
b. The drug has not been tested in infants.
c. The drug is available over the counter, but requires a prescription for use in infants
d. The drug dosage has not been determined for infants.

50. If a drug has Food and Drug Administration (FDA) approval, then a consumer can be sure that

a. It has a long history of use in medicine.
b. The drug comes from a naturally-derived source.
c. It is available over the counter.
d. It has been tested for safety and effectiveness in controlled, scientific studies.

51. In a stressful situation, the sympathetic nervous system becomes more active than the parasympathetic nervous system. Which of the following physiological reactions would be triggered by the sympathetic nervous system?

a. Increased body secretions such as tears and saliva
b. Decreased heart rate
c. Reduced intestinal movement
d. Overall blood vessel dilation

52. Which of the following emotions is not a characteristic result of chronic stress?

a. Increased sexual desire
b. Anxiety
c. Depression
d. Guilt

53. Electroconvulsive therapy, selective serotonin reuptake inhibitors, vagus nerve stimulation, and psychotherapy are all treatments for

a. Parkinson's disease.
b. Depression.
c. Alzheimer's disease.
d. Cerebral palsy.

54. Epilepsy is a common chronic neurological disorder characterized by recurring seizures. Seizures are the result of abnormal or excessive neuronal activity in the brain. Which of the following is not a likely underlying cause of epilepsy?

a. Mutations in ion channel proteins
b. Abnormal levels of the inhibitory neurotransmitter GABA
c. Scar tissue from brain lesions
d. Intense emotional or religious experience

55. Which of the following is a place a person suffering from drug or alcohol addiction could seek treatment?

a. A drug rehabilitation program
b. A hospital emergency room
c. A wilderness retreat
d. A day spa

56. Which of the following factors is likely to be the most significant factor in whether or not an individual receives treatment for a mental health disorder?

a. Gender
b. Socioeconomic background
c. Birth order
d. Marital status

57. Which of the following is a positive symptom of schizophrenia?

a. Lack of motivation
b. Flat or blunted emotions
c. Auditory hallucinations
d. Disorganized, chaotic speech

58. An individual who has just lost his job is deficient at which of the following levels of Maslow's hierarchy of needs?

a. Physiology
b. Safety
c. Esteem
d. Self-actualization

59. The most important factor in being able to survive cancer is

a. A healthy immune system.
b. Access to the best chemotherapy drugs.
c. Having comprehensive health insurance.
d. Early detection.

60. Wellness is the state of health on a continuum from having a high energy level and feeling of well-being to illness and death. Optimal wellness reflects a balanced relationship among physical, mental, and social health. Wellness is primarily determined by

a. A person's genetic makeup.
b. A person's wealth.
c. Lifestyle choices.
d. A person's hygiene.

61. Which of the following is a reason why a person might not be able to be an organ donor?

a. Advanced age
b. A genetic disease like cystic fibrosis
c. Active cancer
d. History of drug use

62. Which of the following is not consistent with good body mechanics when moving a patient?

a. Do not lift anything that can be pushed or pulled
b. Bring the patient close before attempting the move
c. Keep a broad base of stance, with feet 12 to 18 inches apart
d. Turn the body by turning at the waist

63. Which type of therapist works to restore function, relieve pain, and prevent disability after disease, injury, or loss of a body part?

a. Physical therapist
b. Occupational therapist
c. Athletic trainer
d. Respiratory therapist

64. The job of organizing, analyzing, and evaluating medical records is the job of a

a. Medical stenographer.
b. Health science librarian.
c. Medical records administrator.
d. Hospital chief executive officer.

65. One of the functions of the Health Insurance Portability and Accountability Act of 1996 is to

a. Protect individuals from needing to disclose health problems to their employers.
b. Protect health insurance coverage for workers and their families when they change or lose their jobs.
c. Provide universal health insurance to all Americans.
d. Provide health insurance to individuals who have been unemployed for more than 90 days.

66. The acronym RACE describes the plan of action if a fire is discovered in a health care facility. What does RACE stand for?

a. Rely, Alarm, Clean, Evacuate
b. Rescue, Alarm, Combat, Evacuate or Extinguish
c. Rescue, Alarm, Contain, Extinguish or Evacuate
d. Run, Alarm, Combat, Evacuate

67. In a medical emergency with more than one person injured, medical professionals must prioritize patients based on the severity of their condition. This process is called

a. Emergency evaluation.
b. Triage.
c. Pre-hospital sorting.
d. Emergency medicine.

68. A medical lab technician has spilled a container of chloroform on the floor. What would be an appropriate way to clean up the spill?

a. Take up the liquid with paper towels and dispose of the saturated towels in the regular laboratory waste
b. Direct a fan over the spill to hasten evaporation of the liquid, then wipe completely dry with a towel
c. Take up the liquid with a mop and wring the mop into a drain
d. Take up the liquid with sand or another noncombustible absorbent material and store in closed containers for later disposal

69. The standard precautions against infection call for nonsterile gloves to be worn when contact is made with all body fluids except which of the following?

a. Perspiration
b. Saliva
c. Wound drainage
d. Urine

70. The Safety Data Sheet (SDS) is a document that provides information about a chemical, including its fire and explosion hazards, health hazards, reactivity, and protocols for handling spills and disposal. Which federal agency provides the SDS for a product?

a. Office of Management and Budget (OMB)
b. Occupational Safety and Health Administration (OSHA)
c. Centers for Disease Control (CDC)
d. Omnibus Budget Reconciliation Act (OBRA)

71. An important part of fire prevention is identifying fire hazards. Which of the following situations is a preventable fire hazard?

a. Flammable liquids stored in metal cabinets
b. Replacement of used emergency equipment
c. Accumulation of flammable materials in waste containers
d. Continuous use of electrical equipment

72. A patient with viral meningitis would most likely be given what kind of treatment?

a. Isolation
b. Hospitalization and treatment with strong antibiotics
c. Bed rest at home
d. Chemotherapy

73. Which of the following would most likely cause an infectious disease to be transmitted to other people?

a. An HIV positive person swimming in a pool with others
b. A person with respiratory flu flying on an airplane
c. Shaking hands with a person with meningitis
d. Someone with diverticulitis using public restrooms

74. Which of the following is an important strategy in avoiding nosocomial infections?

a. Washing hands before eating
b. Taking antibiotic prescriptions only until symptoms have subsided
c. Thorough hand washing by medical personnel between patients
d. Lengthening hospital stays

75. The most effective way to avoid the spread of serious infections in a hospital is to

a. Immediately dispose of used needles in a container specifically designed for that purpose.
b. Immediately recap needles after use.
c. Double-bag waste.
d. Use disposable eating utensils.

76. The most effective way to avoid the spreading a Human Immunodeficiency Virus (HIV) infection is to

a. Isolate the patient.
b. Get vaccinated against the virus.
c. Avoid unprotected sexual contact and sharing needles.
d. Wear a respiratory mask.

77. A nurse needs to discuss a patient's medical history with a doctor. The most appropriate place for her to have the conversation is

a. On her cellular phone while she is out shopping.
b. In the elevator with other patients present.
c. At the nurses' station with the patient's family present.
d. In the doctor's office with the door closed.

78. All but which of the following are examples of medical malpractice?

a. Performing skills that are beyond the level of a health care worker's training
b. Refusing to prescribe medications a patient has asked for
c. Neglecting to do something that is common practice
d. Prescribing a drug that has contraindications for a particular patient

79. Documentation of health care is important for communicating patient information between health care workers. The written record of health care is called the

a. Chart.
b. Report.
c. Directive.
d. Journal.

80. If a high school student is interested in becoming a doctor, what could be done to help this student learn about medical careers?

a. A doctor could give the student patient charts to study
b. A teacher could recommend television shows featuring doctors for the student to watch
c. A doctor could invite the patient to participate in a medical procedure
d. A doctor could invite the student to volunteer at a hospital, shadowing the doctor and visiting patients

81. Health care workers participate as a team to provide services to patients, and some members of the team must function as leaders in order to accomplish goals. Which of the following is not a characteristic of an effective leader?

a. Confident
b. Does emotional reasoning
c. Assertive
d. Maintains a vision and goals

82. Being a good team member is just as important as having an effective leader in order for a health care team to accomplish its goals. Which of the following is a characteristic of a good team member?

a. Tolerant of differences
b. Blames others when problems arise
c. Depends on others to solve problems
d. Depends on others to examine evidence before making a decision

83. Which of the following careers requires a graduate degree?

a. Registered nurse
b. Veterinary assistant
c. Laboratory manager
d. Physical therapist

84. Continuing education for medical professionals

a. Helps health care providers stay abreast of the latest technological developments in health care.
b. Provides training to underserved populations.
c. Provides training to new staff members at a hospital.
d. Provides educational opportunities after retirement.

85. A student likes working with people, is interested in human health, and wants to start working in her profession as soon as possible. Which would be the best health care career for a career counselor to recommend to her?

a. Dental hygienist
b. Pathologist
c. Nurse practitioner
d. Medical stenographer

86. Which of the following is a new health care career?

a. Doctor of osteopathic medicine
b. Radiologist
c. Genetic counselor
d. Nurse midwife

87. Which of the following is not an essential work habit for a nurse?

a. Punctuality
b. Self-control
c. Good problem-solving abilities
d. Native English speaker

88. Health care workers must be able to do all but which of the following during their careers?

a. Attend professional development training
b. Work from home
c. Communicate well
d. Keep to a schedule

89. The advances in information technology over the past thirty years will most likely dramatically change which career in the health care industry?

a. Radiology technician
b. Medical records manager
c. Dentist
d. Laboratory technician

90. Many hospitals have hotlines where patients can call and speak with a registered nurse about their medical problems. These hotlines are designed to

a. Prevent patients from coming to the emergency room.
b. Help the nurse know what to expect before patients arrive at the hospital.
c. Provide medical information and help patients decide if they should come to the emergency room, call their doctors, or use home care.
d. Begin to replace family practice doctors with nurse practitioners.

91. The Declaration of Helsinki is a document outlining the ethical conduct of research using human subjects. It states that a research investigator's duty is solely to

a. Science.
b. The patient.
c. The research study.
d. The greater good of humankind.

92. If biomedical researchers plan to use hospitalized patients in a study examining the effects of hospitalization on mental health, they must have their study approved by the hospital's

a. Institutional Review Board.
b. General Counsel.
c. Board of Directors.
d. Chief Executive Officer.

93. According to the Health Insurance Portability and Accountability Act (HIPAA),

a. Only members of a health care team have access to medical records, not a patient.
b. Both patients and a patient's family members have access to medical records.
c. Personal medical information can only be shared when necessary for treatment purposes.
d. Confidential information requested by a patient can only be communicated to the patient by mail.

94. Which of the following is the best term to describe the principles and values that determine appropriate behavior for health care professionals?

a. Jurisprudence
b. Ethics
c. Morality
d. Faith

95. Protected Health Information (PHI) must be kept confidential. Which of the following is not an example of PHI?

a. Life insurance coverage
b. Health insurance coverage
c. Medical records
d. Dental records

96. Which of the following is an example of a health care worker operating within the "scope of practice?"

a. A nursing assistant performs dental cleanings
b. A licensed practical nurse records the signs and symptoms of a patient in his medical chart
c. A radiologist administers anesthesia prior to surgery
d. A registered nurse sets a broken bone

97. In 1973 the American Hospital Association adopted a Patient's Bill of Rights. Which of the following rights and responsibilities are not patients' rights, according to this document?

a. Access to emergency services
b. Good faith effort to pay for services
c. Participation in treatment decisions
d. The option to keep medical information completely confidential

98. Which of the following is not true of a durable power of attorney?

a. In order to take effect, a patient must be permanently unconscious or terminally ill
b. It allows for another person to make health care decisions if a person is unable to make them
c. It is an example of an advance directive that allows a patient to express their wishes about health care
d. It is often complemented by a living will

99. A living will allows a person to state in advance which kinds of medical treatment to receive. All but which of the following are issues that could trigger a living will to be invoked?

a. A state of prolonged unconsciousness
b. Death
c. Pain following a surgical procedure
d. Cardiopulmonary resuscitation

100. If a nurse were to leave a paralyzed patient unturned for an entire day this would be considered

a. Liability.
b. Slander.
c. Jurisprudence.
d. Negligence.

Answer Key and Explanations

1. A: The first reproductive cloning of a mammal was announced in 1997. The animal was a sheep named Dolly. Dolly was cloned by placing the nucleus of a somatic cell into an egg cell to create an embryo, which was implanted in the uterus of a sheep and allowed to develop into a newborn. Reproductive cloning, while technically possible, has never been done in humans, and may never be done because of ethical considerations. Research using stem cells derived from cloned human embryos is currently legal and performed in research laboratories. No laws currently govern reproductive human cloning, although it is almost universally opposed. Answers B – D are all historical events in the history of modern health care.

2. C: The World Health Organization (WHO) is a specialized agency of the United Nations and is not an agency of the United States' federal government. WHO performs many worldwide functions such as monitoring outbreaks of infectious diseases and supporting the development and distribution of safe vaccines. The Department of Health and Human Services has over a dozen agencies, all dedicated to the wellbeing of Americans. The CDC monitors and prevents outbreaks of disease, the NIH supports biomedical research, and the FDA regulates the safety of food, cosmetics, pharmaceutical products, and medical devices.

3. D: Fasting interfering with medication schedules and drug absorption is an example of a cultural practice influencing health care delivery. Cultural practices could also influence a patient's receptivity to pain management, adopting a medically necessary diet, likelihood of receiving vaccinations, and overall wellness and health prevention. Cultural considerations can create communication barriers between patients and health care professionals. Different cultures also view important life events such as pregnancy, birth, and death quite differently.

4. B: Eugenics is the study of the control of human characteristics. Devising methods of controlling human characteristics is widely considered unethical and is not a part of modern health care. In vitro fertilization, or joining an egg and sperm in the laboratory, is a technical advance that has been in use since the late 1970s. Gene therapy is a technique in which defective genes are compensated for by giving individuals normal copies of defective genes. It is still in development, but certain gene therapy has been approved for treatment of several disorders, such as cancer, cystic fibrosis, transplant rejection, and heart disease. Low-cost gene sequencing technologies have advanced rapidly in recent years, and individuals can now be screened for genetic disorders by sequencing the gene that could put them at risk.

5. A: A PPO is an insurance plan in which patients pay a monthly insurance premium, and pay either co-payments for office visits or coinsurance (a percentage of health care costs) or both. There is also a yearly deductible. HMOs may have all of these features as well, the difference being that health care providers are in many locations and organized as a network in a PPO whereas HMOs are designated as the staff model, where health care providers work at a designated facility. In fee-for-service plans, patients pay a percentage of the feel incurred. Medicare is a federal health insurance plan for people over age 65, younger people with disabilities, and individuals with advanced renal disease.

6. B: True nutrient deficiencies can be remedied with nutritional supplements. However, it is not accurate to say that most Americans are poorly nourished, and any product that claims such should be viewed with skepticism. A product claiming to make weight loss easy, or similarly claiming that RDAs are set too low, should be viewed with skepticism.

7. A: A low calorie diet will result in low blood glucose levels. This will stimulate glucagon release from the pancreas and will not stimulate insulin release from the pancreas, and glucagon levels will be higher than insulin levels. The body will attempt to compensate for the low blood glucose level by releasing glucose from the liver. A diabetic person fails to release adequate insulin when blood glucose levels are high. Diabetic patients manage this by controlling their diet, so as not to allow blood glucose levels to spike after eating sugary foods, and by taking insulin.

8. B: O negative is the universal donor and would be most valuable to a blood bank. People with the O negative blood type do not have the A, B or Rh antigens on their red blood cells, and so their blood will not cause an immune reaction when given to people of other blood types. O negative people can only receive O negative blood. AB positive is the least useful type of blood because it can only be given to AB positive people. A negative can be given to any blood type except B and AB (Rh positive or negative) types. O positive can be given to any Rh-positive blood type.

9. C: Acidic conditions (low pH) are caused by a high concentration of H^+ ions. When $CaCO_3$ is taken into the stomach, the carbonate ion will neutralize two H^+ ions while the Ca^{2+} ion forms an ionic bond with two chloride ions. This reduces the concentration of H^+ ions and lowers the pH of the digestive juices in the stomach. The overall chemical reaction is as follows:

$$CaCO_3 + 2HCl \rightarrow CaCl_2 + CO_2 + H_2O$$

10. D: When a series of conditions are to be tested in an experiment, a blank should be tested in order to acquire baseline data. This is called a control. In the experiment above, pure water will exert no osmotic pressure, so it is the control for the sucrose solutions. This type of control is also called a negative control. A positive control would be testing a known value in an experimental system to see if the test is working properly. An example of a positive control in this experiment would be to test a sucrose solution where the experimenter already knows the osmotic pressure that it elicits. If the experiment gives the expected results when testing the positive control, then one knows the experimental setup is working (i.e. there are no holes in the membrane).

11. A: The abbreviation q.d. stands for the Latin *quaque die*, or every day. Learning the abbreviation q. is useful because it will help with remembering the abbreviations q.h. (*quaque hora*, every hour), q.i.d. (*quarter in die*, four times a day), and q.o.d. (*quaque altera die*, four times a day). The abbreviation OU stands for the Latin *oculus unitas*, or both eyes. Learning the abbreviations for right (D, for *dexter*), left (S, for *sister*) and both will he helpful in remembering the abbreviations for right/left/both eyes and ears. Ear is abbreviated A for *auris.*

12. B: Post-op or postop is accepted abbreviation for post surgery, or post operation. The prefix hypo- means below or deficient, and the suffix –emia refers to blood. The root "glyc" or "gluc" refers to sugar. Knowing these word parts would allow one to deduce that the word hypoglycemia means low blood sugar. The root "gastr/o" refers to the stomach, and the suffix –ic means "pertaining to," so the word *gastric* means "pertaining to the stomach." Finally, *distension* refers to an enlargement or ballooning effect. The suffixes –algia or –dynia refer to pain.

13. B: WDWN stands for "well-developed/well-nourished," y.o. is the correct abbreviation for year-old, and c/o is the correct abbreviation for "complains of". AS stands for *auris sinistra*, and is a more correct notation than left ear or L ear. 39 degrees Celsius is simply notated 39 C.

14. A: The prefix derma- denotes skin. The suffix –itis means inflammation, so red and swollen (inflamed) skin is called dermatitis. The suffix –emia denotes a blood condition, for example *hyperlipemia* is a blood condition of excessive fat. The suffix –genesis refers to the origin or production of something, for example *pathogenesis* describes the origin or production of disease.

The suffix –pexy refers to suspension or fixation. For example, *gastropexy* means "fixation of the stomach to the abdominal wall."

15. C: This question asks about the meaning of root words. The root "nephr" refers to the kidney, so *nephrology* is the study of the kidney (the suffix –ology means "study of"). The root "path" means disease, so *pathology* is "the study of disease." The root "hemat" means blood, so *hematology* is "the study of blood." The root "osteo" means bone, so *osteology* is "the study of bone." All of these roots can be combined with other suffixes to create different words. For example, *hematopoiesis* is "the formation of blood cells."

16. B: In a normal pregnancy, an egg cell is fertilized by a sperm cell in the fallopian tubes of the uterus, and the egg moves into the uterus, attaching itself to the uterine wall, where it will grow and develop into a fetus. The word *ectopic* means "occurring in an abnormal position or place." The placenta can also be in an abnormal place. For example, if the placenta is covering the cervix, this causes a severe health risk for the mother and baby because the placenta will block the baby from entering the birth canal. This condition is called *placenta previa*.

17. D: Digestion of food takes place in the stomach and small intestine. Digestion begins in the stomach and most absorption of digestive products occurs in the small intestine. Most of the water from food and drink is absorbed back into the blood through the walls of the large intestine, along with vitamins, electrolytes, and bile salts. Problems with reabsorption in the large intestine can cause serious dehydration.

18. C: Cells are the basic unit of life and the basic unit of the human body. Cells divide to produce other cells that are like them, and a tissue is a group of cells that derive from a common source and have similar physical and biochemical properties. A particular kind of tissue will be dedicated to a particular biological function. Organs are composed of more than one kind of tissue and work to perform major body functions. For example, a kidney is composed of distinct kinds of tissues and performs the major function of removing waste from the blood. Kidneys are part of an organ system – the urinary system – that functions to remove waste from the body. Other organs in the urinary system include the bladder, ureters, and urethra.

19. D: The endocrine system is responsible for the hormonal control of the body. Hormones are chemical compounds such as steroids, amino acids, or peptides that monitor and coordinate body activities. Hormones are secreted by the endocrine glands, and each type moves through the blood stream to its own target cells. Hormones guide many body processes, including growth, metabolism, and reproductive functions.

20. A: The synaptic terminal is the end of an axon and opposed to either a muscle cell or a dendrite. Nervous impulses travel down an axon, resulting in depolarization of the electrochemical gradient at the synaptic terminal, followed by release of vesicles containing neurotransmitters. Neurotransmitter molecules are released into the synapse, which is the space between the synaptic terminal and the muscle or dendrite. Axons transmit nervous impulses away from the cell body of a neuron and dendrites receive signals and transmit them to the cell body. Glia, or neuroglia, are special cells that provide support to neurons.

21. B: Normal respiration is called eupnia. Adults respire 16-20 times per minute. The tidal volume is the amount of air normally exchanged with each cycle of inhalation and exhalation, usually about 500 mL per breath for adults. Changes in either the rate or volume of breathing are symptomatic of a problem. Example II is bradypnea (slow breathing), III is tachypnea (fast breathing), and IV is hypopnea (shallow breathing). Other possible abnormal breathing patterns are hyperpnea (deep breathing), dyspnea (difficulty breathing), and apnea (inability to breathe).

22. C: Collagen is a protein that provides elasticity to bone and skin. Bone is a living tissue that must continuously receive food and oxygen. Bone tissue is also composed of inorganic salts, particularly calcium phosphate, as well as blood vessels and bone cells. Because bone contains inorganic components as well as organic components, it does not require as much innervation and connection to the circulatory and nervous systems as do other tissues. Bones grow for the first 18 to 20 years of life, but bone tissue is alive throughout a person's life.

23. D: All kinds of muscle (skeletal, smooth, and cardiac) contract when stimulated by neural impulses. The difference between skeletal muscle and the other kinds of muscle is that skeletal muscle is under voluntary control whereas visceral (or smooth) muscle and cardiac muscle are controlled by the autonomic nervous system, and are thus under involuntary control. Skeletal muscles make up more than 40% of a person's body weight, so it has much greater mass than visceral muscle. Movement is coordinated by two kinds of skeletal muscle: the prime mover contracts, causing movement, while the antagonist muscle relaxes. For example, when moving your hand to your shoulder, the bicep contracts while the triceps relaxes.

24. C: ATP is the basic energy currency of a cell and the direct fuel for muscle contraction. ATP is produced when energy is extracted from glucose through glycolysis and the Krebs cycle – also known as cellular respiration. Glycogen is a polymer of glucose and the body's long-term storage molecule for glucose. Glycogen is stored in the liver; when the body's blood sugar level is low it is broken down to glucose, which is released to the blood stream. Cells can then quickly take up glucose and use it for fuel. Lactic acid is not a fuel source, it is a product of glycolysis in anaerobic conditions.

25. D: The urinary system consists of the kidneys, ureters, bladder, and urethra. The kidneys filter blood which arrives by way of the renal artery. Urine is waste removed from the filtered blood and then carried to the bladder by small tubes of smooth muscle called the ureters. The bladder is a smooth muscle sac that expands as it fills with urine. When the bladder fills, nerves in the muscular wall are stimulated and cause the urge to urinate. Urine moves from the bladder to be excreted through the urethra. If one kidney fails to function, the other kidney can make up for it. If both fail, then waste must be removed from the blood by dialysis. Dialysis is the filtration of blood through a machine containing semipermeable membranes. Ultimately, a patient with kidney failure will need a kidney transplant.

26. C: Infection is a state of disease caused by the presence of pathogenic microorganisms. Some body fluids, such as blood, urine, and internal body systems, are normally sterile and free from microorganisms. The presence of microorganisms in these tissues would constitute an infection. Other parts of the body, specifically the skin, mouth and throat, upper respiratory tract, intestines, and genital tract, normally harbor nonpathogenic microorganisms. These systems can become infected when invaded by pathogenic microorganisms, but the mere presence of microorganisms does not constitute infection.

27. D: Microorganisms are too small to be removed by sedimentation. Microorganisms can often survive freezing, but the ones capable of infecting humans cannot survive boiling, an effective way of killing them. The smallest microscopic pathogens are viruses, which range in size from 0.01 – 0.05 microns. If a filter of this size could be obtained, it would remove viruses. This may not be practical for camping, however, because high pressure may be needed for such a filter. Treating water with chemicals that kill microorganisms would be an effective way of making water safe to drink.

28. A: Microorganisms survive and reproduce well in warm, moist, dark environments that provide a source of food. The mouth provides all of these conditions and many microorganisms colonize the mouth. They are the source of tooth decay and plaque formation. Microorganisms also survive in other areas of the body, such as the skin, scalp, eyes, digestive tract, genital tract, and upper respiratory system. But the areas of the body that provide the most continuously favorable conditions for the growth of microorganisms are internal to the body.

29. B: Sterile technique means preparing growth media and transferring microorganisms in such a way as to not contaminate the environment with the microorganism one is working with while simultaneously avoiding contaminating the sample with other microorganisms from the environment. Care must be taken to sterilize all tools before and after use, as well as sometimes during use.

30. C: Microscopes can easily magnify cells enough to see and count them. Yeast cells are quite different in size and shape from bacteria and protozoa, so a microscope would be an appropriate tool for distinguishing a yeast infection from other kinds of infections. Viruses are much smaller than cells, however, and are too small to be seen with a light microscope, much less distinguished from other kinds of viruses. Some urinary system diseases cause solid particles to be formed in the urine, and these could be seen and detected using a microscope.

31. B: Homeostasis refers to the normal physiological state of a healthy body. Body temperature, pulse rate, blood pressure, and respiratory rate are kept within quite narrow ranges under normal conditions. An increase in body temperature is usually a sign of systemic infection. Changes in the other vital signs can also signal various disease processes. Other changes such as localized redness and swelling, changes in waste elimination, and pain can also signal disease.

32. A: The primary method of protection from infection is good hand-washing technique. Medical professionals should wash their hands at the beginning of their work period, between patient contact, before and after eating, after using the restroom, and before leaving the work environment. The sterilization of work surfaces and the wearing of protective equipment are both important in situations where the risk of infection is particularly high, such as during surgery. Vaccinations are the last line of defense against infection, but other sanitary practices are important in reducing the chance of infection, particularly in cases where no vaccine is available.

33. C: Macrophages are the white blood cells that engulf pathogens, and they are an important line of defense against infection. Increased blood flow at the site of infection helps increase the chances that infecting microorganisms will be found and removed by macrophages. Red blood cells do not play a direct role in the immune response. Epithelial cells form the lining of body cavities and surfaces. They are important in forming a barrier to microorganisms, but if the barrier is ruptured, then the immune system must take action towards preventing infection. Squamous cells are the most superficial layer of an epithelium. They are flat, scale-like cells. For example, the cells lining the inside of the cheek are squamous cells.

34. C: A congenital disorder involves defects or damage to a developing fetus. The cause may be genetic, environmental, behavioral, or unknown. Genetic disorders are all congenital, even if they are not recognized until later in life. A chronic disease is one that is lasting or persistent, often one that has developed slowly. An acute disease is one in which the onset is rapid, as is the recovery. Contagious diseases are those that are caused by communicable agents, especially microorganisms.

Contagious diseases may be either acute or chronic. Occasionally, congenital defects may be caused by contagious disease.

35. D: Unvaccinated people can pass diseases to babies who are too young to be fully immunized. They can also pass diseases to immunosuppressed people like cancer and AIDS patients, as well as the small percentage of children whose immunization did not "take." While it is possible that an unvaccinated child could go through childhood and not get chickenpox at all, or not until adulthood, it is more likely that they will get the disease as children. It is also possible to have multiple chickenpox infections, although not getting the vaccine would not increase the likelihood of serial infections.

36. C: During the incubation phase of an infection, the symptoms of disease are not present yet, although an individual may be contagious. A prodrome is an early, non-specific symptom of disease. For example, a runny nose could be an early symptom of the flu, or could be due to the common cold or allergies. If the runny nose is followed by fever, chills, fatigue, and other flu symptoms, the patient would be considered in the symptomatic phase of disease. The symptomatic phase may be followed by an exacerbation phase, which will then be followed by the remission phase, where symptoms decrease and the cause of the infection is mitigated.

37. A: In order to cause infection, a microorganism must have a human, animal, or environmental reservoir in which it can live, reproduce, and die. It must then have a point of entry into the host. The host must be susceptible to infection, and transport the microorganism it has been infected with to other hosts. There must be a point of exit from the original host, which is likely to be the same as the point of entry. If the host encounters another susceptible host, the infection can then be spread to the other host.

38. B: Parkinson's disease is a brain disorder that primarily affects people after the age of 65. It occurs when certain nerve cells in a part of the brain called the substantia nigra die or become impaired. These nerve cells produce a neurotransmitter called dopamine that controls coordination of the body's muscles and movement. Other common diseases of the elderly are cardiovascular disease and arthritis. The symptoms of poor balance, uncoordinated movement, and tremors are consistent with the pathology of Parkinson's disease.

39. A: Pressure ulcers are areas of damaged tissue where tissues are compressed between bony prominences and hard surfaces. Patients most at risk of getting them are hospitalized, in long-term care facilities, cognitively impaired, or immobile. Elderly patients are particularly at risk because of reduced subcutaneous fat and decreased capillary blood flow. An important role of a health care provider is to prevent pressure ulcers. This can be achieved by making sure the patient is moved every couple of hours, and that padding is placed in areas of particular risk. Pressure ulcers can be very slow to heal in elderly patients, so it is critical that they are prevented.

40. D: When a person is unable to taste, he or she often loses interest in eating. This can place elderly people at a significant risk of becoming malnourished. Malnourishment can mean insufficient caloric intake to meet a person's energy needs, as well as a lack of particular vitamins or minerals necessary for healthy metabolism. An elderly person may need assistance from caregivers in monitoring the quantity and quality of food they take in every day. Other health problems such as Parkinson's disease may be the root cause of some forms of sensory loss but are not symptoms of sensory loss. Sleep problems and dementia have complex roots and a variety of symptoms, but are not directly related to sensory loss.

41. A: An advance health care directive is a document that makes explicit a person's health care preferences, including the type of treatment he or she may want at the end of life. Preferences are given regarding cardiopulmonary resuscitation, organ donation, surgical procedures, and diagnostic testing maybe given. Medical professionals should observe the advanced health care directive, even if it contradicts the wishes of family members. It represents a patient's wishes in the same way as if the patient were able to make the decision for him or herself. The advanced health care directive should designate someone to carry out the person's health care choices.

42. A: Nutrition labels give the quantities of certain nutritional aspects of food, such as calories, fat, cholesterol, protein, and sodium content. Nutrition labels also give the recommended daily amounts for various nutrients. A single serving of a food may have cholesterol content that is within the parameters of a healthy diet, but a person may eat several servings at once, and thereby consume 2 – 3 times the amount of cholesterol contained in a single serving. So in order for the information on a nutrition label to be useful, it is important to observe the size of a serving.

43. C: Therapeutic diets are used to treat specific health conditions. A therapeutic diet must still provide necessary nutrients, but will take into consideration the special needs associated with specific health problems. A low-fat diet will be prescribed for several disorders, one of them being gallbladder disease or gallbladder removal. A restricted residue diet may be prescribed for rectal diseases. A high protein diet may be needed in the case of pregnancy or post-surgery, and a high calorie diet may be prescribed in the case of anorexia nervosa or hyperthyroidism.

44. C: A person may lose weight quickly through severe calorie restriction, but quick weight loss is usually unsuccessful because when the body is deprived of essential nutrients, it stores additional energy in the form of fat. It is generally considered safe and effective to lose 1 pound per week. A pound of fat is equal to 3,500 calories, so consuming 500 calories less per day than is expended will guarantee a loss of one pound of fat per week. A balanced diet provides 15% of the calories from protein. Fat should provide 30% of daily calories, with the remaining 55% provided by carbohydrates. A balanced diet should be maintained throughout a weight loss program.

45. A: Many cultural factors play into dietary preferences, and these cultural factors play a large role in the choices people make about food. Dietary changes take a long time to implement, and if socializing within a culture depends on large family meals with heavy dishes, then cutting back on calories may come at a high social cost to the patient. Understanding the culture a patient comes from will help a health care provider identify ways to help a patient adjust to a new diet. Other considerations, like the ability to read a nutrition label, intake of dietary supplements, and activity level are also important. But cultural factors are foundational and are a primary consideration.

46. A: Food allergies result when the body mistakes food for a harmful substance and produces antibodies against it. The initial contact does not illicit allergy symptoms because there are very few antibodies that recognize the food the first time a person comes in contact with it. On subsequent contact, however, antibodies are ready to react to it. This causes the body to release chemicals that cause allergy symptoms. If the child has not had an allergic reaction to walnuts in the past, he could still have one at a later time. It is less likely that he would have a sudden allergic reaction to something he consumes frequently, like wheat.

47. B: A fast-acting drug would have the best opportunity to work quickly when administered directly to the tissue it is designed to act on. Fast-acting bronchodilators are administered through inhalation so that they come in immediate contact with the bronchi that are inflamed and constricted during an asthma attack. There are many different routes of administration, and for each drug and each indication there is a route of administration that is the safest and most effective.

48. C: Generic drugs are exactly the same chemical compounds at the same concentration and given by the same route of administration as name-brand drugs. They have the same risks and side effects as name brand drugs, and they are subject to the same FDA approval as well. The reason name brand drugs are more expensive is because manufacturers have the expense of developing, testing, and marketing a drug. When a new drug is invented, it is patented for a limited amount of time. When the patent runs out, other manufacturers may apply for permission to make it, and they are able to sell it more cheaply as a generic.

49. A: An indication is a valid reason to use a certain drug or medical procedure. A contraindication is a condition or factor that increases the risks associated with using a particular drug or undergoing a particular medical procedure. For example, pregnant women should avoid getting X-rays because the rapidly dividing cells of the fetus are susceptible to X-ray-induced mutations more than the adult cells of the mother are susceptible to mutation. The mother's cells are susceptible, but to a lesser degree than the fetus'. X-rays are not forbidden for pregnant women, however, and could be used in the case of a serious condition such as a broken bone.

50. D: If a drug has FDA approval, it will be indicated on the drug's labeling. FDA approval requires extensive testing and compliance with regulatory standards to ensure a drug's safety and effectiveness. Many over-the-counter and all prescription drugs carry FDA approval. Some have long been used in medicine, like aspirin. Others are newly designed drugs. Some may have a natural source and others may be synthetic. A nutritional supplement without FDA approval may be effective in treating a health problem, but the dosage and indications for the supplement have not been tested for their safety and effectiveness.

51. C: The autonomic nervous system controls body functions that are beyond our cognitive control. It is divided into the parasympathetic and sympathetic nervous systems. The parasympathetic nervous system conserves energy and increases bodily secretions, including those that help in digestion. The sympathetic nervous system prepares the body for action, and is activated under stressful conditions. It constricts most blood vessels (except those in the heart, leg, and arm muscles) and increases heart rate, blood sugar, perspiration, and mental activity. It reduces intestinal movement, in opposition to the action of the parasympathetic nervous system.

52. A: Emotions associated with chronic stress include anxiety, depression, anger, guilt, hurt, jealousy, shame, and suicidal feelings. The activation of the parasympathetic nervous system during stress often decreases sexual function, resulting in limited sensual and sexual awareness and possibly resulting in sexual dysfunction in both the male and female. Anxiety and depression can have many causes other than stress. Endocrine and neurologic diseases such as diabetes and Parkinson's disease are some other possible causes of anxiety and depression.

53. B: One of the main causes of depression is the imbalance of certain neurotransmitters. Serotonin is one of these neurotransmitters, and selective serotonin reuptake inhibitors are one of the most common treatments for depression. Depression is complex, and many different kinds of treatment, including psychotherapy, electroconvulsive therapy, and vagus nerve stimulation are available to treat it. Other neurological disorders such as Parkinson's disease, Alzheimer's disease, and cerebral palsy are the result of specific neuropathologies and they require treatment specific to the pathology of the particular disease.

54. D: In the past, epileptic seizures were associated with religious experiences, including visions sent by gods or even demonic possession. It is now understood that seizures are caused by specific neurological dysfunction. Epilepsy is not a single disorder, but rather a group of syndromes with different root causes but all involving episodic abnormal electrical activity in the brain. Mutations in ion channels, abnormal levels of neurotransmitters, and lesions in the brain are all possible causes of epilepsy.

55. A: Professional help from doctors, nurses, and therapists is available at drug and alcohol treatment centers, referred to generically as rehabilitation centers. Treatment programs range from short visits for the purpose of diagnosing a problem to full 90-day treatment programs. Treatment for the acute effects of drug and alcohol overdoses is done in a hospital emergency room, but hospitals are generally not the appropriate place to seek treatment for addiction. Recreational retreats and spas do not offer addiction recovery programs.

56. B: Many factors contribute to whether an individual seeks treatment for mental health disorders. Factors like education level, wealth, family background, religion, occupation, and where someone lives all play into mental health treatment far more than they do treatment of physical diseases and disorders. Gender, marital status, and even birth order may come into play, but research has revealed a relationship between socioeconomic status and mental health.

57. C: Schizophrenia is often described in terms of positive and negative symptoms. Positive symptoms are experiences that most people do not have, such as hallucinations, delusions, and thought disorders. Negative symptoms refer to experiences or features that an individual is lacking, for example lack of emotion, lack of motivation, inability to experience pleasure, or reduced verbal ability. Schizophrenia is diagnosed based on symptom profiles rather than diagnosis of physiological pathology.

58. B: Abraham Maslow listed human needs in order of importance using five levels. The lowest level is associated with physiological needs, with the upper levels being associated with psychological needs. Once needs at one level are met, the needs at the next level come into focus. The safety level includes security of body, of employment, of resources, of heath, of property, of the family, and of morality.

59. D: Early detection of cancer is the key for curing it. Early detection involves recognizing symptoms, getting regular check-ups, and performing self-exams. If it is detected early, the number of cancer cells will be small and contained. If cancer is allowed to progress to an advanced stage before detection, it may spread to more than one part of the body, and be much harder to treat. If cancer is not detected early, even the best treatments may not be effective.

60. C: Wellness depends on lifestyle choices like the amount of sleep, type of diet, exercise plan, and habits a person has. Factors affecting the physical aspect of wellness include nutrition, exercise, and access to health care. These factors are all heavily affected by lifestyle choices. Factors affecting wellness regarding mental and social health are learning, critical thinking, stress management, religion, beliefs, and relationships. These things are also affected by in large part by lifestyle choices.

61. C: There are very few reasons why a person would be unable to donate organs of some kind. Active cancer, HIV, and systemic infection are some of the only absolute exclusions. No one is too young or too old. And a genetic disease may affect certain organs or parts of the body and leave others intact. For example, cystic fibrosis affects the lungs, but the lens of the eyes may be perfectly functional. Similarly, a history of drug and alcohol use may damage certain organs, but others will be functional and good candidates for organ donation.

62. D: One should turn the body as a unit by pivoting the feet, not turning at the waist. Other important principles of movement include: squat by bending at the knees, and keep the back straight, and get help if the load is too large. Health care workers that routinely move patients should be aware of the principles of good body mechanics in order to avoid injuries from repetitive movement and bad form. There is a technique to moving patients up in bed, turning to the side, transferring from bed to chair, and other common movements in a health care setting.

63. A: Physical therapists work to restore body function after injury, surgery, disease, or loss of a body part. They may specialize in many areas of practice, including rehabilitation, community health, sports, or industry. An occupational therapist differs from a physical therapist in that an occupational therapist helps patients with birth defects, advanced age, injury, or emotional and/or developmental problems achieve their highest level of independent living. Athletic trainers work mostly with healthy people to prevent injury during athletic activities and treat athletes after injury. A respiratory therapist works specifically to administer respiratory care.

64. C: Administrators and managers are needed in all health care facilities. They do everything from overseeing the institution as a whole to managing specific tasks. The top executive is referred to as the chief executive officer (CEO). The CEO must demonstrate public relations skills and leadership ability in addition to establishing the policies and procedures of a facility. Specific tasks that need to be done by other administrators include managing medical records, transcribing audio medical records, and providing doctors, researchers, and students with access to information. These tasks are performed by, respectively, a medical records administrator, medical stenographer, and health science librarian.

65. B: The Health Insurance Portability and Accountability Act (HIPAA) has two main functions. Title I protects health insurance coverage for people when they change or lose jobs. Title II established national standards for electronic health care transactions and helps keep information private. The privacy rule of HIPAA means that health insurers must disclose information about an individual's medical record or payment history if an individual requests it and when required to do so by law. The health insurer must make reasonable effort to ensure confidentiality, and notify individuals when their information is used.

66. C: The first priority in the case of fire is to make sure everyone gets out safely. A person should be designated as having the responsibility of making sure others are safely removed from the building. People must be rescued and an alarm must be sounded before the fire is contained and extinguished. If the fire cannot be safely extinguished, then one should evacuate and let the fire department extinguish the fire.

67. B: Triage comes from the French verb *trier*, meaning "to separate, sort, or select." Triage helps medical professionals ration patient treatment efficiently when resources are insufficient for all to be treated immediately. Following triage, an injured person will receive first aid, including resuscitation if necessary. Triage is done in emergency rooms and/or at the site of a disaster.

68. D: Chloroform is flammable and toxic in high doses. It is also very volatile, so care should be taken to clean it up before it evaporates into the air. The area in which one uses chloroform should be well ventilated; in the event of a spill, the liquid should be taken up with a noncombustible absorbent material before being stored in a closed container to avoid contaminating the surrounding air with chloroform vapors. Chloroform should not be disposed of in a drain or alongside regular waste, as, like most chemical solvents used in the laboratory, it requires specialized chemical disposal.

69. A: Nonsterile gloves are worn when contact is made with body fluids, mucous membranes, or wet secretions. This precaution is applied at all times to all patients and to all body fluids EXCEPT perspiration. The purpose of this precaution is to reduce transmission of microorganisms from diagnosed and undiagnosed infection sources. Used gloves are placed directly into a designated receptacle and Hands should be washed thoroughly after removing the gloves.

70. B: OSHA has two functions: to establish standards of safety for the workplace, and to enforce those standards. Federal standards require that employees know about potential hazards in their work place, and employers are required to provide a Safety Data Sheet detailing information about the health and safety hazards of products employees work with. OSHA is an agency of the Department of Labor.

71. C: Avoiding accumulation of flammable materials in waste products is one way to reduce fire hazards. Fire hazards common to hospitals and laboratories include improperly stored flammable solvents and chemicals and frayed or bent wires on electrical equipment. Some electrical equipment may require continuous use, but this is safe if the equipment is maintained properly. Fire extinguishers should be kept in easy to find locations and should be in good repair.

72. C: Meningitis is an infection of the fluid and tissue around the brain and spinal cord. It usually results as a complication from another infection and is not contagious. It may be a viral or bacterial infection. Many viral infections cannot be treated with drugs. Viral infections cannot be treated with antibiotics, and chemotherapy drugs are used to treat cancer, not infectious diseases. Because treatment with antibiotics or other drugs is not available for viral meningitis, bed rest at home is generally recommended.

73. B: The symptoms of respiratory flu, like sneezing and coughing, make flu highly contagious. When in an enclosed space, like an airplane, infection may spread quickly. Staying home, washing hands frequently, and sneezing into a tissue can all slow the spread of the flu. HIV can only be spread by means of sexual contact, shared blood, or contaminated needles. Meningitis is not a communicable disease. Diverticulitis is a disorder of the lower intestine and is not an infectious disease.

74. C: A nosocomial infection is one contracted during a hospital stay that is different from the condition the patient was originally admitted to the hospital to be treated for. Nosocomial infections result for many reasons, including the simple fact that medical staff move continuously from patient to patient and bring pathogens with them. Treatment with antibiotics and antiviral medications may be necessary to overcome an infection, whether nosocomial or not. But overuse of antibiotics, or misuse in the form of not finishing a prescription, can increase the selection pressure on emerging antibiotic-resistant strains.

75. A: The most common method of transferring pathogenic organisms that cause the most serious illnesses is through contact with contaminated needles. Needles should never be recapped because this could cause confusion and allow a used needle to be reused. Needles should be considered disposable and should never be reused. Instead, they should be disposed of in a container that is safe for sharps. Methods generally not considered to be effective against spreading disease include disposable eating utensils, double-bagging waste, and fogging an area with disinfectant.

76. C: HIV can only be spread through direct contact with body fluids, which could occur through sexual contact and sharing needles. There is no vaccine against HIV, which is one reason that rate of infection is increasing throughout the world. There is also no cure, which is why acquiring an infection is so dangerous. Isolation is rarely used to prevent the spread of infection. Wearing a respiratory mask is generally only done in cases where a patient is particularly vulnerable to infection, as in the case of surgery.

77. D: Information regarding patient health care, including medical history and treatment plans, is considered confidential. This means that health care workers are legally and ethically responsible for protecting a patient's privacy. Talking about confidential information when other people, including a patient's family, are present would violate confidentiality. Talking about confidential information in a public place where no one is likely to know the patient is also not appropriate. Communication regarding a patient's confidential information need not happen in a private office, but should be done in a way that respects patient privacy.

78. B: A health care worker must understand the limits of his or her particular practice. Performing skills that are outside one's area of training, or failing to do something that is considered common practice within one's training, are both forms of malpractice. Knowing the limits of one's practice may require a health care worker to refuse to perform certain skills or write certain prescriptions, even if a patient requests them. Sometimes patients question the quality or scope of care in a way that results in a lawsuit, and health care providers carry malpractice insurance in case of such situations.

79. A: The chart is the main technique used by health care professionals to communicate about patient care. It must be precise, clear, and concise. A health care worker should chart only the observations they make themselves, not the observations of another person. They should keep any information contained in the chart confidential. The chart also serves as the legal record of the care given to a patient.

80. D: Volunteering opportunities at a local hospital are a good way for a doctor to provide work-based learning experiences for students. The work must be appropriate, however, and the student volunteer must not engage in skills for which he or she is not trained. Patient privacy should also be protected, as volunteers are not privileged to the same kind of information as health care professionals.

81. B: The leader of a group has responsibility for other members of the team. The leader must make decisions, give direction, communicate change, and serve as a role model. Confidence and assertiveness are both useful characteristics in doing these things. Emotional reasoning, or making decisions based on anger, jealousy, or other emotions, gets in the way of the critical thinking that is necessary for effective leadership. A good leader will keep his or her vision and goals in mind as he or she makes decisions and evaluates members of the team.

82. A: An effective team has a common purpose, specific goals, defined roles, and direction. Individual team members are accountable for their own specific responsibilities but must also trust each other. The value of each person's contribution should be recognized, and therefore tolerating differences is an important part of being a good team member. Being part of a team does not mean that someone should blame others for problems that arise or depend on others to make all the decisions and solve all the problems.

83. D: The amount of education required for a career in the health care field varies by position. Nursing is one area in particular that varies widely: Licensed Practical Nurses need an associate's degree, whereas Registered Professional Nurses typically have a four-year bachelor's degree. Nurse practitioners have master's degrees. Assistant-level jobs typically require certification, but an academic degree is not required. The educational path leading to the job of laboratory manager can vary, but most have bachelor's degrees in the biological sciences. According to the Bureau of Labor and Statistics, the entry-level degree for being a physical therapist is a master's degree. Medical professionals such as doctors, optometrists, dentists, and veterinarians have doctorate degrees.

84. A: Advances in medical technology change the field in a rapid manner. Biomedical research routinely uncovers new knowledge necessitating the development of new drugs. Working in a rapidly advancing field requires continuing education for all medical workers. Continuing education could consist of reading professional publications and journals, attending conferences, and attending employee training.

85. A: Many health care careers involve working with people. Pathologists and medical stenographers are two careers with relatively little patient contact, however. Pathologists work primarily in laboratories analyzing samples from biopsies and surgeries. Medial stenographers work in an office transcribing audio medical records. Both dental hygienists and nurse practitioners have a lot of contact with patients. Nurse practitioners must have a master's degree, while dental hygienists need the equivalent of an associate's degree, so a student would begin work in his or her career more quickly as a dental hygienist.

86. C: The sequencing of an individual's genes is a relatively new medical advance. Genetic counselors analyze a patient's DNA sequence. They inform patients of genetic disorders and evaluate their risk of getting a disease based on the genetic defect. Having a mutation in a gene does not necessarily mean that a person will get a disease, so genetic counselors evaluate the risk of a patient getting a particular disease based on genetic and other factors. Doctors of osteopathic medicine, nurse midwives, and radiologists are all professionals whose jobs have been around for quite some time.

87. D: While a nurse must have good communication skills, it is not necessary that he or she be a native speaker of English. A nurse must have good verbal communication skills in order to communicate information about patients to doctors and to be able to communicate medical information to patients. Nurses must also have self-control and good problem-solving abilities in high-pressure situations and be punctual in order to maintain patient schedules that can be strict.

88. B: Few health care careers allow workers to do their jobs from home because so many of them involve patient contact or laboratory work. Professional development is necessary in light of the pace of change and advancement in medical technology. Working with people requires health care workers to be good communicators, and many medical tasks are time sensitive, requiring workers to be punctual and to keep to a schedule.

89. B: Electronic medical records have been slowly adopted in the United States on account of a complex array of factors such as interoperability, older record incorporation, and privacy. Recent legislation encourages hospitals and doctors to switch to electronic medical records, and they will likely become common in the health care industry. This will change the duties a medical records manager performs and require significant retraining for these jobs.

90. C: Ask-a-nurse hotlines are an example of using technology to improve access to information regarding health care. They do not exist to diagnose disease, replace doctors, or prevent patients from coming to the hospital emergency room. Nurse practitioners who answer calls provide information so that patients can make an informed decision about what action they will take regarding their health problems.

91. B: The investigator's responsibility is always to the patient. While there is always a need for research, the patient's welfare must take precedence over science and/or society. Ethical considerations must always take precedence over laws and regulations. When a research subject is unable to give consent or is a minor, then surrogate consent must be given by an individual acting in the subject's best interest.

92. A: In order to ensure that research is conducted in an ethical way, most research institutions have an Institutional Review Board. This is a committee that has been designated to approve, monitor, and review research involving human subjects with the aim to protect the rights and welfare of patients. A hospital's or university's president, chief executive officer, board of directors, and general counsel should be concerned about the ethics of the research conducted at their institutions, but they are not directly involved in evaluating individual research proposals in the way that an Institutional Review Board is.

93. C: HIPAA is a law enacted by Congress in 1996 that protects health insurance coverage for workers and their families when they change jobs while simultaneously providing for the security and privacy of a worker's health data. The privacy rules state that protected medical information can only be shared when necessary for treatment purposes, and that no more information than what is necessary and relevant should be shared. HIPAA allows the patient to determine which telephone number he or she wishes to be contacted with. Patients are allowed full access to their own medical records, but other people, even if they are related to the patient, are not.

94. B: Ethics describes the principles and values that determine appropriate human behavior. It is a branch of philosophy that seeks to determine how moral values should be determined and how a moral outcome can be achieved in a given situation. Ethics and morality seem similar, but morality usually refers to a specific code of conduct as taught by a particular religion or philosophy. Faith is the belief that something is true, and usually refers to belief in religious ideas. Jurisprudence is the theory and philosophy of law. Health care workers should be aware of the law, but it is much more important that they behave in an ethical manner.

95. A: Whether a person has life insurance and what kind of insurance the person has is not considered protected health information. Workers' compensation claims are similarly unprotected. Life insurance and workers' compensation providers are allowed to use and reuse patient information without prior consent. This is not true of medical records, dental records, or other private health information, which the law states must be kept confidential.

96. B: Health care workers must stay within a "scope of practice." This means they use the methods and procedures in which they are trained and do not perform skills in which they are not trained. Doing work outside of one's scope of practice is illegal as well as unethical. A nursing assistant is not trained or licensed in dental care, and therefore cannot perform dental cleanings. A radiologist is not trained or licensed in anesthesia administration, and therefore cannot engage in it. A registered nurse has a defined scope of practice for her job: setting broken bones would be within the scope of practice for a physician, not a nurse.

97. D: Confidentiality and personal privacy are important parts of the Patient's Bill of Rights. However, medical information can never be kept completely confidential, as the team of health care workers responsible for a patient's care will have access to the patient's private medical information. The information is kept confidential outside the health care team, however. Quality care without mistreatment, neglect, or abuse is also part of the Patient's Bill of Rights, as is the ability to participate in treatment decisions. Patients have responsibilities as well, such as the responsibility to make a good faith effort to pay for services.

98. A: A durable power of attorney and a living will are both examples of advanced health care directives. The durable power of attorney allows for another person to make health care decisions if a person is unable to make them for him or herself; a living will allows a person to state in advance what kinds of medical treatment he or she would like to receive. A person need not be permanently unconscious or terminally ill in order for a durable power of attorney to be invoked. They need only be temporarily unable to make decisions for themselves.

99. C: If a person is capable of communicating their wishes, then a living will need not and must not be invoked. Only serious circumstances such as a prolonged state of unconsciousness or resuscitation following a heart attack would trigger a living will to be invoked. Simply being in pain or temporarily incapacitated would not invoke a living will. Death would invoke a living will regarding issues like whether or not an individual wants their organs and tissues to be donated.

100. D: Failing to do something that is considered common practice is considered both negligence and malpractice. A health care worker could be legally liable for malpractice, and many health care workers carry individual or group insurance against malpractice lawsuits. Slander is when the spoken word is used to give an individual or organization a negative image.

Thank You

We at Mometrix would like to extend our heartfelt thanks to you, our friend and patron, for allowing us to play a part in your journey. It is a privilege to serve people from all walks of life who are unified in their commitment to building the best future they can for themselves.

The preparation you devote to these important testing milestones may be the most valuable educational opportunity you have for making a real difference in your life. We encourage you to put your heart into it—that feeling of succeeding, overcoming, and yes, conquering will be well worth the hours you've invested.

We want to hear your story, your struggles and your successes, and if you see any opportunities for us to improve our materials so we can help others even more effectively in the future, please share that with us as well. **The team at Mometrix would be absolutely thrilled to hear from you!** So please, send us an email (support@mometrix.com) and let's stay in touch.

If you'd like some additional help, check out these other resources we offer for your exam:
http://mometrixflashcards.com/TExES

Online Resources

Due to our efforts to try to keep this book to a manageable length, we've created a link that will give you access to all of your online resources:

mometrix.com/resources719/texeshealsci

It's Your Moment, Let's Celebrate It!

Share your story @mometrixtestpreparation